A CASEBOOK ON

*Shakespeare's
Sonnets*

A CASEBOOK ON

Shakespeare's Sonnets

EDITED BY

Gerald Willen & Victor B. Reed

Hunter College of the City University of New York

NEW YORK

Thomas Y. Crowell Company

ESTABLISHED 1834

First Printing, June, 1964
Second Printing, June, 1965

Copyright © 1964 by
THOMAS Y. CROWELL COMPANY
All Rights Reserved

Library of Congress Catalog Card Number: 64-14573

Designed by GUY FLEMING

Manufactured in the United States of America

Preface

WHEN SHAKESPEARE'S SONNETS first appeared in 1609, their publisher, Thomas Thorpe, dedicated them to "the onlie begetter of these ensuing sonnets, Mr. W. H." Had he deliberately set out to obscure the poems from serious criticism, he could not have found a more successful formula. Like the conjurer's empty gesture that leads our eyes away from his real work, Thorpe's preface diverted generations of scholars to a barren search for the identity of Mr. W. H. and away from the magic by which Shakespeare created a world out of something no more substantial than breath.

The *Sonnets* received very little attention of any kind until 1780, when Edmond Malone decided "to do them that justice to which they seem entitled." But justice, in great part because of Thorpe's dedication, was not forthcoming until the twentieth century. The nineteenth century's abundant scholarship consisted chiefly of inane speculations on "the problem" of the *Sonnets*—a problem, neither critical nor literary except in the most peripheral sense, of identity: Who were W. H., the rival poet, the dark lady, the young man who figures so prominently in these poems? The poems themselves mattered only as evidence in the debate on "the problem."

In the twentieth century we have learned that seeing the pattern of the poem exceeds in pleasure even the most interesting investigations of the poet's private life. This volume therefore presents, with a newly edited text of the *Sonnets*, essays focusing on the sonnets themselves, rather than on biographical puzzles. Our decision to limit the selections to six full-length essays and eight explications is dictated both by considerations of space and availability (we exclude, for example, William

Empson's remarks on the *Sonnets*, since *Seven Types of Ambiguity* is widely available) and by our own critical preferences.

We begin with an essay by Laura Riding and Robert Graves that deals directly and intelligently with the original text. The reading of Shakespeare's sonnets has been much affected by this essay and by Mr. Empson's observation that the pleasure to be had from poetry derives in great measure from its richness of meaning—its "ambiguity," as he would say. Ours is an approximation to an "Empsonian" text, aimed at exhibiting the multiple meanings of the phrases of the poems. (The useful meanings, that is, for there are pernicious ambiguities and vacuous ambiguities as well as constructive Empsonian ambiguities in all poetry.) Naturally the limitations of space make it impossible to provide all such meanings. We have tried simply to fill those gaps in the reader's responses that are due to changes in the language since Shakespeare's time.

Everyone will have his own notion of what phrases need to be dealt with in the notes. We have chosen to risk being too inclusive; and the reader will—indeed, if we have done our work properly, should—sometimes feel that we are explaining things that are already perfectly plain. If the reader thinks we should have commented where we have not, one of two explanations is likely: he is not looking at the line in the way that most other readers may be expected to, and the problem will clear up if he does; or he sees something we do not, as some readers doubtless will.

No changes whatever have been made in Shakespeare's text, which in this book is precisely that of 1609, except that we have used modern *s* and *W* instead of their Elizabethan equivalents and have followed the modern practice of distinguishing between *u* and *v* and between *i* and *j*. Similarly, no changes in the texts of the essays or explications have been made except in two respects: footnotes not numbered consecutively have been renumbered; and, when necessary, sonnet numbers have been changed from roman to arabic. Superscript numbers in brackets indicate the end of the page on which the selection appeared in the original source.

We should like to thank the many friends and colleagues who have helped us. Above all, we are most grateful to the authors and the publishers of the essays reprinted here.

G. W. and V. B. R.

New York City
March, 1964

Contents

Contents

I

The Sonnets

TO.THE.ONLIE.BEGETTER.OF.
THESE.INSVING.SONNETS.
M^r.W.H. ALL.HAPPINESSE.
AND.THAT.ETERNITIE.
PROMISED.
BY.
OVR.EVER-LIVING.POET.
WISHETH.
THE.WELL-WISHING.
ADVENTVRER.IN.
SETTING.
FORTH.

T. T.

A NOTE ON THE METHOD OF ANNOTATION

When one of the meanings of a word is obvious to the twentieth-century reader, that meaning is not given in the notes; we go on immediately to the obsolete meaning. Thus, if a note begins with a "(b)" meaning, we have assumed that the "(a)" meaning is self-evident.

I

From fairest creatures we desire increase,
That thereby beauties *Rose* might never die,
But as the riper should by time decease,
His tender heire might beare his memory: 4
But thou contracted to thine owne bright eyes,
Feed'st thy lights flame with selfe substantiall fewell,
Making a famine where aboundance lies,
Thy selfe thy foe, to thy sweet selfe too cruell: 8
Thou that art now the worlds fresh ornament,
And only herauld to the gaudy spring,
Within thine owne bud buriest thy content,
And tender chorle makst wast in niggarding: 12
    Pitty the world, or else this glutton be,
    To eate the worlds due, by the grave and thee.

---

1 *increase* (b) offspring (Cf. *Coriolanus* 3.3.114: "her womb's increase") 2 *beauties* beauty's (The apostrophe was not used in the possessive case until the second half of the seventeenth century) 3 *as the riper* i.e., when the ripe rose *by time* in time, in good time (= "betime"; OED cites from 1565: "let us turne and amende by time") 4 *tender* young, immature (Cf. *Richard II* 2.3.42: "tender, raw and young") 5 *contracted* (b) engaged to marry (Cf. *Measure for Measure* 5.1.380: "Say, wast thou e'er contracted to this woman?") 6 *selfe substantiall* made of your own substance (The phrase does not appear elsewhere in Elizabethan English, but cf. Plotinus' similar *autoousia*, echoed in various Latin Neo-Platonic texts) 11 *content* (a) happiness (Cf. 119.13) (b) contents 12 *tender* (b) sensitive (Cf. 141.6) *chorle* churl, a base, miserly fellow (Cf. Coverdale's *Bible*, Isaiah 32.5: "Then shall the niggard be no more called gentle, nor the churl liberal") 13 *this glutton be* you will be such a glutton as (Cf. *Twelfth Night* 3.4.281: "Do me this courteous office, as to know . . .") 14 *eate the worlds due, by the grave and thee* i.e., devour what death and you owe the world

3

2

When fortie Winters shall beseige thy brow,
And digge deep trenches in thy beauties field,
Thy youthes proud livery so gaz'd on now,
Wil be a totter'd weed of smal worth held: 4
Then being askt, where all thy beautie lies,
Where all the treasure of thy lusty daies;
To say within thine owne deepe sunken eyes,
Were an all-eating shame, and thriftlesse praise.   8
How much more praise deserv'd thy beauties use,
If thou couldst answere this faire child of mine
Shall sum my count, and make my old excuse
Prooving his beautie by succession thine.   12
   This were to be new made when thou art ould,
   And see thy blood warme when thou feel'st it could,

---

4 *totter'd weed* tattered garment (but note that *field* in line 2 also suggests the sense of "worthless plant" for *weed*) 8 *thriftlesse* (a) unprofitable, worthless (b) wasteful (parallel to *all-eating*) 9 *use* (a) investment (Cf. 134.10) (b) employment for sexual purposes (Cf. 20.14) 11 *sum* (a) complete (OED cites Marlowe, *Jew of Malta* 1.1.3: "There was the venture summ'd and satisfied") (b) reckon up *count* account *old excuse* excuse for being old 12 *by succession* according to the rules of inheritance

3

Looke in thy glasse and tell the face thou vewest,
Now is the time that face should forme an other,
Whose fresh repaire if now thou not renewest,
Thou doo'st beguile the world, unblesse some mother.   4
For where is she so faire whose un-eard wombe
Disdaines the tillage of thy husbandry?
Or who is he so fond will be the tombe,
Of his selfe love to stop posterity?   8
Thou art thy mothers glasse and she in thee
Calls backe the lovely Aprill of her prime,
So thou through windowes of thine age shalt see,
Dispight of wrinkles this thy goulden time.   12
    But if thou live remembred not to be,
    Die single and thine Image dies with thee.

---

3 *repaire* state, condition   4 *unblesse some mother* deprive some
woman of the blessings of being a mother   5 *un-eard* unploughed,
unfertilized (OED: "Ear . . . [ultimately derived from] W. Aryan
root *ar* to plough"; "un-eard" was close in pronunciation to "un-
heired")   6 *husbandry* (a) farming   (b) acting as a husband   7
fond foolish   *will be* that he will be   8 *to stop* by debarring   9 *glasse*
(a) mirror (Cf. *Lucrece* 1758: "Poor broken glass, I often did behold
In thy sweet semblance my old age new-born")   (b) window (rare in
Elizabethan English, but OED quotes from c. 1566: "faire eyes that
are the windowes of all the bodie, and glasses of the soule"; cf. *Richard II* 1.3.208: "Even in the glasses of thine eyes I see thy grieved
heart." We are probably meant to see the parallel to *windowes* in line
11)   9–10 *in thee calls backe* in seeing you recalls   13 *remembred
not to be* intending not to be remembered

4

Unthrifty lovelinesse why dost thou spend,
Upon thy selfe thy beauties legacy?
Natures bequest gives nothing but doth lend,
And being franck she lends to those are free: 4
Then beautious nigard why doost thou abuse,
The bountious largesse given thee to give?
Profitles userer why doost thou use
So great a summe of summes yet can'st not live?   8
For having traffike with thy selfe alone,
Thou of thy selfe thy sweet selfe dost deceave,
Then how when nature calls thee to be gone,
What acceptable *Audit* can'st thou leave?   12
    Thy unus'd beauty must be tomb'd with thee,
    Which used lives th'executor to be.

---

1 *unthrifty* (a) unprofitable (b) wasteful (Cf. 2.8) 4 *franck, free*
liberal, generous (OED cites several examples of the customary legal
redundancy "frank and free") *those are* those who are 7 *use* (a)
use up (b) invest, draw profit from 8 *so great a summe of* so many
summes principal sums? (i.e., investments) *summe of summes* grand
total (Cf. Nashe, *Strange Newes* H2v [McKerrow ed.] 305: "The sum
of sums is this"; this common Elizabethan phrase derives from the
equally common Latin *summa summarum*, as in Lucretius, *De Rerum
Natura* 5.361) *live* (a) make a living (b) live on (in your child) 9
traffike commerce (in both mercantile and sexual senses) 10 *thou of
thy selfe thy sweet selfe dost deceave* (a) you cheat yourself out of
yourself (i.e., your second self, your son) (b) by yourself you are
false to yourself 14 *lives* i.e., in your son

5

Those howers that with gentle worke did frame,
The lovely gaze where every eye doth dwell
Will play the tirants to the very same,
And that unfaire which fairely doth excell: 4
For never resting time leads Summer on,
To hidious winter and confounds him there,
Sap checkt with frost and lustie leav's quite gon.
Beauty ore-snow'd and barenes every where,   8
Then were not summers distillation left
A liquid prisoner pent in walls of glasse,
Beauties effect with beauty were bereft,
Nor it nor noe remembrance what it was.   12
    But flowers distil'd though they with winter meete,
    Leese but their show, their substance still lives sweet.

---

1 *howers* hours *frame* (a) form (b) serve as a frame for? (This
antedates by two centuries the OED's first record of such usage, but
the corresponding noun appears in 24.3, and the *gaze* of the next line,
like a painting an object of scrutiny, suggests that Shakespeare intends
the reader to see the cultured hours of the youth as a frame for his
beauty) 2 *gaze* (b) thing that is gazed at (Cf. *Macbeth* 5.7.53: "the
show and gaze o' the time") 4 *unfaire* rob of beauty *fairely* in
beauty 6 *confounds* destroys (Cf. 63.10) 9 *summers distillation*
perfumes distilled from summer flowers 11 *bereft* removed 12 *nor
it nor noe* (leaving) neither itself nor any 14 *leese* lose (Cf. Bacon,
Essays, "Empire": "that he wins in the Hundred, he leeseth in the
Shire")

6

Then let not winters wragged hand deface,
In thee thy summer ere thou be distil'd:
Make sweet some viall; treasure thou some place,
With beautits treasure ere it be selfe kil'd: 4
That use is not forbidden useiy,
Which happies those that pay the willing lone;
That's for thy selfe to breed an other thee,
Or ten times happier be it ten for one,   8
Ten times thy selfe were happier then thou art,
If ten of thine ten times refigur'd thee,
Then what could death doe if thou should'st depart,
Leaving thee living in posterity?   12
  Be not selfe-wild for thou art much too faire,
   To be deaths conquest and make wormes thine heire.

---

1 *wragged* (ragged) rough (Cf. *Titus Andronicus* 5.3.133: "ragged
stones")   3 *treasure* enrich 4 *beautits* beauty's (misprint for "beauties")   *selfe kil'd* (a) self-killed   (b) killed itself? (OED lists no
identical usage, but quotes from 1532: "Thys is the thing selfe that is
in debate")   5 *use* (b) lending money at interest (Cf. 2.9)   6 *willing lone* loan assumed willingly   7 *that's* that (a loan that makes the
borrower happy) is what it would be   10 *thine* i.e., your children
13 *selfe-wild* (a) willful, stubborn (Cf. *1 Henry IV* 3.1.198: "a pee-
vish self-willed harlotry")   (b) yourself your legacy

7

Loe in the Orient when the gracious light,
Lifts up his burning head, each under eye
Doth homage to his new appearing sight,
Serving with lookes his sacred majesty,   4
And having climb'd the steepe up heavenly hill,
Resembling strong youth in his middle age,
Yet mortall lookes adore his beauty still,
Attending on his goulden pilgrimage: 8
But when from high-most pich with wery car,
Like feeble age he reeleth from the day,
The eyes (fore dutious) now converted are
From his low tract and looke an other way: 12
     So thou, thy selfe out-going in thy noon:
     Unlok'd on diest unlesse thou get a sonne.

---

2 *under eye* eye on earth below (Cf. *King Lear* 2.2.170: "This under globe")   3 *new appearing* (a) new-appearing, having the appearance of freshness (b) newly appearing (Cf. 30.12: "Which I new pay")   5 *steepe up* steeply ascending (Cf. *Passionate Pilgrim* 9.5: "upon a steep up hill")   8 *attending on* (often used in relation to royal personages)   9 *high-most pich* zenith (Cf. Milton, *Paradise Lost* 2.77: "Down ... from the pitch of Heaven")   *car* chariot   11 *fore* formerly *converted* (b) turned aside (Cf. *As You Like It* 5.4.168: "converted from his enterprise")   12 *tract* track, path   13 *out-going* passing beyond   *thy selfe out-going in thy noon* continuing beyond the moment of your prime

8

Musick to heare, why hear'st thou musick sadly,
Sweets with sweets warre not, joy delights in joy:
Why lov'st thou that which thou receavst not gladly,
Or else receav'st with pleasure thine annoy?⠀⠀⠀⠀⠀⠀4
If the true concord of well tuned sounds,
By unions married do offend thine eare,
They do but sweetly chide thee, who confounds
In singlenesse the parts that thou should'st beare:⠀⠀⠀⠀8
Marke how one string sweet husband to an other,
Strikes each in each by mutuall ordering;
Resembling sier, and child, and happy mother,
Who all in one, one pleasing note do sing:⠀⠀⠀⠀⠀12
⠀⠀Whose speechlesse song being many seeming one,
⠀⠀Sings this to thee thou single wilt prove none.

---

1 *musick to heare* i.e., you who are yourself music to hear⠀⠀6 *by unions married* (b) i.e., married by being sounded together⠀⠀7 *confounds* (a) mixes together⠀⠀(b) destroys (Cf. 63.10)⠀⠀8 *parts* (a) separate melodies of a harmony⠀⠀(b) virtues, talents (Cf. 17.4)⠀⠀*beare* sustain ("To bear a part" was the common Elizabethan way of saying "to sing one voice in a polyphonic song," as in *Lucrece* 1327)⠀⠀10 *strikes* sounds (Cf. Thomas Morley, *Introduction to Music:* "I greatly mislike your causing the treble strike a sharp eight to the base")⠀⠀*each in each* together with the other? on the other? (Cf. *Midsummer Night's Dream* 4.1.129: "each under each")⠀⠀11 *sier* sire

9

Is it for feare to wet a widdowes eye,
That thou consum'st thy selfe in single life?
Ah; if thou issulesse shalt hap to die,
The world will waile thee like a makelesse wife,   4
The world wilbe thy widdow and still weepe,
That thou no forme of thee hast left behind,
When every privat widdow well may keepe,
By childrens eyes, her husbands shape in minde: 8
Looke what an unthrift in the world doth spend
Shifts but his place, for still the world injoyes it
But beauties waste hath in the world an end,
And kept unusde the user so destroyes it: 12
    No love toward others in that bosome sits
    That on himselfe such murdrous shame commits.

---

4 *makelesse* mateless 5 *wilbe* will be 6 *forme* image, likeness (OED cites from 1611: "An escutcheon is the form or representation of a shield") 9 *looke what* whatever (Cf. 37.13: "Looke what is best, that best I wish in thee") *unthrift* spendthrift 10 *his* its 11 *beauties waste* i.e., wasted beauty 12 *unusde* (a) unemployed (b) unconsumed (in opposition to *waste* above) 14 *on himselfe* against himself *murdrous shame commits* (Although a wider range of nouns was used with "commit" in the sixteenth century than modern English allows—as in *Winter's Tale* 2.3.49: "committing honour"— "commits shame" is an odd phrase for Shakespeare, and it is likely that by *murdrous shame* he meant "shameful murder," following the pattern of an ancient figure of rhetoric. Cf. 36.6)

For shame deny that thou bear'st love to any
Who for thy selfe art so unprovident
Graunt if thou wilt, thou art belov'd of many,
But that thou none lov'st is most evident: 4
For thou art so possest with murdrous hate,
That gainst thy selfe thou stickst not to conspire,
Seeking that beautious roofe to ruinate
Which to repaire should be thy chiefe desire: 8
O change thy thought, that I may change my minde,
Shall hate be fairer log'd then gentle love?
Be as thy presence is gracious and kind,
Or to thy selfe at least kind harted prove, 12
    Make thee an other selfe for love of me,
    That beauty still may live in thine or thee.

---

1 *for shame* (a) from a sense of shame (b) (ejaculation of reproof)
6 *thou stickst not* you do not hesitate (Cf. *2 Henry IV* 1.2.24: "he
will not stick to say his face is a face-royal") 7 *roofe* (a) i.e., of
your house, or family (b) your body 10 *log'd* lodged 11 *presence*
appearance (Cf. *Comedy of Errors* 3.2.13: "Bear a fair presence,
though your heart be tainted") *gracious* (pronounced as a trisyl-
lable)

As fast as thou shalt wane so fast thou grow'st,
In one of thine, from that which thou departest,
And that fresh bloud which yongly thou bestow'st,
Thou maist call thine, when thou from youth convertest,   4
Herein lives wisdome, beauty, and increase,
Without this follie, age, and could decay,
If all were minded so, the times should cease,
And threescoore yeare would make the world away: 8
Let those whom nature hath not made for store,
Harsh, featurelesse, and rude, barrenly perrish,
Looke whom she best indow'd, she gave the more;
Which bountious guift thou shouldst in bounty cherrish,   12
  She carv'd thee for her seale, and ment therby,
  Thou shouldst print more, not let that coppy die.

---

2 *one of thine* i.e., your son   *departest* (a) quit, leave (b) share
with others (Shakespeare does not use this sense of "depart" elsewhere; but, though obsolescent, it was good sixteenth-century English. The Geneva Bible has for John 19.24: "They departed my rai-
ment among them")   3 *yongly* as a young man   4 *convertest* (a)
change (b) turn away (Cf. 7.11)   6 *could* cold   9 *store* (a) re-
plenishment (Cf. 14.12) (b) abundance (Cf. Sidney, *Psalms* 25.11:
"Behold my foes, what store they be")   11 *looke whom* whomever
(Cf. 9.9)   14 *coppy* (copy) (a) pattern (Cf. *All's Well That Ends
Well* 1.2.46: "such a man Might be a copy to these younger times")
(b) manuscript ready for printing   (c) plenty, abundance (OED
cites from 1593: "such as have coppy of new coined words")

I 2

When I doe count the clock that tels the time,
And see the brave day sunck in hidious night,
When I behold the violet past prime,
And sable curls or silver'd ore with white:⠀⠀⠀⠀⠀⠀⠀4
When lofty trees I see barren of leaves,
Which erst from heat did canopie the herd
And Sommers greene all girded up in sheaves
Borne on the beare with white and bristly beard:⠀⠀⠀8
Then of thy beauty do I question make
That thou among the wastes of time must goe,
Since sweets and beauties do them-selves forsake,
And die as fast as they see others grow,⠀⠀⠀⠀⠀⠀⠀12
⠀⠀⠀And nothing gainst Times sieth can make defence
⠀⠀⠀Save breed to brave him, when he takes thee hence.

---

1 *count* count the chimes of (Cf. *Julius Caesar* 2.1.192: "Peace! count the clock. . . . The clock hath stricken three") 2 *brave* splendid (Cf. 15.8) 4 *sable* black (used especially as a heraldic term) *or* (Most modern editors read "all." "Or" itself is a heraldic term for gold) *ore* o'er (over) 6 *erst* formerly 7 *girded* tied 8 *beare* (bier) (b) frame for carrying harvested grain, hand barrow *beard* (b) awn of wheat or similar grain 13 *sieth* scythe 14 *brave* (a) defy (b) adorn (Cf. *Richard III* 5.3.280: "He [the sun] should have braved the east an hour ago")

O that you were your selfe, but love you are
No longer yours, then you your selfe here live,
Against this cumming end you should prepare,
And your sweet semblance to some other give.   4
So should that beauty which you hold in lease
Find no determination, then you were
You selfe again after your selfes decease,
When your sweet issue your sweet forme should beare.   8
Who lets so faire a house fall to decay,
Which husbandry in honour might uphold,
Against the stormy gusts of winters day
And barren rage of deaths eternall cold?   12
   O none but unthrifts, deare my love you know,
   You had a Father, let your Son say so.

---

2 *here* (homonymous with "heir"?) *your selfe here* (a) yourself
here (b) your self-heir, your own heir? (6) *determination* termination (associated in legal phraseology with the cessation of leases and
estates) *were* would be   7 *you selfe* yourself (misprint)   10 *husbandry* (a) careful management (Cf. *Macbeth* 2.1.4: "There's husbandry in heaven: Their candles are all out") (b) (punning suggestion of "being a husband"; cf. 3.6)   13 *unthrifts* spendthrifts
(Modern punctuation would put a period or exclamation point after
unthrifts, love, or *know*)

Not from the stars do I my judgement plucke,
And yet me thinkes I have Astronomy,
But not to tell of good, or evil lucke,
Of plagues, of dearths, or seasons quallity,   4
Nor can I fortune to breefe mynuits tell;
Pointing to each his thunder, raine and winde,
Or say with Princes if it shal go wel
By oft predict that I in heaven finde.   8
But from thine eies my knowledge I derive,
And constant stars in them I read such art
As truth and beautie shal together thrive
If from thy selfe, to store thou wouldst convert: 12
   Or else of thee this I prognosticate,
   Thy end is Truthes and Beauties doome and date.

---

2 *me thinkes* (methinks) I think   *Astronomy* (in Shakespeare's day, chiefly astrology)   5 *to breefe mynuits* (a) to the exact minute (b) in precise detail? (Cf. Jonson, *Staple of News* 1.5.138: "Let me heare from thee every minute of Newes")   6 *pointing* appointing, pointing out   *his* its   8 *oft* frequent? (perhaps a misprint, but cf. Milton, *Samson Agonistes* 382: "Warn'd by oft experience")   *predict* (perhaps a coinage for "prediction," perhaps a misprint for some technical term of astrology)   10 *art* learning   11 *as* as that   12 *convert* (a) change (b) turn your attention? (OED cites from 1615: "Now convert we to the Person and Court of this Sultan")   14 *doome* (a) destruction (b) doomsday *date* day of termination (Cf. 30.6 and *Lucrece* 26)

15

When I consider every thing that growes
Holds in perfection but a little moment.
That this huge stage presenteth nought but showes
Whereon the Stars in secret influence comment.   4
When I perceive that men as plants increase,
Cheared and checkt even by the selfe-same skie:
Vaunt in their youthfull sap, at height decrease,
And were their brave state out of memory.   8
Then the conceit of this inconstant stay,
Sets you most rich in youth before my sight,
Where wastfull time debateth with decay
To change your day of youth to sullied night,   12
   And all in war with Time for love of you
   As he takes from you, I ingraft you new.

---

2 *holds* remains, lasts (Cf. *Winter's Tale* 4.4.36: "Your resolution cannot hold") *holds in* keeps in, retains 6 *cheared* (cheered) (b) encouraged *checkt* stopped 7 *vaunt* boast 8 *were* wear (in the senses of both "dress in" and "use up") *brave* handsome, showy (Cf. 12.2) *out of memory* until forgotten 9 *conceit* thought (especially of a deluded sort; cf. *Othello* 3.3.115: "As if thou then hadst shut up in thy brain Some horrible conceit") 11 *debateth* (b) contends (Cf. *Lucrece* 1421: "debate with angry swords"; note that the following *with* can be taken in the opposed senses of "against" and "in alliance with")

16

But wherefore do not you a mightier waie
Make warre uppon this bloudie tirant time?
And fortifie your selfe in your decay
With meanes more blessed then my barren rime?   4
Now stand you on the top of happie houres,
And many maiden gardens yet unset,
With vertuous wish would beare your living flowers,
Much liker then your painted counterfeit: 8
So should the lines of life that life repaire
Which this (Times pensel or my pupill pen)
Neither in inward worth nor outward faire
Can make you live your selfe in eies of men,   12
   To give away your selfe, keeps your selfe still,
   And you must live drawne by your owne sweet skill,

---

6 *unset* unplanted (Cf. Marlowe, *Dr. Faustus* [Louis Wright ed.] 7.19: "banks are set with groves of fruitful vines") 8 *liker* more like (you) *counterfeit* portrait (Cf. *Merchant of Venice* 3.2.115: "What find I here? Fair Portia's counterfeit!") 9 *lines of life* (a) i.e., the child as portrait of the father (b) lineage *repaire* restore, revive (Cf. *Two Gentlemen of Verona* 5.4.11: "Repair me with thy presence, Sylvia") 10 (*Times . . . pen*) (Most modern editors omit both these parentheses) 11 *faire* beauty (Cf. 18.7)

I 7

Who will beleeve my verse in time to come
If it were fild with your most high deserts?
Though yet heaven knowes it is but as a tombe
Which hides your life, and shewes not halfe your parts: 4
If I could write the beauty of your eyes,
And in fresh numbers number all your graces,
The age to come would say this Poet lies,
Such heavenly touches nere toucht earthly faces.   8
So should my papers (yellowed with their age)
Be scorn'd, like old men of lesse truth then tongue,
And your true rights be termd a Poets rage,
And stretched miter of an Antique song.   12
    But were some childe of yours alive that time,
    You should live twise in it, and in my rime.

---

4 *parts* qualities (Cf. 8.8) 6 *numbers* meters, verses 11 *rage* inspired irrationality (Cf. Chapman, *Iliad* 1.66: "his prophetic rage Given by Apollo") 12 *stretched* exaggerated, strained (OED cites from 1674: "If this answer seems harsh or stretched, we shall . . . soften it by a clear instance") *miter* meter (i.e., poetry) *Antique* (b) antic, fantastic (Cf. *Hamlet* 1.5.172: "To put an antic disposition on")

1 8

Shall I compare thee to a Summers day?
Thou art more lovely and more temperate:
Rough windes do shake the darling buds of Maie,
And Sommers lease hath all too short a date: 4
Sometime too hot the eye of heaven shines,
And often is his gold complexion dimm'd,
And every faire from faire some-time declines,
By chance, or natures changing course untrim'd: 8
But thy eternall Sommer shall not fade,
Nor loose possession of that faire thou ow'st,
Nor shall death brag thou wandr'st in his shade,
When in eternall lines to time thou grow'st,.   12
    So long as men can breath or eyes can see,
    So long lives this, and this gives life to thee,

---

1 *compare* (used both in the modern sense and for its relation to "comparison," an Elizabethan word for simile)   4 *date* duration (a technical term of the law of contracts, as in Countess of Pembroke, *Psalms* 81.6: "A lease of bliss with endless date")   7 *faire from faire* fair thing from beauty (Cf. 16.11)   8 *untrim'd* (a) (nautical) with sails not properly set for a new course (b) lacking elegance or ornament (Cf. *King John* 3.1.209: "a new untrimmed bride")   10 *ow'st* ownest   12 *lines* i.e., of verse   *grow'st* (a) are part of, belong to (as in *2 Henry IV* 1.2.100: "lay aside that which grows to me") (b) become rooted in, grow fast to (as in *Richard II* 5.3.30: "May my knees grow to the earth")

1 9

Devouring time blunt thou the Lyons pawes,
And make the earth devoure her owne sweet brood,
Plucke the keene teeth from the fierce Tygers yawes,
And burne the long liv'd Phænix in her blood,   4
Make glad and sorry seasons as thou fleet'st,
And do what ere thou wilt swift-footed time
To the wide world and all her fading sweets:
But I forbid thee one most hainous crime,   8
O carve not with thy howers my loves faire brow,
Nor draw noe lines there with thine antique pen,
Him in thy course untainted doe allow,
For beauties patterne to succeding men.   12
　　Yet doe thy worst ould Time dispight thy wrong,
　　My love shall in my verse ever live young.

---

3 *yawes* jaws 10 *antique* (b) antic, grotesque (Cf. 17.12) 11 *course* (b) charge of combatants in a tournament (OED cites from 1568: "set hys speare in the rest to . . . runne the first course") *untainted* (b) untouched in a joust (Cf. the OED quotation from 1551: "a match . . . at tilt . . . wane by 4 taintes")

mans face with natures owne hand painted,
thou the Master Mistris of my passion,
ans gentle hart but not acquainted
With shifting change as is false womens fashion,   4
An eye more bright then theirs, lesse false in rowling:
Gilding the object where-upon it gazeth,
A man in hew all *Hews* in his controwling,
Which steales mens eyes and womens soules amaseth.   8
And for a woman wert thou first created,
Till nature as she wrought thee fell a dotinge,
And by addition me of thee defeated,
By adding one thing to my purpose nothing.   12
  But since she prickt thee out for womens pleasure,
  Mine be thy love and thy loves use their treasure.

---

1 *painted* (b) colored with cosmetic   2 *haste* hast   4, 5 *false* fickle, unfaithful   7 *hew* (hue) (a) form (OED cites Greene, *Orlando Furioso:* "Thrice hath Cynthia chang'd her hue") (b) complexion (The curious phrasing of the line and the capitalization of *Hews* have led some commentators to see a series of puns here, possibly on the name of the person addressed. "Hew" was pronounced in Elizabethan English very much like "you" and "hews" very much like "use," both noun and verb forms of which were spoken with a sounded *s*)   *controwling* (a) dominating (b) restraining   11 *defeated* deprived, cheated (Milton, *Paradise Lost* 11.254 has: "Death . . . Defeated of his seisure")   13 *prickt thee out* (a) gave you male genitals (b) marked you out, chose you (as in Jonson, *Cynthia's Revels* 5.2: "Why did the ladies prick out me?")   14 *use* (b) employment for sexual purposes (Cf. Tourneur, *Revenger's Tragedy* 2.2: "Her tongue has turned my sister into use")

2 I

So is it not with me as with that Muse,
Stird by a painted beauty to his verse,
Who heaven it selfe for ornament doth use,
And every faire with his faire doth reherse,   4
Making a coopelment of proud compare
With Sunne and Moone, with earth and seas rich gems:
With Aprills first borne flowers and all things rare,
That heavens ayre in this huge rondure hems,   8
O let me true in love but truly write,
And then beleeve me, my love is as faire,
As any mothers childe, though not so bright
As those gould candells fixt in heavens ayer: 12
   Let them say more that like of heare-say well,
   I will not prayse that purpose not to sell.

---

1 *Muse* poet (Cf. Milton, *Lycidas* 19: "So may some gentle Muse
With lucky words favour my destin'd Urn, And as he passes turn")
3 *ornament* (b) figure of speech (Cf. Puttenham, *Arte of English
Poesie*, "Of Ornament") 4 *faire with his faire* fair thing with his
fair one *reherse* name one after another (Cf. *Taming of the Shrew*
1.2.124: "Those defects I have before rehearsed") 5 *coopelment*
couplement, union *compare* comparison (Cf. 35.6 and 130.14) 8
rondure sphere (Cotgrave's French-English *Dictionary*, 1611, defines
rondeur as "roundness, globiness") 13 *like of* like *heare-say* un-
founded statements? 14 *that purpose* who intend

22

My glasse shall not perswade me I am ould,
So long as youth and thou are of one date,
But when in thee times forrwes I behould,
Then look I death my daies should expiate.　　　4
For all that beauty that doth cover thee,
Is but the seemely rayment of my heart,
Which in thy brest doth live, as thine in me,
How can I then be elder then thou art?　　　8
O therefore love be of thy selfe so wary,
As I not for my selfe, but for thee will,
Bearing thy heart which I will keepe so chary
As tender nurse her babe from faring ill,　　　12
　　Presume not on thy heart when mine is slaine,
　　Thou gav'st me thine not to give backe againe.

---

2 of *one date* of the same duration (Cf. 123.5)　3 *forrwes* furrows
4 *look I* I foresee, expect　*expiate* end (Cf. the somewhat similar
Richard III 3.3.23: "The hour of death is expiate")　11 *chary* carefully (Cf. Marlowe, *Dr. Faustus* 6.175: "This will I keep as chary as
my life")　13 *presume not on* do not count on, do not expect

As an unperfect actor on the stage,
Who with his feare is put besides his part,
Or some fierce thing repleat with too much rage,
Whose strengths abondance weakens his owne heart;   4
So I for feare of trust, forget to say,
The perfect ceremony of loves right,
And in mine owne loves strength seeme to decay,
Ore-charg'd with burthen of mine owne loves might: 8
O let my books be then the eloquence,
And domb presagers of my speaking brest,
Who pleade for love, and look for recompence,
More then that tonge that more hath more exprest.   12
    O learne to read what silent love hath writ,
    To heare wit eies belongs to loves fine wiht.

---

2 *put besides* put out of, made to forget (Cf. *1 Henry IV* 3.1.179: "you . . . have done enough To put him quite besides his patience") 5 *for feare of trust* (a) fearing distrust (Cf. *Passionate Pilgrim* 7.10: "How many tales to please me hath she coined, Dreading my love") (b) fearing to trust myself? (The curious phrasing here is probably partly owing to Shakespeare's interest in the paradoxical conjunction of "fear" and "trust") 6 *right* (b) rite 8 *ore-charg'd* overloaded 9 *books* (Most modern editors follow Capell's emendation, *looks*) 10 *presagers* (b) revealers? (Cf. Spenser, *Faerie Queene* 1.10.61: "Then seek this path that I to thee presage, Which after all to heaven shall thee send") 12 *that tonge* (See sonnet 21) 14 *wit* with (misprint) *wiht* wit (misprint)

24

Mine eye hath play'd the painter and hath steeld,
Thy beauties forme in table of my heart,
My body is the frame wherein ti's held,
And perspective it is best Painters art.   4
For through the Painter must you see his skill,
To finde where your true Image pictur'd lies,
Which in my bosomes shop is hanging stil,
That hath his windowes glazed with thine eyes: 8
Now see what good-turnes eyes for eies have done,
Mine eyes have drawne thy shape, and thine for me
Are windowes to my brest, where-through the Sun
Delights to peepe, to gaze therein on thee   12
　　Yet eyes this cunning want to grace their art
　　They draw but what they see, know not the hart.

---

1 *steeld* (Modern editors accept Capell's emendation *stell'd*, meaning
"portrayed." Cf. *Lucrece* 1444: "a face where all distress is stelled")
2 *table* board on which a picture is painted (Cf. *All's Well* 1.1.107:
"draw His arched brows . . . In our heart's table")   4 *perspective*
(pronounced with primary accent on the first syllable, as in *All's
Well* 5.3.48) the art of making a painting appear three-dimensional?
(The word was also used for an optical device which produced
startling and distorted images. The line may very well be corrupt,
but the word *perspective*, stemming from the Latin for "see through,"
is given some slight support by the following line)   8 *glazed* furnished with glass   13 *want* lack (with *this cunning* for object)

2 5

Let those who are in favor with their stars,
Of publike honour and proud titles bost,
Whilst I whome fortune of such tryumph bars
Unlookt for joy in that I honour most;   4
Great Princes favorites their faire leaves spread,
But as the Marygold at the suns eye,
And in them-selves their pride lies buried,
For at a frowne they in their glory die.   8
The painefull warrier famosed for worth,
After a thousand victories once foild,
Is from the booke of honour rased quite,
And all the rest forgot for which he toild: 12
   Then happy I that love and am beloved
   Where I may not remove, nor be removed.

---

3 *of* from (Cf. *Cymbeline* 3.3.102: "Thinking to bar thee of succession") 4 *unlookt for* (a) unexpectedly (b) not sought out (by public honor) *that* that which 7 *pride* (b) magnificent display, splendor (as in the traditional phrase "peacock in his pride") (c) flourishing state, prime (Cf. *1 Henry VI* 4.7.16: "There died . . . my blossom, in his pride") 9 *painefull* suffering from wounds (OED cites from 1612: "They see themselves . . . painful and deformed with scabs") *worth* (Theobald suggested that, for the sake of the rhyme, either *worth* should be emended to "fight" or *quite* in line 11 should be emended to "forth"; most modern editors choose one of these alternatives, but some emend *worth* to "might") 11 *rased* erased 14 *remove* move, depart

2 6

Lord of my love, to whome in vassalage
Thy merrit hath my dutie strongly knit;
To thee I send this written ambassage
To witnesse duty, not to shew my wit.   4
Duty so great, which wit so poore as mine
May make seeme bare, in wanting words to shew it;
But that I hope some good conceipt of thine
In thy soules thought (all naked) will bestow it: 8
Til whatsoever star that guides my moving,
Points on me gratiously with faire aspect,
And puts apparrell on my tottered loving,
To show me worthy of their sweet respect,   12
    Then may I dare to boast how I doe love thee,
    Til then, not show my head where thou maist prove me

COMPARE this sonnet with the dedication to *Lucrece:* "To the Right
Honourable Henry Wriothesley, Earl of Southampton. . . . The
warrant I have of your Honourable disposition, not the worth of my
untutored lines, makes [this book] assured of acceptance. . . . Were
my worth greater, my duty would show greater; meantime, as it is,
it is bound to your Lordship. . . ."

2 *dutie* reverence, respect   3 *ambassage* message carried by an am-
bassador   4 *witnesse* bear witness to   7 *conceipt* (a) conception
(b) image, figurative language   *good conceipt* high opinion (Cf. *Two
Gentlemen of Verona* 3.2.17: "The good conceit I hold of thee")
8 *bestow* put, place   10 *points on* shines on (Cf. *Richard II* 1.3.147:
"his golden beams . . . Shall point on me and gild my banishment."
In *Julius Caesar* 1.3.32: "they are portentous things Unto the climate
that they point upon," the phrase seems also to imply the marking
out of something as the object of supernatural influence)   *with faire
aspect* (b) in an astrological configuration that signifies beneficial influence   11 *tottered* tattered (Cf. 2.4)   12 *their* thy? (misprint?)
14 *prove me* put me to the test

27

Weary with toyle, I hast me to my bed,
The deare repose for lims with travaill tired,
But then begins a journy in my head
To worke my mind, when boddies work's expired.   4
For then my thoughts (from far where I abide)
Intend a zelous pilgrimage to thee;
And keepe my drooping eye-lids open wide,
Looking on darknes which the blind doe see.   8
Save that my soules imaginary sight
Presents their shaddoe to my sightles view,
Which like a jewell (hunge in gastly night)
Makes blacke night beautious, and her old face new. 12
    Loe thus by day my lims, by night my mind,
    For thee, and for my selfe, noe quiet finde.

––––––––––

2 *travaill* (a) travel (Cf. 50.2) (b) travail 3 *journy* (journey)
(b) a day's work 5 *from far* from afar, from the far place 6 *intend* (a) proceed on (as in *Pericles* 1.2.116: "I now . . . to Tarsus
Intend my travel") (b) mean (to make) 9 *imaginary* (b) imaginative, image-making (Cf. *King John* 4.2.265: "foul imaginary eyes
of blood Presented thee more hideous than thou art") 10 *their* thy?
(misprint? Or does *their* stand for *my thoughts?*) *shaddoe* (shadow)
(b) image 12 *blacke* (b) ugly (The OED does not recognize this
signification, but note the many lines in Shakespeare that depend for
their effect upon a punning opposition between "black" and "beauteous," like *Two Gentlemen of Verona* 5.2.112: "Black men are pearls,
in beauteous ladies' eyes") 14 *for* (b) because of

2 8

How can I then returne in happy plight
That am debard the benifit of rest?
When daies oppression is not eazd by night,
But day by night and night by day oprest.   4
And each (though enimes to ethers raigne)
Doe in consent shake hands to torture me,
The one by toyle, the other to complaine
How far I toyle, still farther off from thee.   8
I tell the Day to please him thou art bright,
And do'st him grace when clouds doe blot the heaven:
So flatter I the swart complexiond night,
When sparkling stars twire not thou guil'st th' eaven.   12
  But day doth daily draw my sorrowes longer,
  And night doth nightly make greefes length seeme
    stronger

-----

5 *ethers* (either's) each other's 6 *shake hands* i.e., join forces 12
twire (a) peep out (Cf. Jonson, *Sad Shepherd* 2.2: "Which maids
will twire at, 'tween their fingers") (b) wink (OED cites from
1601: "So hard a matter is it for a man to keepe his eies from twiring,
and many men naturally cannot chuse but be evermore winking and
twinckling with their eies") *guil'st* gildest *eaven* even, evening 14
length (Many modern editors unnecessarily emend to "strength")

When in disgrace with Fortune and mens eyes,
I all alone beweepe my out-cast state,
And trouble deafe heaven with my bootlesse cries,
And looke upon my selfe and curse my fate.　　　4
Wishing me like to one more rich in hope,
Featur'd like him, like him with friends possest,
Desiring this mans art, and that mans skope,
With what I most injoy contented least,　　　8
Yet in these thoughts my selfe almost despising,
Haplye I thinke on thee, and then my state,
(Like to the Larke at breake of daye arising)
From sullen earth sings himns at Heavens gate,　　　12
　　For thy sweet love remembred such welth brings,
　　That then I skorne to change my state with Kings.

2, 10, 14 *state* (a) condition (b) state of mind (c) fortune, estate
(Cf. *Merry Wives of Windsor* 3.4.5: "my state being galled with my
expense") (d) status, high rank (Cf. *Richard III* 3.7.204: "unfit for
state and majesty") 6 *featur'd* (a) fashioned, having features (b)
handsome (In George Turberville's 1567 translation of Ovid's *Hero-
ides,* a phrase meaning "beauty" is rendered as "featured face") 8 *injoy* (enjoy) (b) possess 10 *haplye* (a) by chance, perhaps (b)
happily 12 *sullen* (b) dark (Cf. *1 Henry IV* 1.2.234: "like bright
metal on a sullen ground")

3 0

When to the Sessions of sweet silent thought,
I sommon up remembrance of things past,
I sigh the lacke of many a thing I sought,
And with old woes new waile my deare times waste: 4
Then can I drowne an eye (un-us'd to flow)
For precious friends hid in deaths dateles night,
And weepe a fresh loves long since canceld woe,
And mone th'expence of many a vannisht sight.   8
Then can I greeve at greevances fore-gon,
And heavily from woe to woe tell ore
The sad account of fore-bemoned mone,
Which I new pay, as if not payd before.   12
    But if the while I thinke on thee (deare friend)
    All losses are restord, and sorrowes end.

---

1 *Sessions* (b) sittings of a law court 2 *sommon* call before a court
sommon up call to one's aid 4 *waste* (b) loss, destruction (*times
waste* implying both "waste of time" and "that which is destroyed by
time") 6 *dateles* (b) endless, without fixed limit (Cf. "date" as a
technical term in the law of contracts, 18.4 and *Lucrece* 26) 7 *woe*
(sometimes homonymous with "woo") 8 *expence* (b) loss (Cf.
Tourneur, *Revenger's Tragedy* 1.3: "Enter upon . . . her chastity,
And bring it into expense") 9 *fore-gon* past, gone before 10 *tell*
(b) count, reckon (Cf. *Venus & Adonis* 277: "trots, as if he told the
steps")

Thy bosome is indeared with all hearts,
Which I by lacking have supposed dead,
And there raignes Love and all Loves loving parts,
And all those friends which I thought buried.   4
How many a holy and obsequious teare
Hath deare religious love stolne from mine eye,
As interest of the dead, which now appeare,
But things remov'd that hidden in there lie.   8
Thou art the grave where buried love doth live,
Hung with the tropheis of my lovers gon,
Who all their parts of me to thee did give,
That due of many, now is thine alone.   12
　　Their images I lov'd, I view in thee,
　　And thou (all they) hast all the all of me.

---

1 *indeared* (b) made precious (OED cites from 1594: "Love . . .
endeareth the meanest things, and doubleth the estimate of things that
are precious") 2 *by lacking* because I lacked them 3 *parts* (b)
qualities (Cf. 17.4 and 37.7) (c) acts? (Cf. Sir Walter Ralegh, *Dis-
coverie of Guiana*: "For your . . . friendly parts, I have hitherto only
returned promises") 5 *obsequious* funereal, appropriate to obsequies
(Cf. *Titus Andronicus* 5.3.152: "shed obsequious tears upon this
trunk") 7 *interest* rightful due 7–8 *appeare, but* appear to be only
8 *there* (Most modern editors emend to *thee*) 11 *parts of me* shares
of me, claims upon me

If thou survive my well contented daie,
When that churle death my bones with dust shall cover
And shalt by fortune once more re-survay:
These poore rude lines of thy deceased Lover: 4
Compare them with the bett'ring of the time,
And though they be out-stript by every pen,
Reserve them for my love, not for their rime,
Exceeded by the hight of happier men.   8
Oh then voutsafe me but this loving thought,
Had my friends Muse growne with this growing age,
A dearer birth then this his love had brought
To march in ranckes of better equipage: 12
    But since he died and Poets better prove,
    Theirs for their stile ile read, his for his love.

---

1 *my well contented daie* (a) the day that will content me well
(b) the day on which I give full satisfaction for my debts (OED cites
a legal document of 1531: "the sommes now be not paide or otherwise contented") 3 *by fortune* (b) perchance, perhaps 7 *reserve*
keep (Cf. *Twelfth Night* 1.5.201: "for what is yours to bestow is not
yours to reserve") *rime* poetry (Cf. 17.14, 55.2, and 106.3) 8 *happier* more fortunate 9 *voutsafe* vouchsafe

33

Full many a glorious morning have I seene,
Flatter the mountaine tops with soveraine eie,
Kissing with golden face the meddowes greene;
Guilding pale streames with heavenly alcumy: 4
Anon permit the basest cloudes to ride,
With ougly rack on his celestiall face,
And from the for-lorne world his visage hide
Stealing unseene to west with this disgrace: 8
Even so my Sunne one early morne did shine,
With all triumphant splendor on my brow,
But out alack, he was but one houre mine,
The region cloude hath mask'd him from me now.   12
   Yet him for this, my love no whit disdaineth,
   Suns of the world may staine, whē heavens sun stainteh.

---

4 *alcumy* alchemy (by which ordinary materials are converted to gold) 5 *anon* soon 6 *ougly* ugly *rack* high cloud driven by the wind (Cf. *Hamlet* 2.2.505: "as we often see, against some storm . . . the rack stand still") 11 *out alack* alas 12 *region* (b) sky, air (usually with a qualifying adjective, as in "airy region," the airy part of the universe; but cf. *Hamlet* 2.2.509: "the dreadful thunder Doth rend the region") *region cloude* (a) cloud of the upper air? (The "upper" is added hopefully by commentators in order to avoid the vacantly obvious "cloud of the air," but the philological evidence for such a reading is not reassuring) (b) cloud covering the whole area in which I am located? (That is, "region" may be used here with its common modern signification of "area" but may be understood as the old uninflected genitive equivalent to "region's"—cf. "sun rise" and "heart throb." So too *Hamlet* 2.2.607: "I should have fatted all the region kites With this slave's offal.") 14 *whē* when *stainteh* staineth (misprint)

3 4

Why didst thou promise such a beautious day,
And make me travaile forth without my cloake,
To let bace cloudes ore-take me in my way,
Hiding thy brav'ry in their rotten smoke.   4
Tis not enough that through the cloude thou breake,
To dry the raine on my storme-beaten face,
For no man well of such a salve can speake,
That heales the wound, and cures not the disgrace: 8
Nor can thy shame give phisicke to my griefe,
Though thou repent, yet I have still the losse,
Th' offenders sorrow lends but weake reliefe
To him that beares the strong offenses losse.   12
    Ah but those teares are pearle which thy love sheeds,
    And they are ritch, and ransome all ill deeds.

---

2 *travaile* travel   3 *bace*   (b) somber, dark? (Cf. 100.4)   4 *brav'ry*
fine clothes (Cf. *Taming of the Shrew* 4.3.57: "scarfs and fans and
double change of bravery")   *rotten*   (b) unwholesome (Cf. *Coriolanus* 2.3.35: "rotten dews")   12 *losse* (Modern editors read "cross";
cf. 42.12)   13 *sheeds* sheds   14 *ransome* redeem, atone for (Cf.
120.14)

3 5

No more bee greev'd at that which thou hast done,
Roses have thornes, and silver fountaines mud,
Cloudes and eclipses staine both Moone and Sunne,
And loathsome canker lives in sweetest bud.   4
All men make faults, and even I in this,
Authorizing thy trespas with compare,
My selfe corrupting salving thy amisse,
Excusing their sins more then their sins are: 8
For to thy sensuall fault I bring in sence,
Thy adverse party is thy Advocate,
And gainst my selfe a lawfull plea commence,
Such civill war is in my love and hate,   12
    That I an accessary needs must be,
    To that sweet theefe which sourely robs from me,

---

3 *staine* (b) obscure the luster of (OED cites from 1594: "A small cloude in a cleare day may somewhat stayne, not wholy stop the Sunnes light") 4 *canker* a worm that devours blossoms 5 *make faults* commit offenses (Cf. *Richard II* 1.2.5: "those hands Which made the fault that we cannot correct") 6 *compare* metaphorical comparison (Cf. 21.5) 7 *amisse* misdeed (Cf. 151.3 and *Hamlet* 4.5.18: "Each toy seems Prologue to some great amiss") 8 *their . . . their* (usually emended to "thy . . . thy," although some editors prefer not to emend, taking *men* in line 5 to be the antecedent) 9 *in sence* (b) incense? 10 *adverse party* adversary

36

Let me confesse that we two must be twaine,
Although our undevided loves are one:
So shall those blots that do with me remaine,
Without thy helpe, by me be borne alone.   4
In our two loves there is but one respect,
Though in our lives a seperable spight,
Which though it alter not loves sole effect,
Yet doth it steale sweet houres from loves delight,   8
I may not ever-more acknowledge thee,
Least my bewailed guilt should do thee shame,
Nor thou with publike kindnesse honour me,
Unlesse thou take that honour from thy name: 12
   But doe not so, I love thee in such sort,
   As thou being mine, mine is thy good report.

---

1 *twaine* separated, estranged (Cf. *Troilus & Cressida* 3.1.111: "she'll none of him. They two are twain") 3 *blots* (b) disgraces (OED cites from 1587: "Without the blots of everlasting blame") 5 *but one respect* an undivided regard for one another 6 *seperable* sundering, that separates us *spight* (b) annoying matter, source of irritation (Cf. Jonson, *Every Man in His Humor* 1.3: "I ha' no boots, that's the spite on't") *seperable spight* (b) spiteful separation (For similar reversals of normal noun-adjective relationships, cf. 9.14, 51.1, 51.6, and 77.7) 14 *report* (a) reputation (Cf. *Much Ado About Nothing* 3.1.97: "foremost in report through Italy") (b) commendation (Cf. 83.5)

37

As a decrepit father takes delight,
To see his active childe do deeds of youth,
So I, made lame by Fortunes dearest spight
Take all my comfort of thy worth and truth.   4
For whether beauty, birth, or wealth, or wit,
Or any of these all, or all, or more
Intitled in their parts, do crowned sit,
I make my love ingrafted to this store: 8
So then I am not lame, poore, nor dispis'd,
Whilst that this shadow doth such substance give,
That I in thy abundance am suffic'd,
And by a part of all thy glory live: 12
    Looke what is best, that best I wish in thee,
    This wish I have, then ten times happy me.

---

4 *of* from   *truth* (b) loyalty, fidelity (Cf. 41.12)   7 *intitled in* (a) ennobled in (b) having a claim to (Cf. *Love's Labor's Lost* 5.2.821: "If this thou do deny, let our hands part, Neither intitled in the other's heart")   *their* (emended in most but not all editions to "thy") *parts* endowments, qualities (Cf. 17.4)   8 *store* abundance, wealth (Cf. 11.9)   13 *looke what* whatever (Cf. 9.9)

How can my Muse want subject to invent
While thou dost breath that poor'st into my verse,
Thine owne sweet argument, to excellent,
For every vulgar paper to rehearse: 4
Oh give thy selfe the thankes if ought in me,
Worthy perusal stand against thy sight,
For who's so dumbe that cannot write to thee,
When thou thy selfe dost give invention light?   8
Be thou the tenth Muse, ten times more in worth
Then those old nine which rimers invocate,
And he that calls on thee, let him bring forth
Eternal numbers to out-live long date.   12
   If my slight Muse doe please these curious daies,
   The paine be mine, but thine shal be the praise.

---

1 *want subject to invent* lack subject matter 2 *breath* breathe
poor'st pourest 3 *argument* theme, subject (Cf. 76.10) *to* too 4
paper piece of writing (Cf. 17.9) *rehearse* relate (Cf. *Winter's Tale*
5.2.68: "Like an old tale still, which will have matter to rehearse")
8 *invention* imagination (Cf. 103.7) 12 *numbers* verses (Cf. 17.6)
date term of existence (Cf. 123.5 and Lydgate, *Secrees of Old Phi-
lisoffres* 421: "to persevere and lastyn a long date") 13 *curious*
fastidious (OED cites from 1592: "Christ was not curious in his diet")

39

Oh how thy worth with manners may I singe,
When thou art all the better part of me?
What can mine owne praise to mine owne selfe bring;
And what is't but mine owne when I praise thee,   4
Even for this, let us devided live,
And our deare love loose name of single one,
That by this seperation I may give:
That due to thee which thou deserv'st alone: 8
Oh absence what a torment wouldst thou prove,
Were it not thy soure leisure gave sweet leave,
To entertaine the time with thoughts of love,
Which time and thoughts so sweetly dost deceive.   12
    And that thou teachest how to make one twaine,
    By praising him here who doth hence remaine.

---

6 *loose* lose   10 *soure* unpleasant (Cf. *2 Henry VI* 3.2.301: "Heart's discontent and sour affliction")   11 *entertaine* occupy, make entertaining (Cf. *Lucrece* 1361: "The weary time she cannot entertain") 12 *dost* (Some editions emend to "doth" or, oddly, to "do"; others understand *thou* of line 9 as the subject) *deceive* (b) wile away (Cf. Florio, *Second Frutes* 65: "Let us do something to deceive the time, and that we may not think it long")

40

Take all my loves, my love, yea take them all,
What hast thou then more then thou hadst before?
No love, my love, that thou maist true love call,
All mine was thine, before thou hadst this more: 4
Then if for my love, thou my love receivest,
I cannot blame thee, for my love thou usest,
But yet be blam'd, if thou this selfe deceavest
By wilfull taste of what thy selfe refusest.   8
I doe forgive thy robb'rie gentle theefe
Although thou steale thee all my poverty:
And yet love knowes it is a greater griefe
To beare loves wrong, then hates knowne injury.   12
   Lascivious grace in whom all il wel showes,
   Kill me with spights yet we must not be foes.

---

5 *for* (b) because of (Cf. 99.6)   6 *usest* (b) have sexual relations
with (Cf. 20.14)   8 *taste* (b) test, trial (Cf. *King Lear* 1.2.47: "he
wrote this but as an essay or taste of my virtue")   *what thy selfe refusest* i.e., what you actually disdain (Cf. *Much Ado* 4.1.186: "Refuse
me, hate me, torture me to death")

4 1

Those pretty wrongs that liberty commits,
When I am some-time absent from thy heart,
Thy beautie, and thy yeares full well befits,
For still temptation followes where thou art.   4
Gentle thou art, and therefore to be wonne,
Beautious thou art, therefore to be assailed.
And when a woman woes, what womans sonne,
Will sourely leave her till he have prevailed.   8
Aye me, but yet thou mighst my seate forbeare,
And chide thy beauty, and thy straying youth,
Who lead thee in their ryot even there
Where thou art forst to breake a two-fold truth: 12
   Hers by thy beauty tempting her to thee,
   Thine by thy beautie beeing false to me.

---

1 *pretty* (b) petty, trifling (Cf. Sir Thomas More, "Confutacyon of Tyndales Answere," *Works* 423.2: "I found in the tone some pretty peccadilians" [peccadilloes])   3 *befits* befit   4 *still* always (Cf. 47.12)   7 *woes* woos   8 *sourely* harshly, ill-naturedly (Cf. 35.14)   9 *seate* place (as in modern "country seat"; here used in a sexual sense. Cf. *Othello* 2.1.305: "I do suspect the lusty Moor Hath leaped into my seat")   *forbeare* leave alone (Cf. *Antony & Cleopatra* 2.7.44: "Forbear me till anon")   12 *truth* troth, loyalty (Cf. 152.10)

42

That thou hast her it is not all my griefe,
And yet it may be said I lov'd her deerely,
That she hath thee is of my wayling cheefe,
A losse in love that touches me more neerely.   4
Loving offendors thus I will excuse yee,
Thou doost love her, because thou knowst I love her,
And for my sake even so doth she abuse me,
Suffring my friend for my sake to approove her,   8
If I loose thee, my losse is my loves gaine,
And loosing her, my friend hath found that losse,
Both finde each other, and I loose both twaine,
And both for my sake lay on me this crosse,   12
    But here's the joy, my friend and I are one,
    Sweete flattery, then she loves but me alone.

---

3 *cheefe* i.e., chief cause, the most important part (OED cites a some-what similar passage from 1509: "The chefe is gone of all thy mel-ody")   4 *neerely* deeply (Cf. *Two Gentlemen of Verona* 3.1.60: "some affairs that touch me near")   7 *abuse* (b) betray, cuckold (Cf. *Othello* 3.3.267: "She's gone; I am abused; and my relief Must be to loathe her")   8 *approove* (b) test, try (OED cites from 1532: "approvinge it by experience")   14 *flattery* (b) wishful thinking, deception (Cf. 87.13)

43

When most I winke then doe mine eyes best see,
For all the day they view things unrespected,
But when I sleepe, in dreames they looke on thee,
And darkely bright, are bright in darke directed.   4
Then thou whose shaddow shaddowes doth make bright,
How would thy shadowes forme, forme happy show,
To the cleere day with thy much cleerer light,
When to un-seeing eyes thy shade shines so?   8
How would (I say) mine eyes be blessed made,
By looking on thee in the living day?
When in dead night their faire imperfect shade,
Through heavy sleepe on sightlesse eyes doth stay?   12
    All dayes are nights to see till I see thee,
    And nights bright daies when dreams do shew thee me,

---

1 *winke* close my eyes (Cf. Lyly, *Campaspe* 4.4: "Though I wink, I sleep not")   2 *unrespected* (b) unregarded, unnoticed (Cf. Sidney, *Arcadia* 3.28: "The last groan of his brother was the only answer he could get to his unrespected eloquence"; cf. also 54.10)   4 *darkely* (b) blindly (OED cites from 1576: "my dimme and darke eyesight") (c) mysteriously (OED cites from 1576: "This booke was . . . written of sett purpose very darkely")   5 *shaddow* dream-image (Cf. 27.10)   6 *shaddowes forme* i.e., body, the form that casts the shadow *forme happy show* create a delightful appearance (Cf. *Henry V* 3.6.88: "he would gladly make show to the world")   11 *their* (Most modern editors emend to "thy")   14 *me* to me

44

If the dull substance of my flesh were thought,
Injurious distance should not stop my way,
For then dispight of space I would be brought,
From limits farre remote, where thou doost stay,   4
No matter then although my foote did stand
Upon the farthest earth remoov'd from thee,
For nimble thought can jumpe both sea and land,
As soone as thinke the place where he would be.   8
But ah, thought kills me that I am not thought
To leape large lengths of miles when thou art gone,
But that so much of earth and water wrought,
I must attend, times leasure with my mone.   12
    Receiving naughts by elements so sloe,
    But heavie teares, badges of eithers woe.

---

1 *dull* sluggish (because composed of earth and water—see line 11; and cf. 51.2)   2 *stop my way* prevent me from coming (Cf. *Taming of the Shrew* 3.2.237: "I'll bring my action on the proudest he That stops my way")   3 *dispight of* in spite of (Cf. 3.12)   4 *where* to the place where   13 *naughts* nothing (Modern editors emend to "nought," but OED cites from 1586: "Thy crop of corn is tares availing naughts") *elements* i.e., earth and water   14 *eithers* (a) earth's and water's (because heavy and wet) (b) your and my

45

The other two, slight ayre, and purging fire,
Are both with thee, where ever I abide,
The first my thought, the other my desire,
These present absent with swift motion slide.   4
For when these quicker Elements are gone
In tender Embassie of love to thee,
My life being made of foure, with two alone,
Sinkes downe to death, opprest with melancholie.   8
Untill lives composition be recured,
By those swift messengers return'd from thee,
Who even but now come back againe assured,
Of their faire health, recounting it to me.   12
  This told, I joy, but then no longer glad,
  I send them back againe and straight grow sad.

---

1 *other two* (of the four "elements": earth, water, air, fire. The first
two are mentioned at the end of 44) *slight* insubstantial (Cf. Nashe,
Unfortunate Traveller 18: "he that could make a garment slightest
and thinnest") 4 *present absent* present-absent, now present and now
absent 7 *life* living being (Cf. *Macbeth* 5.8.2: "whiles I see lives")
8 *opprest* (b) weighed down (Cf. 28.3–4) *melancholie* (b) black
bile (one of the four essential fluids of the body, associated in Elizabethan medical theory with the element of earth; cf. *Much Ado*
2.1.357: "There's little of the melancholy element in her") 9 *lives*
life's *composition* constitution, make-up (Cf. Lyly, *Euphues* [Arber
ed.] 143: "A good composition of the body layeth a good foundation
of old age") *recured* restored (Cf. Spenser, *Faerie Queene* 1.9.2:
"When their powres . . . With dew repast they had recured well")
11 *even but now* at this very moment 12 *their* (Modern editors
emend to "thy")

46

Mine eye and heart are at a mortall warre,
How to devide the conquest of thy sight,
Mine eye, my heart their pictures sight would barre,
My heart, mine eye the freeedome of that right,   4
My heart doth plead that thou in him doost lye,
(A closet never pearst with christall eyes)
But the defendant doth that plea deny,
And sayes in him their faire appearance lyes.   8
To side this title is impannelled
A quest of thoughts, all tennants to the heart,
And by their verdict is determined
The cleere eyes moyitie, and the deare hearts part.   12
    As thus, mine eyes due is their outward part,
    And my hearts right, their inward love of heart.

---

2 *thy sight* the sight of you (Cf. 75.9) 3 *my heart . . . would barre*
i.e., would debar my heart from *their* (Modern editors emend to
"thy") 4 *mine eye* i.e., would debar my eye from *freeedome of*
(misprint) privilege of exercising 5 *plead* (b) argue, allege (as if
before a court; cf. other legal references in this sonnet) 8 *their* thy
(Cf. line 3) 9 *side* (a) decide (abbreviated form like "citall" for
"recital" in *1 Henry IV* 5.2.62: "He made a blushing citall of himselfe"; cf. also 53.8) (b) assign to one side or the other? (OED cites
only this example, but cf. other transitive uses of the verb, as in *Coriolanus* 1.1.197: "They'll . . . side factions . . . making parties strong")
10 *quest* inquest, jury (Cf. *Richard III* 1.4.193: "What lawful quest
have given their verdict up") 12 *moyitie* portion (not necessarily a
half; cf. *King Lear* 1.1.7: "neither can make choice of either's moiety")
13, 14 *their* thy (Cf. line 3)

47

Betwixt mine eye and heart a league is tooke,
And each doth good turnes now unto the other,
When that mine eye is famisht for a looke,
Or heart in love with sighes himselfe doth smother;　　4
With my loves picture then my eye doth feast,
And to the painted banquet bids my heart:
An other time mine eye is my hearts guest,
And in his thoughts of love doth share a part.　　8
So either by thy picture or my love,
Thy seife away, are present still with me,
For thou nor farther then my thoughts canst move,
And I am still with them, and they with thee.　　12
　　Or if they sleepe, thy picture in my sight
　　Awakes my heart, to hearts and eyes delight.

---

1 *league is tooke* alliance is made (Cf. *Richard III* 1.3.280: "I'll kiss thy hand In sign of league and amity with thee," and *King John* 3.1.17: "take a truce")　4 *or heart* or when my heart　10 *seife* self (misprint)　*are* art　11 *nor* no　12 *still* always (Cf. 126.10)

48

How carefull was I when I tooke my way,
Each trifle under truest barres to thrust,
That to my use it might un-used stay
From hands of falsehood, in sure wards of trust?   4
But thou, to whom my jewels trifles are,
Most worthy comfort, now my greatest griefe,
Thou best of deerest, and mine onely care,
Art left the prey of every vulgar theefe.   8
Thee have I not lockt up in any chest,
Save where thou art not, though I feele thou art,
Within the gentle closure of my brest,
From whence at pleasure thou maist come and part,   12
   And even thence thou wilt be stolne I feare,
   For truth prooves theevish for a prize so deare.

---

1 *tooke my way* set out on my journey (Cf. Chaucer, *Tale of Melibee*
[Robinson ed.] 1806: "And right anon they tooken hire wey to the
court")   2 *truest* most reliable (Cf. *Troilus & Cressida* 1.3.238:
"strong joints, true swords")   3 *to* for   4 *hands of falsehood* perfidi-
ous hands   5 *to* in comparison to (Cf. *Macbeth* 3.4.63: "flaws and
starts, Impostors to true fear")   7 *mine onely care* (a) my only
worry (b) the only thing I care about (The play of words depends
partly on the fact that *carus*, the Latin origin of "care," means "dear")
8 *vulgar* common   11 *closure* enclosure (Cf. the similar line in *Venus
& Adonis* 782: "Into the quiet closure of my breast")   14 *truth* honesty (Cf. *Venus & Adonis* 724: "Rich preys make true men thieves")

49

Against that time (if ever that time come)
When I shall see thee frowne on my defects,
When as thy love hath cast his utmost summe,
Cauld to that audite by advis'd respects,   4
Against that time when thou shalt strangely passe,
And scarcely greete me with that sunne thine eye,
When love converted from the thing it was
Shall reasons finde of setled gravitie.   8
Against that time do I insconce me here
Within the knowledge of mine owne desart,
And this my hand, against my selfe upreare,
To guard the lawfull reasons on thy part,   12
    To leave poore me, thou hast the strength of lawes,
    Since why to love, I can alledge no cause.

---

1 *against* in anticipation of (Cf. 13.3)   3 *when as* when   *cast* (a) calculated (Cf. *2 Henry VI* 4.2.97: "write and read and cast accompt") (b) thrown away (Cf. *Othello* 1.1.150: "the state . . . Cannot with safety cast him")   4 *Cauld* called   *advis'd* (b) cautious, careful *respects* (a) reflections, considerations (Cf. *King John* 4.2.214: "perchance it frowns More upon humour than advised respect") (b) marks of deference for high rank (Cf. Bacon's essay "Of Ceremonies and Respects")   5 *strangely* (b) as a stranger, coldly (Cf. *2 Henry IV* 5.2.63: "You all look strangely on me")   7 *converted* (a) changed (b) turned away (Cf. 7.11)   8 *of* (b) for (Cf. *Henry V* 4.1.113: "he sees reason of fears")   9 *insconce* (b) shelter behind a fortication (A "sconce" was a small earthwork, as in *Henry V* 3.6.78)   11 *hand* handwriting *upreare* (a) raise in taking an oath as a witness (b) raise in violence (Cf. *2 Henry IV* 4.1.214: "the arm That was upreared to execution")

5 0

How heavie doe I journey on the way,
When what I seeke (my wearie travels end)
Doth teach that ease and that repose to say
Thus farre the miles are measurde from thy friend.　　4
The beast that beares me, tired with my woe,
Plods duly on, to beare that waight in me,
As if by some instinct the wretch did know
His rider lov'd not speed being made from thee:　　8
The bloody spurre cannot provoke him on,
That some-times anger thrusts into his hide,
Which heavily he answers with a grone,
More sharpe to me then spurring to his side,　　12
　　For that same grone doth put this in my mind,
　　My greefe lies onward and my joy behind.

---

1 *heavie* (a) sadly (Cf. *Love's Labor's Lost* 5.2.14: "He made her
melancholy, sad, and heavy") (b) slowly (Cf. *Midsummer Night's
Dream* 5.1.377: "The heavy gait of night") 2 *travels* (b) travail's
(Cf. 27.2; both words were spelled both ways in Elizabethan English) 6 *duly* (dully) slowly (Cf. 51.2)

5 I

Thus can my love excuse the slow offence,
Of my dull bearer, when from thee I speed,
From where thou art, why shoulld I hast me thence,
Till I returne of posting is noe need.   4
O what excuse will my poore beast then find,
When swift extremity can seeme but slow,
Then should I spurre though mounted on the wind,
In winged speed no motion shall I know,   8
Then can no horse with my desire keepe pace,
Therefore desire (of perfects love being made)
Shall naigh noe dull flesh in his fiery race,
But love, for love, thus shall excuse my jade,   12
    Since from thee going he went wilfull slow,
    Towards thee ile run, and give him leave to goe.

---

1 *slow offence* (b) offensive slowness (Cf. 36.6) 2 *bearer* horse (Cf. 50.5) 4 *posting* riding with great speed (Cf. *Comedy of Errors* 3.2.152: "Go hie thee presently, post to the road." The modern meaning of "rising rhythmically in the saddle" was unknown to Shakespeare) 6 *swift extremity* (b) extreme swiftness (Cf. 36.6) 8 *know* perceive 10 *perfects* perfect'st? perfect? (misprint) 11 *naigh* (doubtless a misprint for something akin to "need" or "wait for") 14 *goe* walk (Cf. 130.11)

5 2

So am I as the rich whose blessed key,
Can bring him to his sweet up-locked treasure,
The which he will not ev'ry hower survay,
For blunting the fine point of seldome pleasure.   4
Therefore are feasts so sollemne and so rare,
Since sildom comming in the long yeare set,
Like stones of worth they thinly placed are,
Or captaine Jewells in the carconet.   8
So is the time that keepes you as my chest,
Or as the ward-robe which the robe doth hide,
To make some speciall instant speciall blest,
By new unfoulding his imprison'd pride.   12
    Blessed are you whose worthinesse gives skope,
    Being had to tryumph, being lackt to hope.

---

1 *rich* rich man (Cf. *King James Bible,* Proverbs 14.20: "The poor is hated even of his own neighbor, but the rich hath many friends") 4 *for* for fear of (Cf. *Two Gentlemen of Verona* 1.2.133: "here they shall not lie, for catching cold") *seldome* infrequent 5 *sollemne* (b) marked by special ceremonies (Cf. *Two Gentlemen of Verona* 5.4.161: "triumphs, mirth, and rare solemnity") 8 *captaine* principal (OED cites from 1566: "A manifest and Captain Untruthe") *carconet* (carcanet) necklace 12 *his* its

53

What is your substance, whereof are you made,
That millions of strange shaddowes on you tend?
Since every one, hath every one, one shade,
And you but one, can every shaddow lend: 4
Describe *Adonis* and the counterfet,
Is poorely immitated after you,
On *Hellens* cheeke all art of beautie set,
And you in *Grecian* tires are painted new: 8
Speake of the spring, and foyzon of the yeare,
The one doth shaddow of your beautie show,
The other as your bountie doth appeare,
And you in every blessed shape we know.   12
    In all externall grace you have some part,
    But you like none, none you for constant heart.

---

2 *strange* (b) not your own (Cf. *Love's Labor's Lost* 4.2.134: "One Monsieur Berowne, one of the strange queen's lords") *shaddowes* (b) images, likenesses (Cf. *Lucrece* 1366 and 1457: "a piece Of skilful painting"; "On this sad shadow Lucrece spends her eyes") *on you tend* wait on you, follow you like servants (Cf. 57.1)   3 *one, hath* one hath,   4 *you but* you, but   5 *counterfet* (Read without comma) image, description (Cf. 16.8)   8 *tires* clothing, attire? (Cf. similar instances of aphaeresis in "bove" for "above," *Macbeth* 3.5.31, and "bout" for "about," *Tempest* 1.2.220; cf. also 46.9)   9 *foyzon* rich harvest

55

54

Oh how much more doth beautie beautious seeme,
By that sweet ornament which truth doth give,
The Rose lookes faire, but fairer we it deeme
For that sweet odor, which doth in it live: 4
The Canker bloomes have full as deepe a die,
As the perfumed tincture of the Roses,
Hang on such thornes, and play as wantonly,
When sommers breath their masked buds discloses: 8
But for their virtue only is their show,
They live unwoo'd, and unrespected fade,
Die to themselves. Sweet Roses doe not so,
Of their sweet deathes, are sweetest odors made: 12
    And so of you, beautious and lovely youth,
    When that shall vade, by verse distils your truth.

---

2 *by* because of (Cf. *3 Henry VI* 4.4.12: "The bishop of York, Fell
Warwick's brother and, by that, our foe") *truth* (b) fidelity (Cf.
14.11) 5 *Canker bloomes* canker roses, scentless wild roses (Cf.
Much Ado 1.3.28: "I had rather be a canker in a hedge than a rose in
his grace") 7 *such* like, similar *wantonly* (b) sportively, playfully
(Cf. *Love's Labor's Lost* 5.2.771: "All wanton as a child") (c) luxuri-
antly (Cf. *Midsummer Night's Dream* 2.1.99: "quaint mazes in the
wanton green") 8 *discloses* (b) unfolds (Cf. *Hamlet* 1.3.40: "before their buttons be disclosed") 9 *for* because (Cf. 40.6) 10 *unrespected* (b) unnoticed (Cf. 43.2) 11 *to themselves* (a) alone, in
isolation (b) without benefit to others (Cf. 94.10 and Clarendon, *Collection of Several Tracts* 293: "They live to and within themselves")
14 *vade* (a) perish (Cf. Lady Mary Wroth, *Countesse of Mount-
gomeries Urania* 22: "the flowers vade, and grass die") (b) fade (Cf.
Richard II 1.2.20: "his summer leaves all vaded") *by* (Most modern
editors emend to "my")

5 5

Not marble, nor the guilded monument,
Of Princes shall out-live this powrefull rime,
But you shall shine more bright in these contents
Then unswept stone, besmeer'd with sluttish time.　　　　4
When wastefull warre shall *Statues* over-turne,
And broiles roote out the worke of masonry,
Nor *Mars* his sword, nor warres quick fire shall burne:
The living record of your memory.　　　　8
Gainst death, and all oblivious emnity
Shall you pace forth, your praise shall stil finde roome,
Even in the eyes of all posterity
That weare this world out to the ending doome.　　　　12
　　So til the judgement that your selfe arise,
　　You live in this, and dwell in lovers eies.

---

2 *rime* poetry　4 *besmeer'd* besmeared (Cf. *Lucrece* 939–945: "Time's
glory is to . . . smear with dust their glittering golden towers")
sluttish filthy, disgustingly untidy　5 *wastefull* destructive　6 *broiles*
conflicts　7 *Mars his* Mars's (a fairly common Elizabethan genitive,
as in Jonson's phrase about his son: "Ben Jonson his best piece of poetry")　9 *oblivious emnity* enmity (misprint) which causes oblivion
(Cf. *Macbeth* 5.3.43: "some sweet oblivious antidote")　12 *doome*
(a) doomsday　(b) sentence, judgment (Cf. 107.4)　13 *that* (b)
when (Cf. *Midsummer Night's Dream* 4.1.133: "Now it is the time of
night That the graves all gaping wide, Every one lets forth his sprite")

56

Sweet love renew thy force, be it not said
Thy edge should blunter be then apetite,
Which but too daie by feeding is alaied,
To morrow sharpned in his former might.   4
So love be thou, although too daie thou fill
Thy hungrie eies, even till they winck with fulnesse,
Too morrow see againe, and doe not kill
The spirit of Love, with a perpetual dulnesse: 8
Let this sad *Intrim* like the Ocean be
Which parts the shore, where two contracted new,
Come daily to the banckes, that when they see:
Returne of love, more blest may be the view.   12
    As cal it Winter, which being ful of care,
    Makes Sõmers welcome, thrice more wish'd, more rare.

------

3 *but* only for *too daie* today *alaied* allayed 4 *in* to 6 *winck*
(b) close (Cf. 43.1) 10 *contracted new* newly betrothed (Cf. 1.5)
13 *as* or

57

Being your slave what should I doe but tend,
Upon the houres, and times of your desire?
I have no precious time at al to spend;
Nor services to doe til you require.   4
Nor dare I chide the world without end houre,
Whilst I (my soveraine) watch the clock for you,
Nor thinke the bitternesse of absence sowre,
When you have bid your servant once adieue.   8
Nor dare I question with my jealious thought,
Where you may be, or your affaires suppose,
But like a sad slave stay and thinke of nought
Save where you are, how happy you make those.   12
    So true a foole is love, that in your Will,
    (Though you doe any thing) he thinkes no ill.

---

1 *tend* wait (with servile associations; cf. *Hamlet* 1.3.83: "Go, your servants tend") 5 *world without end* endless (usually printed as a hyphenated compound; cf. *Love's Labor's Lost* 5.2.799. Cf. also *Book of Common Prayer*, Matins: "As it was in the beginning, is now, and ever shall be, world without end") 9 *jealious* (jealous) (b) suspicious 13 *Will* (b) sexual appetite (Cf. *Lucrece* 247: "Thus . . . holds he disputation, 'Tween frozen conscience and hot burning will") (c) William (Note the double grammar that permits the two readings of "love thinks there is no ill in your will" and "William's love thinks no ill, no matter what you do")

5 8

That God forbid, that made me first your slave,
I should in thought controule your times of pleasure,
Or at your hand th' account of houres to crave,
Being your vassail bound to staie your leisure. 4
Oh let me suffer (being at your beck)
Th' imprison'd absence of your libertie,
And patience tame, to sufferance bide each check,
Without accusing you of injury. 8
Be where you list, your charter is so strong,
That you your selfe may priviledge your time
To what you will, to you it doth belong,
Your selfe to pardon of selfe-doing crime. 12
   I am to waite, though waiting so be hell,
   Not blame your pleasure be it ill or well.

---

3 *th' account of* accounting for *to crave* should ask to know 4 *staie* wait for, wait upon (Cf. *Midsummer Night's Dream* 2.1.235: "I will not stay thy questions; let me go") 7 *patience . . . check* (Most editors repunctuate, setting *tame to sufferance* off with commas. The MS almost certainly had no punctuation at all in the line; hence both readings are possible) *bide* endure 9 *charter* privilege, right (Cf. *As You Like It* 2.7.48: "I must have liberty Withal, as large a charter as the wind" 10–11 *priviledge . . . to* authorize to be used for 12 *selfe-doing* (a) committed by yourself (b) done to yourself

59

If their bee nothing new, but that which is,
Hath beene before, how are our braines beguild,
Which laboring for invention beare amisse
The second burthen of a former child? 4
Oh that record could with a back-ward looke,
Even of five hundreth courses of the Sunne,
Show me your image in some antique booke,
Since minde at first in carrecter was done. 8
That I might see what the old world could say,
To this composed wonder of your frame,
Whether we are mended, or where better they,
Or whether revolution be the same. 12
    Oh sure I am the wits of former daies,
    To subjects worse have given admiring praise.

---

1 *is* (Read without comma) 3 *invention* creation of something new
(Cf. 105.11) *amisse* (a) mistakenly (b) improperly (*beare amisse*
thus meaning "miscarry") 5 *record* memory (Cf. *Twelfth Night*
5.1.253: "O that record is lively in my soul") 6 *hundreth* hundred
8 *carrecter* (character) writing 10 *composed* well put together (Cf.
Two Gentlemen of Verona 3.2.69: "By wailful sonnets whose composed rhymes Should be fraught with serviceable vows") 11 *where*
(b) whether (Cf. *Venus & Adonis* 304: "And where he run or fly,
They know not whether") 12 *revolution* change (i.e., supposedly
different things; cf. *2 Henry IV* 3.1.45: "O God, that one might
read the book of fate And see the revolution of the times")

60

Like as the waves make towards the pibled shore,
So do our minuites hasten to their end,
Each changing place with that which goes before,
In sequent toile all forwards do contend.   4
Nativity once in the maine of light.
Crawles to maturity, wherewith being crown'd,
Crooked eclipses gainst his glory fight,
And time that gave, doth now his gift confound.   8
Time doth transfixe the florish set on youth,
And delves the paralels in beauties brow,
Feedes on the rarities of natures truth,
And nothing stands but for his sieth to mow.   12
    And yet to times in hope, my verse shall stand
    Praising thy worth, dispight his cruell hand.

---

1 *pibled* pebbled   4 *sequent* following one after another   5 *nativity*
(a) birth (Cf. *Comedy of Errors* 4.4.32: "I have served him from the
hour of my nativity")   (b) the newborn child? (Shakespeare often
used the abstract in place of the concrete, as in 138.12: "And age in
love, loves not t'have years told")   (c) the fortune determined by the
stars at birth, the horoscope (Cf. *King Lear* 1.2.140: "My nativity was
under Ursa Major")   *maine* (a) sea   (b) main body (Cf. *Hamlet*
4.4.15: "against the main of Poland")   7 *crooked* malignant   8 *confound* destroy   9 *transfixe* pierce through   *florish* (a) bloom (OED
cites: "The tree is first seene in the budde and then in the flourish")
(b) embellishment (particularly in calligraphy)   11 *rarities* (b)
wonders   *truth* (perhaps a corruption in the text, but note that
"true" sometimes means "well-proportioned," as in 62.6)   13 *in hope*
i.e., of the future

6 1

Is it thy wil, thy Image should keepe open
My heavy eielids to the weary night?
Dost thou desire my slumbers should be broken,
While shadowes like to thee do mocke my sight?   4
Is it thy spirit that thou send'st from thee
So farre from home into my deeds to prye,
To find out shames and idle houres in me,
The skope and tenure of thy Jelousie?   8
O no, thy love though much, is not so great,
It is my love that keepes mine eie awake,
Mine owne true love that doth my rest defeat,
To plaie the watch-man ever for thy sake.   12
    For thee watch I, whilst thou dost wake elsewhere,
    From me farre of, with others all to neere.

---

7 *shames* things to be ashamed of 8 *skope* (b) object, aim (Cf.
Richard II 3.3.112: "His coming hither hath no further scope Than
. . .) *tenure* purport, intent (Cf. *2 Henry IV* 4.1.8: "letters from
Northumberland; Their cold intent, tenure and substance, thus")
11 *defeat* ruin (Cf. *Othello* 4.2.160: "His unkindness may defeat my
life")

62

Sinne of selfe-love possesseth al mine eie,
And all my soule, and al my every part;
And for this sinne there is no remedie,
It is so grounded inward in my heart.   4
Me thinkes no face so gratious is as mine,
No shape so true, no truth of such account,
And for my selfe mine owne worth do define,
As I all other in all worths surmount.   8
But when my glasse shewes me my selfe indeed
Beated and chopt with tand antiquitie,
Mine owne selfe love quite contrary I read
Selfe, so selfe loving were iniquity,   12
   T'is thee (my selfe) that for my selfe I praise,
   Painting my age with beauty of thy daies,

---

6 *true* well-proportioned (Cf. *King Lear* 1.2.8: "my shape as true As honest madam's issue") 8 *as* in such a way that 10 *beated* (a) beaten, battered? (This form appears nowhere else in Shakespeare) (b) scraped, flayed? (Cf. the agricultural usage, "to slice off the rough sod from the ground"; OED cites from 1534: "They must go beate theyr landes with mattockes." But note that "beat" was sometimes pronounced like "bate" and "bait," and cf. OED articles on those words for other apposite meanings) 10 *tand* tanned, leathery 12 *selfe* (Read without comma)

63

Against my love shall be as I am now
With times injurious hand chrusht and ore-worne,
When houres have dreind his blood and fild his brow
With lines and wrincles, when his youthfull morne   4
Hath travaild on to Ages steepie night,
And all those beauties whereof now he's King
Are vanishing, or vanisht out of sight,
Stealing away the treasure of his Spring.   8
For such a time do I now fortifie
Against confounding Ages cruell knife,
That he shall never cut from memory
My sweet loves beauty, though my lovers life.   12
   His beautie shall in these blacke lines be seene,
   And they shall live, and he in them still greene.

---

1 *against* in provision for the time when (Cf. 49.1) 2 *chrusht* crushed
ore-worne worn out 5 *travaild* (a) traveled (b) travailed (for the
double meaning, cf. 27.2) *steepie* steep, precipitous (Cf. Donne,
Biathanatos [1644 ed.] 216: "the limits are obscure, and steepy, and
slippery, and narrow." M. M. Mahood suggests that the meaning
"steeped in die" is also implied here) 9 *fortifie* establish a position
of defense (OED cites from 1576: "Sailing up the River of Thamise,
he fortifieth at Middleton") 10 *confounding* destroying, defeating
(Cf. 60.8) 12 *though* i.e., even though he cuts 13 *blacke* (b) ugly
(paradoxical with *beautie;* cf. 27.12) 14 *still* always *greene* (shall)
be green (OED cites from 1612: "Freestone greeneth presently with
the first wet and raine")

When I have seene by times fell hand defaced
The rich proud cost of outworne buried age,
When sometime loftie towers I see downe rased,
And brasse eternall slave to mortall rage. 4
When I have seene the hungry Ocean gaine
Advantage on the Kingdome of the shoare,
And the firme soile win of the watry maine,
Increasing store with losse, and losse with store. 8
When I have seene such interchange of state,
Or state it selfe confounded, to decay,
Ruine hath taught me thus to ruminate
That Time will come and take my love away. 12
   This thought is as a death which cannot choose
   But weepe to have, that which it feares to loose.

---

2 *cost* costly creation (Cf. *2 Henry IV* 1.3.60: "leaves his part-created cost A naked subject to the weeping clouds") 3 *sometime loftie* (a) sometimes lofty (b) sometime-lofty 4 *mortall* (b) deadly 7 *win of* gain an advantage over (Cf. *Cymbeline* 1.1.121: "So in our trifles I still win of you") 8 *store* the amount possessed 10 *state* stateliness, grandeur (Cf. 29) *confounded* deteriorated (Cf. *Henry V* 3.1.13: "as doth a galled rock O'erhang and jutty his confounded base") 14 *to have* that it has

65

Since brasse, nor stone, nor earth, nor boundlesse sea,
But sad mortallity ore-swaies their power,
How with this rage shall beautie hold a plea,
Whose action is no stronger then a flower?   4
O how shall summers hunny breath hold out,
Against the wrackfull siedge of battring dayes,
When rocks impregnable are not so stoute,
Nor gates of steele so strong but time decayes?   8
O fearefull meditation, where alack,
Shall times best Jewell from times chest lie hid?
Or what strong hand can hold his swift foote back,
Or who his spoile or beautie can forbid?   12
    O none, unlesse this miracle have might,
    That in black inck my love may still shine bright.

---

1 *since* i.e., since there is no (Cf. *Richard III* 2.1.84: "and no one in
this presence But his red color hath forsook his cheeks")   3 *rage* (a)
violent force (OED cites from 1562: "The rage of fyre is swaged with
water")   (b) sensual appetite (Cf. folio version of *Richard III*
3.5.82: "his raging eye," for which the quarto has "lustful")   *hold a
plea* (b) try a legal action (OED cites from 1576: "a court in which
they hold plea of all causes and actions")   4 *action* (a) force   (b)
legal cases, legal grounds (Cf. preceding quotation)   5 *hunny* honey
6 *wrackfull* destructive, wrecking (Cf. Spenser, *Faerie Queene* 6.8.36:
"wreckful wind")   10 *chest* (a) coffer, jewel casket (Cf. 52.9)   (b)
coffin (Cf. the anonymous *Return from Parnassus* 1.2.13: "Let all
his faults sleep with his mournful chest")   12 *spoile* (a) ruin, destruction (Cf. *1 Henry IV* 3.3.11: "Company, villainous company,
hath been the spoil of me")   (b) plunder (Cf. *1 Henry IV* 1.1.74: "Is
not this an honorable spoil? A gallant prize?")   *or* of (misprint)   14
still always

66

Tyr'd with all these for restfull death I cry,
As to behold desert a begger borne,
And needie Nothing trimd in jollitie,
And purest faith unhappily forsworne,⠀⠀⠀⠀⠀⠀⠀⠀4
And gilded honor shamefully misplast,
And maiden vertue rudely strumpeted,
And right perfection wrongfully disgrac'd,
And strength by limping sway disabled,⠀⠀⠀⠀⠀⠀8
And arte made tung-tide by authoritie,
And Folly (Doctor-like) controuling skill,
And simple-Truth miscalde Simplicitie,
And captive-good attending Captaine ill.⠀⠀⠀⠀⠀12
⠀⠀Tyr'd with all these, from these would I be gone,
⠀⠀Save that to dye, I leave my love alone.

---

2 *desert* i.e., those deserving of a reward⠀⠀3 *Nothing* worthless person (Cf. *Cymbeline* 3.4.135: "That harsh, noble, simple nothing, That Cloten")⠀⠀*trimd* arrayed⠀⠀*jollitie* finery (OED cites from 1698: "The Jollity and Pomp of the Heathens is much allayed by the Puritanism . . . of the Moors")⠀⠀4 *unhappily* maliciously (OED cites from 1549: "They thynke unhappeliest in their herts whan they speake smotheliest with their toungs")⠀⠀*forsworne* (a) abandoned, renounced (Cf. *Passionate Pilgrim* 33: "A woman I forswore") (b) perjured, guilty of breaking an oath⠀⠀5 *misplast* misplaced⠀⠀7 *right* real, true (Lyly writes in *Euphues* 191: "A right gentleman is sooner seen by the trial of his virtue")⠀⠀8 *sway* management, direction⠀⠀11 *Simplicitie* simple-mindedness⠀⠀14 *to dye* by dying

67

Ah wherefore with infection should he live,
And with his presence grace impietie,
That sinne by him advantage should atchive,
And lace it selfe with his societie?   4
Why should false painting immitate his cheeke,
And steale dead seeing of his living hew?
Why should poore beautie indirectly seeke,
Roses of shaddow, since his Rose is true?   8
Why should he live, now nature banckrout is,
Beggerd of blood to blush through lively vaines,
For she hath no exchecker now but his,
And proud of many, lives upon his gaines?   12
    O him she stores, to show what welth she had,
    In daies long since, before these last so bad.

---

1 *infection* corruption   3 *atchive* achieve   5 *painting* cosmetics (Cf.
20.1)   6 *dead seeing* the lifeless semblance (Some editors emend to
"seeming")   8 *roses of shaddow* mere images of roses?   9 *banckrout*
bankrupt   10 *beggerd of* destitute of, lacking (Cf. *Hamlet* 4.5.92:
"necessity, of matter beggered")   12 *proud of many* i.e., proud of a
multitude of beautiful things   13 *stores* preserves (Cf. 68.13)

Thus is his cheeke the map of daies out-worne,
When beauty liv'd and dy'ed as flowers do now,
Before these bastard signes of faire were borne,
Or durst inhabit on a living brow: 4
Before the goulden tresses of the dead,
The right of sepulchers, were shorne away,
To live a scond life on second head,
Ere beauties dead fleece made another gay: 8
In him those holy antique howers are seene,
Without all ornament, it selfe and true,
Making no summer of an others greene,
Robbing no ould to dresse his beauty new,   12
   And him as for a map doth Nature store,
   To shew faulse Art what beauty was of yore.

---

1 *out-worne* past (Cf. 64.2)   3 *bastard* counterfeit (Cf. *Comedy of Errors* 3.2.19: "Shame hath a bastard fame")   *faire* beauty (Cf. 18.7) 6 *the right of* rightfully belonging to (Cf. 46.14)   7 *scond* second (misprint)   9 *howers* hours   13 *store* keep (Cf. 67.13)

69

Those parts of thee that the worlds eye doth view,
Want nothing that the thought of hearts can mend:
All toungs (the voice of soules) give thee that end,
Uttring bare truth, even so as foes Commend.   4
Their outward thus with outward praise is crownd,
But those same toungs that give thee so thine owne,
In other accents doe this praise confound
By seeing farther then the eye hath showne.   8
They looke into the beauty of thy mind,
And that in guesse they measure by thy deeds,
Then churls their thoughts (although their eies were kind)
To thy faire flower ad the rancke smell of weeds,   12
   But why thy odor matcheth not thy show,
   The solye is this, that thou doest common grow.

---

3 *end* (probably a printer's error for the MS "due"; usually so emended)   4 *even so as foes Commend* exactly as enemies praise (i.e., faintly)   5 *their* (almost always emended to "thy")   6 *thine owne* i.e., your due   7 *confound* (b) destroy (OED cites from 1570: "Archimedes . . . utterly confounded the Roman Navy")   14 *solye* fault? (a misprint that has been variously but never happily emended to "soil," "sole," or "solve")

That thou are blam'd shall not be thy defect,
For slanders marke was ever yet the faire,
The ornament of beauty is suspect,
A Crow that flies in heavens sweetest ayre.   4
So thou be good, slander doth but approve,
Their worth the greater beeing woo'd of time,
For Canker vice the sweetest buds doth love,
And thou present'st a pure unstayined prime.   8
Thou hast past by the ambush of young daies,
Either not assayld, or victor beeing charg'd,
Yet this thy praise cannot be soe thy praise,
To tye up envy, evermore inlarged,   12
    If some suspect of ill maskt not thy show,
    Then thou alone kingdomes of hearts shouldst owe.

---

1 *defect* fault 3 *suspect* suspicion (Cf. *Comedy of Errors* 3.1.87:
"draw within the compass of suspect The . . . honor of your wife")
5 *approve* prove (Cf. *Merchant of Venice* 3.2.79: "approve it with a
text") 6 *their* thy (misprint) 7 *Canker vice* disease of flowers
thought to be caused by canker worm (Cf. 35.4) 8 *unstayined* un-
stained 10 *charg'd* attacked 11 *soe* so much 12 *to* as to (Cf.
Henry VIII 3.1.85: "Though he be grown so desperate to be honest")
inlarged at liberty (Cf. *Henry V* 2.2.40: "Enlarge the man committed
yesterday") 13 *show* appearance (Cf. 43.6) 14 *owe* own (Cf.
18.10)

Noe Longer mourne for me when I am dead,
Then you shall heare the surly sullen bell
Give warning to the world that I am fled
From this vile world with vildest wormes to dwell: 4
Nay if you read this line, remember not,
The hand that writ it, for I love you so,
That I in your sweet thoughts would be forgot,
If thinking on me then should make you woe.   8
O if (I say) you looke upon this verse,
When I (perhaps) compounded am with clay,
Do not so much as my poore name reherse;
But let your love even with my life decay.   12
   Least the wise world should looke into your mone,
   And mocke you with me after I am gon.

———————

2 *then* than   4 *vildest* vilest (Both forms were common in Elizabethan English)   8 *woe* woeful (Cf. *Tempest* 5.1.139: "I am woe
for't")   11 *reherse* utter (Cf. *Richard II* 5.3.128: "Pity may move
thee 'pardon' to rehearse")   13 *least* lest   *mone* (moan) grief (Cf.
1 Henry VI 2.3.44: "Thy mirth shall turn to moan")

72

O least the world should taske you to recite,
What merit liv'd in me that you should love
After my death (deare love) for get me quite,
For you in me can nothing worthy prove.   4
Unlesse you would devise some vertuous lye,
To doe more for me then mine owne desert,
And hang more praise upon deceased I,
Then nigard truth would willingly impart: 8
O least your true love may seeme falce in this,
That you for love speake well of me untrue,
My name be buried where my body is,
And live no more to shame nor me, nor you.   12
 For I am shamd by that which I bring forth,
 And so should you, to love things nothing worth.

----

1 *least* lest (Cf. 71.13) *taske* challenge (Cf. *Richard II* 4.1.52: "I task the earth to the like") 10 *untrue* untruly 14 *should you* should you be

That time of yeeare thou maist in me behold,
  When yellow leaves, or none, or few doe hange
  Upon those boughes which shake against the could,
  Bare rn'wd quiers, where late the sweet birds sang.   4
In me thou seest the twi-light of such day,
  As after Sun-set fadeth in the West,
  Which by and by blacke night doth take away,
  Deaths second selfe that seals up all in rest.   8
In me thou seest the glowing of such fire,
  That on the ashes of his youth doth lye,
  As the death bed, whereon it must expire,
  Consum'd with that which it was nurrisht by.   12
    This thou percev'st, which makes thy love more strong.
    To love that well, which thou must leave ere long.

---

4 *rn'wd* ruin'd (misprint)   *quiers* choirs (of churches, where services are sung)   10 *that* as (Cf. *Hamlet* 3.4.40: "Such an act That blurs the grace and blush of modesty")   *his* its

74

But be contented when that fell arest,
With out all bayle shall carry me away,
My life hath in this line some interest,
Which for memoriall still with thee shall stay.   4
When thou revewest this, thou doest revew,
The very part was consecrate to thee,
The earth can have but earth, which is his due,
My spirit is thine the better part of me,   8
So then thou hast but lost the dregs of life,
The pray of wormes, my body being dead,
The coward conquest of a wretches knife,
To base of thee to be remembred,   12
    The worth of that, is that which it containes,
    And that is this, and this with thee remaines.

---

1 *fell* cruel (Cf. *3 Henry VI* 2.6.72: "we devise fell tortures for thy faults") *arest* arrest (i.e., death; cf. *Hamlet* 5.2.347: "this fell sergeant, Death, Is strict in his arrest") 3 *this line* i.e., these lines of poetry (Cf. 71.5) *interest* (b) part, share (Cf. *Richard III* 2.2.47: "so much interest have I in thy sorrow") 4 *still* always (Cf. 55.10) 12 *to* too 13 *that* i.e., the body 14 *this* i.e., my spirit (the part *consecrate to thee*, which is expressed in the poem)

7 5

So are you to my thoughts as food to life,
Or as sweet season'd shewers are to the ground;
And for the peace of you I hold such strife,
As twixt a miser and his wealth is found.   4
Now proud as an injoyer, and anon
Doubting the filching age will steale his treasure,
Now counting best to be with you alone,
Then betterd that the world may see my pleasure,   8
Some-time all ful with feasting on your sight,
And by and by cleane starved for a looke,
Possessing or pursuing no delight
Save what is had, or must from you be tooke.   12
    Thus do I pine and surfet day by day,
      Or gluttoning on all, or all away,

---

2 *sweet season'd* (a) sweet-spiced, sweet-scented (b) of the sweet season, springtime *shewers* showers   3 *peace* (puns on "piece," a coin; cf. Jonson, *Devil Is an Ass* 1.1.5: "I'll warrant you for half a piece")   *of you* i.e., that I derive from you   5 *anon* soon, presently   6 *doubting* fearing (Cf. *Hamlet* 1.2.255: "I doubt some foul play")   7 *counting* counting it, thinking it   12 *had* i.e., had from you   14 *or . . . or* either . . . or   *all away* i.e., with all (food) taken away

76

Why is my verse so barren of new pride?
So far from variation or quicke change?
Why with the time do I not glance aside
To new found methods, and to compounds strange?   4
Why write I still all one, ever the same,
And keepe invention in a noted weed,
That every word doth almost fel my name,
Shewing their birth, and where they did proceed?   8
O know sweet love I alwaies write of you,
And you and love are still my argument:
So all my best is dressing old words new,
Spending againe what is already spent: 12
   For as the Sun is daily new and old,
   So is my love still telling what is told,

---

1 *pride* ostentatious adornment (Cf. *Lucrece* 1809: "to clothe his wit
in state and pride")   3 *the time* the times, the fashion   4 *compounds*
(a) mixtures, concoctions (perhaps catachrestic imagery, as in the
poetry of Chapman, Marston, and Donne; cf. 118.2) (b) compound
words (OED cites from 1605: "Wee retaine it in the compound 'Husband'")   5 *all one* the same way   6 *invention* imagination, creativity
(Cf. 59.3)   *noted* (b) well-known (Cf. *Hamlet* 2.1.23: "companions
noted and most known")   *weed* garment (Cf. 2.4)   7 *fel* tell (misprint)   10 *argument* theme (Cf. 38.3)

Thy glasse will shew thee how thy beauties were,
Thy dyall how thy pretious mynuits waste,
The vacant leaves thy mindes imprint will beare,
And of this booke, this learning maist thou taste.   4
The wrinckles which thy glasse will truly show,
Of mouthed graves will give thee memorie,
Thou by thy dyals shady stealth maist know,
Times theevish progresse to eternitie.   8
Looke what thy memorie cannot containe,
Commit to these waste blacks, and thou shalt finde
Those children nurst, deliverd from thy braine,
To take a new acquaintance of thy minde.   12
    These offices, so oft as thou wilt looke,
    Shall profit thee, and much inrich thy booke.

---

1 *glasse* mirror *were* (b) wear 3 *vacant leaves* blank pages (of a notebook) 4 *learning* lesson *taste* experience (Cf. *Tempest* 5.1.123: "you do yet taste Some subtleties o' the isle") 6 *mouthed* gaping, open-mouthed (Cf. *1 Henry IV* 1.3.97: "mouthed wounds") 7 *shady stealth* stealthy shadow (Cf. 36.6) 8 *theevish* stealthy (Cf. *All's Well* 2.1.69: "the thievish minutes") 9 *looke what* whatever (Cf. 9.9) 10 *waste* empty *blacks* blanks (i.e., blank pages) 11 *nurst* nursed, taken care of 13 *offices* exercises, actions (Cf. *Macbeth* 2.3.136: "To show an unfelt sorrow is an office Which the false man does easy")

78

So oft have I invok'd thee for my Muse,
And found such faire assistance in my verse,
As every *Alien* pen hath got my use,
And under thee their poesie disperse.   4
Thine eyes, that taught the dumbe on high to sing,
And heavie ignorance aloft to flie,
Have added fethers to the learneds wing,
And given grace a double Majestie.   8
Yet be most proud of that which I compile,
Whose influence is thine, and borne of thee,
In others workes thou doost but mend the stile,
And Arts with thy sweete graces graced be.   12
  But thou art all my art, and doost advance
  As high as learning, my rude ignorance.

---

3 *as* that *got my use* adopted my practice (Cf. *All's Well* 5.1.24:
"with more haste Than is his use") 4 *disperse* (b) publish (OED
cites from 1612: "By their owne divulged and dispersed ignominie")
5 *on high* (b) aloud (OED cites from 1519: "If we call any thing
on high, The taverner will answer") 9 *compile* compose (Cf. *Love's
Labor's Lost* 4.3.134: "Did never sonnet for her sake compile") 13
advance lift up (Cf. *Richard III* 1.2.40: "Advance thy halberd higher
than my breast")

79

Whilst I alone did call upon thy ayde,
My verse alone had all thy gentle grace,
But now my gracious numbers are decayde,
And my sick Muse doth give an other place.   4
I grant (sweet love) thy lovely argument
Deserves the travaile of a worthier pen,
Yet what of thee thy Poet doth invent,
He robs thee of, and payes it thee againe,   8
He lends thee vertue, and he stole that word,
From thy behaviour, beautie doth he give
And found it in thy cheeke: he can affoord
No praise to thee, but what in thee doth live.   12
   Then thanke him not for that which he doth say,
   Since what he owes thee, thou thy selfe doost pay,

---

3 *numbers* verses (Cf. 38.12) *decayde* fallen off in quality (OED
cites from 1511: "Archerie . . . is right litell used, but dayly . . .
decayth and abateth")   4 *give an other place* make room for another
(poet)   5 *lovely argument* (b) the theme of your beauty (Cf. 76.10)
11 *affoord* give, offer (Cf. *Love's Labor's Lost* 4.1.40: "praise we
may afford To any lady that subdues a lord")

8 0

O how I faint when I of you do write,
Knowing a better spirit doth use your name,
And in the praise thereof spends all his might,
To make me toung-tide speaking of your fame.   4
But since your worth (wide as the Ocean is)
The humble as the proudest saile doth beare,
My sawsie barke (inferior farre to his)
On your broad maine doth wilfully appeare.   8
Your shallowest helpe will hold me up a floate,
Whilst he upon your soundlesse deepe doth ride,
Or (being wrackt) I am a worthlesse bote,
He of tall building, and of goodly pride.   12
   Then If he thrive and I be cast away,
   The worst was this, my love was my decay.

---

1 *faint* become weak, lose heart (Cf. "faint-hearted") 6 *as* as well as
7 *sawsie* (saucy) presumptuous (Cf. *Troilus & Cressida* 1.3.42:
"where's then the saucy boat Whose weak untimber'd sides but even
now Co-rivall'd greatness?") 8 *wilfully* (b) freely (OED cites
from 1475: "Thys hors so went wylfully here and there over all where
at hys lust wold") 9 *a floate* afloat 10 *soundlesse* unfathomable
11 *wrackt* wrecked (Cf. 126.5) 12 *pride* (b) magnificence (Cf.
Romeo & Juliet 1.2.10: "Let two more summers wither in their pride")
14 *decay* downfall (Cf. *King John* 4.3.154: "The imminent decay of
wrested pomp")

8 1

Or I shall live your Epitaph to make,
Or you survive when I in earth am rotten,
From hence your memory death cannot take,
Although in me each part will be forgotten.   4
Your name from hence immortall life shall have,
Though I (once gone) to all the world must dye,
The earth can yeeld me but a common grave,
When you intombed in mens eyes shall lye,   8
Your monument shall be my gentle verse,
Which eyes not yet created shall ore-read,
And toungs to be, your beeing shall rehearse,
When all the breathers of this world are dead,   12
    You still shall live (such vertue hath my Pen)
    Where breath most breaths, even in the mouths of men.

———————

1 *or* either (Cf. 114.1) 4 *part* personal quality, attribute (Cf. 17.4 and *Winter's Tale* 5.1.64: "for what dull part in't You choose her") 5 *from hence* (a) henceforth, hereafter (Cf. *Othello* 3.3.380: "from hence I'll love no friend") (b) from these poems 10 *ore-read* read through (Cf. *Measure for Measure* 4.2.212: "You shall anon over-read it at your pleasure") 11 *rehearse* relate (Cf. *Winter's Tale* 5.2.68: "Like an old tale still, which will have matter to rehearse") 13 *vertue* (b) power (Cf. *Merchant of Venice* 5.1.199: "If you had known the virtue of the ring") 14 *breaths* breathes

82

I grant thou wert not married to my Muse,
And therefore maiest without attaint ore-looke
The dedicated words which writers use
Of their faire subject, blessing every booke.   4
Thou art as faire in knowledge as in hew,
Finding thy worth a limmit past my praise,
And therefore art inforc'd to seeke anew,
Some fresher stampe of the time bettering dayes.   8
And do so love, yet when they have devisde,
What strained touches Rhethorick can lend,
Thou truly faire, wert truly simpathizde,
In true plaine words, by thy true telling friend.   12
  And their grosse painting might be better us'd,
  Where cheekes need blood, in thee it is abus'd.

---

2 *attaint* disgrace (Cf. *Lucrece* 824: "reproach to him allotted That is as clear from this attaint of mine") *ore-looke* examine, read (Cf. *Two Gentlemen of Verona* 1.2.48: "I would I had overlooked the letter") 5 *hew* hue, complexion 6 *limmit* (b) region (Cf. *1 Henry IV* 3.1.74: "The Archdeacon hath divided it [the map] Into three limits very equally") 8 *time bettering dayes* (a) days that improve on the past? (b) improving times? (Cf. 32.5) 11 *simpathizde* matched, portrayed (Cf. *Lucrece* 1113: "True sorrow . . . When with like semblance it is sympathized") 13 *painting* (b) make-up, rouge (Cf. 20.1)

I never saw that you did painting need,
And therefore to your faire no painting set,
I found (or thought I found) you did exceed,
The barren tender of a Poets debt: 4
And therefore have I slept in your report,
That you your selfe being extant well might show,
How farre a moderne quill doth come to short,
Speaking of worth, what worth in you doth grow,   8
This silence for my sinne you did impute,
Which shall be most my glory being dombe,
For I impaire not beautie being mute,
When others would give life, and bring a tombe.   12
    There lives more life in one of your faire eyes,
    Then both your Poets can in praise devise.

---

1 *painting* (b) cosmetics (Cf. 82.13) (c) flattering (Cf. *Love's Labor's Lost* 4.1.16: "Nay, never paint me now! When fair is not, praise cannot mend the brow") 2 *faire* beauty (Cf. 18.7) *set* applied 4 *tender* offering 5 *slept* been slow *report* commendation (Cf. *Love's Labor' Lost* 2.1.63: "Much too little . . . Is my report to his great worthiness") 7 *moderne* (b) ordinary (OED cites from 1591: "It . . . maketh him blinde and inconsiderate in matters as well moderne, as necessarie to his salvation") 9 *for* as *impute* consider (OED cites from 1611: "[King Henry VI] for his holy life was imputed a Saint")

84

Who is it that sayes most, which can say more,
Then this rich praise, that you alone, are you,
In whose confine immured is the store,
Which should example where your equall grew, 4
Leane penurie within that Pen doth dwell,
That to his subject lends not some small glory,
But he that writes of you, if he can tell,
That you are you, so dignifies his story. 8
Let him but coppy what in you is writ,
Not making worse what nature made so cleere,
And such a counter-part shall fame his wit,
Making his stile admired every where. 12
    You to your beautious blessings adde a curse,
    Being fond on praise, which makes your praises worse.

---

1 *which* who (Cf. "Our Father, which art in Heaven," and Abbot, *Shakespearian Grammar* 265) 3 *store* supply, treasury (Cf. 146.10) 4 *example* show, provide an example of (Cf. *Love's Labor's Lost* 3.1.85: "I will example it") 11 *counter-part* copy (OED cites from 1676: "They seem to be . . . copies or counterparts of one another") *fame* make famous (Cf. Jonson, *Epigrams* 1.43: "Her foes enough would fame thee in their hate") 14 *on* of (Cf. *Tempest* 4.1.157: "such stuff As dreams are made on")

8 5

My toung-tide Muse in manners holds her still,
While comments of your praise richly compil'd,
Reserve their Character with goulden quill,
And precious phrase by all the Muses fil'd.   4
I thinke good thoughts, whilst other write good wordes,
And like unlettered clarke still crie Amen,
To every Himne that able spirit affords,
In polisht forme of well refined pen.   8
Hearing you praisd, I say 'tis so, 'tis true,
And to the most of praise adde some-thing more,
But that is in my thought, whose love to you
(Though words come hind-most) holds his ranke before,   12
  Then others, for the breath of words respect,
  Me for my dombe thoughts, speaking in effect.

---

1 *in manners* out of politeness, modesty (Cf. *Twelfth Night* 2.1.15: "it charges me in manners the rather to express myself") *holds her still* keeps still 3 *reserve* preserve? (OED cites from 1605: "The Egyptians embalmed and filled them with odoriferous spices, reserving them in glasse or coffins") *Character* (b) writing 4 *fil'd* polished, refined 5 *other* others 6 *clarke* clerk(s) 7 *Himne* hymn *affords* offers (Cf. 79.11) 12 *holds . . . before* keeps his front rank, yields to no one else's love (For "before" meaning "in front," cf. 60.3) 13 *breath of words* language, speech

86

Was it the proud full saile of his great verse,
Bound for the prize of (all-to-precious) you,
That did my ripe thoughts in my braine inhearce,
Making their tombe the wombe wherein they grew?   4
Was it his spirit, by spirits taught to write,
Above a mortall pitch, that struck me dead?
No, neither he, nor his compiers by night
Giving him ayde, my verse astonished.   8
He nor that affable familiar ghost
Which nightly gulls him with intelligence,
As victors of my silence cannot boast,
I was not sick of any feare from thence.   12
    But when your countinance fild up his line,
    Then lackt I matter, that infeebled mine.

---

3 *inhearce* entomb, seal up in death (Cf. *1 Henry VI* 4.7.45: "See
where he lies inhearsed")   6 *pitch* height (used especially of the highest point of a falcon's flight before it drops on the prey; cf. *2 Henry
VI* 2.1.12: "bears his thoughts above his falcon's pitch")   *struck* (b.)
darted at and seized (said of falcons; OED cites from 1687: "th'eager
Hawk makes sure of's prize, Strikes with full might")   7 *compiers*
compeers, companions   8 *astonished* stunned with fear (Cf. *Lucrece*
1730: "Stone-still, astonished with this deadly deed")   9 *he nor*
neither he nor (Cf. 141.9)   10 *gulls* fools (Cf. *Henry V* 2.2.121:
"That same demon that hath gulled thee thus")   *intelligence* (b)
knowledge, secret information (Cf. *1 Henry IV* 4.3.98: "Sought to
entrap me by intelligence")   11 *cannot* can (Elizabethan double negative)   13 *countinance* (a) face   (b) support, approval, patronage
(Cf. *1 Henry IV* 1.2.33: "Under whose countenance we steal")   *fild
up* (b) i.e., filled up what was lacking

Farewell thou art too deare for my possessing,
And like enough thou knowst thy estimate,
The Charter of thy worth gives thee releasing:
My bonds in thee are all determinate.   4
For how do I hold thee but by thy granting,
And for that ritches where is my deserving?
The cause of this faire guift in me is wanting,
And so my pattent back againe is swerving.   8
Thy selfe thou gav'st, thy owne worth then not knowing,
Or mee to whom thou gav'st it, else mistaking,
So thy great guift upon misprision growing,
Comes home againe, on better judgement making.   12
    Thus have I had thee as a dreame doth flatter,
    In sleepe a King, but waking no such matter.

---

1 *deare* (b) expensive   2 *estimate* value   3 *Charter* (a) deed, contract   (b) privilege, immunity (Cf. *As You Like It* 2.7.48: "I must have liberty Withal, as large a charter as the wind")   *of thy worth* (a) to your worth   (b) provided by your worth   *releasing* freedom from obligation (especially from a contract)   4 *bonds* (a) ties (of affection)   (b) contracts   *determinate* of limited duration (Cf. the verb form in *Richard II* 1.3.150: "The sly slow hours shall not determinate The dateless limit of thy dear exile")   8 *pattent* title of possession   10 *mistaking* misjudging   11 *guift* gift   *misprision* misunderstanding   13 *flatter* (b) delude (Cf. 42.14)

88

When thou shalt be dispode to set me light,
And place my merrit in the eie of skorne,
Upon thy side, against my selfe ile fight,
And prove thee virtuous, tho thou art forsworne: 4
With mine owne weakenesse being best acquainted,
Upon thy part I can set downe a story
Of faults conceald, wherein I am attainted:
That thou in loosing me, shall win much glory: 8
And I by this wil be a gainer too,
For bending all my loving thoughts on thee,
The injuries that to my selfe I doe,
Doing thee vantage, duble vantage me. 12
    Such is my love, to thee I so belong,
    That for thy right, my selfe will beare all wrong.

---

1 *dispode* disposed (misprint) *set me light* hold me in low esteem
(Cf. *Richard II* 1.3.293: "For gnarling sorrow hath less power to bite
The man that mocks at it and sets it light") 4 *art forsworne* have
broken your oath (Cf. 152.1) 6 *upon thy part* in your behalf (Cf.
49.12) 7 *attainted* dishonored, disgraced (Cf. 82.2) 8 *that* so that
loosing losing 10 *bending . . . on* fixing . . . on, attaching . . . to
(OED cites from 1510: "On whom so ever he hath his heart Ibente")
12 *vantage* benefit *duble* double

Say that thou didst forsake mee for some falt,
And I will comment upon that offence,
Speake of my lamenesse, and I straight will halt:
Against thy reasons making no defence.   4
Thou canst not (love) disgrace me halfe so ill,
To set a forme upon desired change,
As ile my selfe disgrace, knowing thy wil,
I will acquaintance strangle and looke strange: 8
Be absent from thy walkes and in my tongue,
Thy sweet beloved name no more shall dwell,
Least I (too much prophane) should do it wronge:
And haplie of our old acquaintance tell.   12
    For thee, against my selfe ile vow debate,
    For I must nere love him whom thou dost hate.

---

3 *halt* (b) be lame (Cf. *Timon of Athens* 4.1.24: "Cripple our senators, that their limbs may halt As lamely as their manners") 6 *set a forme upon* (a) give shape to, establish the form of (Cf. *King John* 5.7.26: "you are born To set a form upon that indigest . . . so shapeless and so rude") (b) give a respectable appearance to (by analogy to phrases of the sort seen in *1 Henry VI* 4.1.103: "To set a gloss upon his bold intent") *change* i.e., alteration in our relationship 8 *strange* like a stranger, as though I did not know you (Cf. *Comedy of Errors* 5.1.295: "Why look you strange on me?") 12 *haplie* by chance 13 *debate* hostility, a quarrel (Cf. *Midsummer Night's Dream* 2.1.116: "And this same progeny of evils comes From our debate, from our dissension")

90

Then hate me when thou wilt, if ever, now,
Now while the world is bent my deeds to crosse,
Joyne with the spight of fortune, make me bow,
And doe not drop in for an after losse: 4
Ah doe not, when my heart hath scapte this sorrow,
Come in the rereward of a conquerd woe,
Give not a windy night a rainie morrow,
To linger out a purposd over-throw.   8
If thou wilt leave me, do not leave me last,
When other pettie griefes have done their spight,
But in the onset come, so stall I taste
At first the very worst of fortunes might.   12
    And other straines of woe, which now seeme woe,
    Compar'd with losse of thee, will not seeme so.

---

2 *to crosse* on frustrating (Cf. 133.8)   4 *after* later   5 *scapte* escaped
6 *rereward* rearward, rear van (OED cites from 1601: "There stands
in The Rere-ward of This Booke a Troope of straunge Discourses")
8 *linger out* prolong (Cf. *2 Henry VI* 1.2.266: "Borrowing only lingers and lingers it out")   11 *in the onset* (a) at the beginning (b)
in the attack (as opposed to the rear van)   *stall* shall (misprint)   13
straines (a) sorts (Cf. *Merry Wives of Windsor* 3.3.196: "I would all
of the same strain were in the same distress") (b) extremes (Cf. *2
Henry V* 4.5.171: "swell my thoughts to any strain of pride")

9 1

Some glory in their birth, some in their skill,
Some in their wealth, some in their bodies force,
Some in their garments though new-fangled ill:
Some in their Hawkes and Hounds, some in their Horse.   4
And every humor hath his adjunct pleasure,
Wherein it findes a joy above the rest,
But these perticulers are not my measure,
All these I better in one generall best.   8
Thy love is bitter then high birth to me,
Richer then wealth, prouder then garments cost,
Of more delight then Hawkes or Horses bee:
And having thee, of all mens pride I boast.   12
    Wretched in this alone, that thou maist take,
    All this away, and me most wretched make.

---

5 *humor* temperament (Cf. *Julius Caesar* 4.3.119: "That rash humor which my mother gave me Makes me forgetful") *adjunct* corresponding   6 *above the rest* (b) especially (Cf. *King Lear* 4.1.50: "Do as I bid thee, or rather do thy pleasure; Above the rest, be gone")   9 *bitter* better (misprint)   12 *all mens pride* all the things other men are proud of

9 2

But doe thy worst to steale thy selfe away,
For tearme of life thou art assured mine,
And life no longer then thy love will stay,
For it depends upon that love of thine.   4
Then need I not to feare the worst of wrongs,
When in the least of them my life hath end,
I see, a better state to me belongs
Then that, which on thy humor doth depend.   8
Thou canst not vex me with inconstant minde,
Since that my life on thy revolt doth lie,
Oh what a happy title do I finde,
Happy to have thy love, happy to die!   12
    But whats so blessed faire that feares no blot,
    Thou maist be falce, and yet I know it not.

---

2 *tearme* (term) duration   8 *humor* (b) caprice (Cf. 91.5)   9
minde (b) intention, desire (Cf. *Titus Andronicus* 5.3.1: "it is my
father's mind That I repair to Rome")   10 *since that* since *revolt*
change of opinion (OED cites from 1596: "She did observe his soon
Revolt from friend to friend")   *lie* [*on*] hinges on (Cf. *Antony &*
Cleopatra 3.8.5: "our fortune lies Upon this jump")

93

So shall I live, supposing thou art true,
Like a deceived husband, so loves face,
May still seeme love to me, though alter'd new:
Thy lookes with me, thy heart in other place.   4
For their can live no hatred in thine eye,
Therefore in that I cannot know thy change,
In manies lookes, the falce hearts history
Is writ in moods and frounes and wrinckles strange.   8
But heaven in thy creation did decree,
That in thy face sweet love should ever dwell,
What ere thy thoughts, or thy hearts workings be,
Thy lookes should nothing thence, but sweetnesse tell.   12
  How like *Eaves* apple doth thy beauty grow,
  If thy sweet vertue answere not thy show.

---

3 *new* newly, recently (Cf. 56.10)   7 *manies* many's   *falce* false   11
what ere whate'er, whatever   13 *Eaves* Eve's   14 *vertue* (b) power
(Cf. 81.13)   *answere not* does not correspond to   *show* appearance
(Cf. 70.12)

94

They that have powre to hurt, and will doe none,
That doe not do the thing, they most do showe,
Who moving others, are themselves as stone,
Unmooved, could, and to temptation slow: 4
They rightly do inherrit heavens graces,
And husband natures ritches from expence,
They are the Lords and owners of their faces,
Others, but stewards of their excellence: 8
The sommers flowre is to the sommer sweet,
Though to it selfe, it onely live and die,
But if that flowre with base infection meete,
The basest wccd out-braves his dignity: 12
    For sweetest things turne sowrest by their deedes,
    Lillies that fester, smell far worse then weeds.

---

1 *will* (emphatic, equivalent to "choose to") *doe none* i.e., do no hurt 2 *showe* seem capable of doing 6 *husband* save (Cf. *Hamlet* 4.5.137: "I'll husband them so well, They shall go far") *expence* (a) expenditure (b) waste 8 *stewards* custodians (those charged with controlling or dispensing their masters' goods) 10 *to it selfe* for itself (Cf. *King James Bible*, Romans 14.7–8: "none of us liveth to himself, and no man dieth to himself . . . . we die unto the Lord") 12 *out-braves* surpasses in splendor (Cf. 15.8, *brave*)

9 5

How sweet and lovely dost thou make the shame,
Which like a canker in the fragrant Rose,
Doth spot the beautie of thy budding name?
Oh in what sweets doest thou thy sinnes inclose!   4
That tongue that tells the story of thy daies,
(Making lascivious comments on thy sport)
Cannot dispraise, but in a kinde of praise,
Naming thy name, blesses an ill report.   8
Oh what a mansion have those vices got,
Which for their habitation chose out thee,
Where beauties vaile doth cover every blot,
And all things turnes to faire, that eies can see!   12
   Take heed (deare heart) of this large priviledge,
   The hardest knife ill us'd doth loose his edge.

---

2 *canker* canker worm (Cf. 35.4)   6 *sport* (b) sexual activities (Cf. *Titus Andronicus* 2.3.79: "foul desire . . . conducted you.—And, being intercepted in your sport")   13 *large* (b) licentious (Cf. *Antony & Cleopatra* 3.6.93: "large in his abominations")

96

Some say thy fault is youth, some wantonesse,
Some say thy grace is youth and gentle sport,
Both grace and faults are lov'd of more and lesse:
Thou makst faults graces, that to thee resort: 4
As on the finger of a throned Queene,
The basest Jewell wil be well esteem'd:
So are those errors that in thee are seene,
To truths translated, and for true things deem'd.   8
How many Lambs might the sterne Wolfe betray,
If like a Lambe he could his lookes translate.
How many gazers mighst thou lead away,
If thou wouldst use the strength of all thy state?   12
    But doe not so, I love thee in such sort,
    As thou being mine, mine is thy good report.

---

1 *wantonesse* (a) promiscuity, lasciviousness (Cf. 97.7) (b) capriciousness, sportiveness (Cf. *King John* 4.1.16: "Yet, I remember, when I was in France, Young gentlemen would be as sad as night Only for wantonness") 2 *sport* (b) sexual behavior (Cf. 95.6) 3 *more and lesse* persons of all ranks (Cf. *1 Henry IV* 4.3.68: "The more and less came in with cap and knee") 8 *translated* transformed (Cf. *Midsummer Night's Dream* 3.1.125: "Bottom . . . thou art translated") 10 *like* into those of 12 *state* (b) majesty, grandeur (Cf. *Richard III* 3.7.204: "unfit for state and majesty") 13–14 *but . . . report* (Cf. 36.13–14) 14 *report* reputation (Cf. *Measure for Measure* 2.3.12: "Hath blistered her report")

97

How like a Winter hath my absence beene
From thee, the pleasure of the fleeting yeare?
What freezings have I felt, what darke daies seene?
What old Decembers barenesse every where?   4
And yet this time remov'd was sommers time,
The teeming Autumne big with ritch increase,
Bearing the wanton burthen of the prime,
Like widdowed wombes after their Lords decease: 8
Yet this aboundant issue seem'd to me,
But hope of Orphans, and un-fathered fruite,
For Sommer and his pleasures waite on thee,
And thou away, the very birds are mute.   12
   Or if they sing, tis with so dull a cheere,
   That leaves looke pale, dreading the Winters neere.

---

5 *remov'd* when I was absent 6 *teeming* pregnant, fruitful (Cf. *King Lear* 1.4.305: "If she must teem, Create her child of spleen") *increase* produce 7 *bearing the . . . burthen* (a) bearing the child (Cf. *King John* 3.1.90: "Let wives with child Pray that their burthens may not fall") (b) bearing the weight of the beloved in a sexual embrace (Cf. *Romeo & Juliet* 2.5.78: "But you shall bear the burden soon at night") *prime* spring (As an adjective, the word meant "lecherous") 13 *cheere* spirit (Cf. *All's Well* 3.2.67: "have a better cheer")

9 8

From you have I beene absent in the spring,
When proud pide Aprill (drest in all his trim)
Hath put a spirit of youth in every thing:
That heavie *Saturne* laught and leapt with him.   4
Yet nor the laies of birds, nor the sweet smell
Of different flowers in odor and in hew,
Could make me any summers story tell:
Or from their proud lap pluck them where they grew: 8
Nor did I wonder at the Lillies white,
Nor praise the deepe vermillion in the Rose,
They weare but sweet, but figures of delight:
Drawne after you, you patterne of all those.   12
  Yet seem'd it Winter still, and you away,
  As with your shaddow I with these did play.

---

2 *proud* (b) proudly (c) magnificently, splendidly (Cf. 99.3, 12,
pride) *pide* pied *trim* fine attire (Cf. *1 Henry IV* 4.1.113: "They
come like sacrifices in their trim") 4 *heavie* (b) melancholy (Cf.
50.1) *Saturne* (considered the planet whose influence produced melancholy; cf. modern "saturnine") 5 *nor . . . nor* neither . . . nor
6 *different flowers* flowers different (Cf. word order in 44.6) 7 *summers* i.e., joyful 9 *wonder at* (b) admire 11 *weare* (a) were (Cf.
77.1) (b) wear? 14 *shaddow* image (Cf. *1 Henry VI* 2.3.36: "Long
time thy shadow hath been thrall to me, For in my gallery thy picture
hangs")

99

The forward violet thus did I chide,
Sweet theefe whence didst thou steale thy sweet that smels
If not from my loves breath, the purple pride,
Which on thy soft cheeke for complexion dwells?   4
In my loves veines thou hast too grosely died,
The Lillie I condemned for thy hand,
And buds of marjerom had stolne thy haire,
The Roses fearefully on thornes did stand,   8
Our blushing shame, an other white dispaire:
A third nor red, nor white, had stolne of both,
And to his robbry had annext thy breath,
But for his theft in pride of all his growth   12
A vengfull canker eate him up to death.
  More flowers I noted, yet I none could see,
  But sweet, or culler it had stolne from thee.

---

1 *forward* (b) early (Cf. *Two Gentlemen of Verona* 1.1.45: "the most forward bud Is eaten by the canker ere it blow") 3 *pride* (a) adornment (Cf. 76.1) (b) magnificence (Cf. 80.12) 5 *grosely* (grossly) (a) obviously (b) excessively (OED cites from 1547: "They do fede grossly") *died* dyed 6 *condemned for* i.e., condemned for having stolen the whiteness of 7 *marjerom* marjoram 9 *our* one (misprint) 12 *pride* (b) prime (Cf. *1 Henry IV* 1.1.60: "in the very heat And pride of their contention") 13 *canker* canker worm (Cf. 95.2) 15 *culler* color

Where art thou Muse that thou forgetst so long,
To speake of that which gives thee all thy might?
Spendst thou thy furie on some worthlesse songe,
Darkning thy powre to lend base subjects light.   4
Returne forgetfull Muse, and straight redeeme,
In gentle numbers time so idely spent,
Sing to the eare that doth thy laies esteeme,
And gives thy pen both skill and argument.   8
Rise resty Muse, my loves sweet face survay,
If time have any wrincle graven there,
If any, be a *Satire* to decay,
And make times spoiles dispised every where.   12
    Give my love fame faster then time wasts life,
    So thou prevenst his sieth, and crooked knife.

---

3 *furie* ecstasy of inspiration (Cf. *Othello* 3.4.73: "in her prophetic fury") 4 *base* (b) dark? (OED cites from 1586: "well colored, not too high or base"; but the usage seems to have been primarily restricted to certain technical phrases, and it is uncertain whether an Elizabethan reader would have seen a pun here) 6 *gentle* suited to a person of high birth (Cf. "gentleman") *numbers* verse (Cf. 17.6) 8 *argument* subject matter (Cf. 38.3) 9 *resty* sluggish (Cf. *Cymbeline* 3.6.34: "resty sloth Finds the down pillow hard") 11 *to* on 12 *spoiles* (b) spoliations, destructions 13 *wasts* destroys (Cf. 55.4) 14 *thou prevenst* (a) you foil (b) you anticipate *sieth* scythe

Oh truant Muse what shalbe thy amends,
For thy neglect of truth in beauty di'd?
Both truth and beauty on my love depends:
So dost thou too, and therein dignifi'd: 4
Make answere Muse, wilt thou not haply saie,
Truth needs no collour with his collour fixt,
Beautie no pensell, beauties truth to lay:
But best is best, if never intermixt.   8
Because he needs no praise, wilt thou be dumb?
Excuse not silence so, for't lies in thee,
To make him much out-live a gilded tombe:
And to be praisd of ages yet to be.   12
   Then do thy office Muse, I teach thee how,
   To make him seeme long hence, as he showes now.

---

2 *truth* (b) fidelity (Cf. 41.12 and 138.1) *di'd* dyed   4 *therein dignifi'd* therein are dignified (For grammar, cf. 121.3)   5 *haply* perhaps   6 *collour* (color) (b) pretense, pretext (Cf. *Antony & Cleopatra* 1.3.32: "seek no color for your going")   7 *lay* lay on, apply?
(Cf. for sense *Twelfth Night* 1.5.258: "beauty . . . whose red and
white Nature's own sweet and cunning hand laid on") (b) alloy, mix
with something inferior? ("Lay" was a rare shortened form of "allay,"
which sometimes meant "alloy"; but the OED finds no example of this
usage for "lay" after 1572)

My love is strengthned though more weake in seeming
I love not lesse, thogh lesse the show appeare,
That love is marchandiz'd, whose ritch esteeming,
The owners tongue doth publish every where.　　　　4
Our love was new, and then but in the spring,
When I was wont to greet it with my laies,
As *Philomell* in summers front doth singe,
And stops his pipe in growth of riper daies:　　　　8
Not that the summer is lesse pleasant now
Then when her mournefull himns did hush the night,
But that wild musick burthens every bow,
And sweets growne common loose their deare delight.　　12
　　Therefore like her, I some-time hold my tongue:
　　Because I would not dull you with my songe.

---

1 *seeming* appearance   2 *show* outward manifestation   3 *esteeming* valuation (Cf. *Cymbeline* 1.4.90: "What do you esteem it at?")   7 *Philomell* Philomela, the nightingale (from the Greek myth)   12 *deare* (b) precious (c) rare (Cf. Coverdale's *Bible*, I Samuel 3.1: "The word of the Lord was dear at the same time," where the signification is "scarce")   14 *dull* bore (OED cites from 1576: "My desire is not to dull you, if I cannot delight you")

103

Alack what poverty my Muse brings forth,
That having such a skope to show her pride,
The argument all bare is of more worth
Then when it hath my added praise beside.   4
Oh blame me not if I no more can write!
Looke in your glasse and there appeares a face,
That over-goes my blunt invention quite,
Dulling my lines, and doing me disgrace.   8
Were it not sinfull then striving to mend,
To marre the subject that before was well,
For to no other passe my verses tend,
Then of your graces and your gifts to tell.   12
    And more, much more then in my verse can sit,
    Your owne glasse showes you, when you looke in it.

---

1 *poverty* poor stuff (Cf. 40.10) 2 *pride* (b) grandeur (Cf. 80.12
and 104.4) 3 *argument* subject matter (Cf. 76.10 and 100.8) 7 *over-
goes* (a) exceeds (Cf. *Richard III* 2.2.61: "What cause have I . . . To
overgo thy woes and drown thy cries?") (b) overwhelms (Cf. *3 Henry VI* 2.5.123: "Sad-hearted men, much overgone with care") *blunt*
(a) dull-witted (b) unpolished *invention* (a) imagination (Cf.
Venus & Adonis, Dedication 5: "first heir of my invention") (b)
work, creation (Cf. *Twelfth Night* 5.1.341: "that letter . . . say 'tis
not . . . your invention") 11 *passe* end, issue (Cf. Milton, *Eikono-
klastes* 9.86: "his consents and his denials come all to one pass") 13
sit be contained

To me faire friend you never can be old,
For as you were when first your eye I eyde,
Such seemes your beautie still: Three Winters colde,
Have from the forrests shooke three summers pride,   4
Three beautious springs to yellow *Autumne* turn'd,
In processe of the seasons have I seene,
Three Aprill perfumes in three hot Junes burn'd,
Since first I saw you fresh which yet are greene.   8
Ah yet doth beauty like a Dyall hand,
Steale from his figure, and no pace perceiv'd,
So your sweete hew, which me thinkes still doth stand
Hath motion, and mine eye may be deceaved.   12
   For feare of which, heare this thou age unbred,
   Ere you were borne was beauties summer dead.

---

6 *processe* the progression   7 *perfumes* incenses (the original meaning of the word; note its etymology)   9 *Dyall* sundial or watch (For
the latter, cf. *As You Like It* 2.7.20: "And then he drew a dial from
his poke")   10 *steale from* (b) move stealthily away from   *his figure* (a) the numeral of the dial (b) the bodily shape of the beloved
no pace (there is) no movement (Cf. Chapman, *Iliad* 1.394: "The
Pow'r whose pace doth move The round earth")   11 *hew* (a) complexion (b) form (Cf. 20.7)   *still doth stand* (a) stands still, stands
motionless (b) still remains (Cf. *Macbeth* 3.1.4: "it was said It should
not stand in thy posterity")

105

Let not my love be cal'd Idolatrie,
Nor my beloved as an Idoll show,
Since all alike my songs and praises be
To one, of one, still such, and ever so.   4
Kinde is my love to day, to morrow kinde,
Still constant in a wondrous excellence,
Therefore my verse to constancie confin'de,
One thing expressing, leaves out difference.   8
Faire, kinde, and true, is all my argument,
Faire, kinde and true, varrying to other words,
And in this change is my invention spent,
Three theams in one, which wondrous scope affords.   12
  Faire, kinde, and true, have often liv'd alone.
  Which three till now, never kept seate in one.

---

1 *Idolatrie* (b) polytheism (Cf. Donne, "To the Countesse of Salisbury" 38: "And if things like these have been said by me Of others, call not that Idolatry") 2 *show* appear, seem 8 *difference* diversity (Cf. *Pericles* 4.2.85: "indeed shall you . . . taste gentlemen of all fashions; . . . you shall have the difference of all complexions") 9 *argument* theme (Cf. 103.3) 10 *varrying* restating in different words (OED quotes Gabriel Harvey: "I gave him this Theame out of Ovid, to translate, and varie after his best fashion") 14 *kept seate* dwelt

When in the Chronicle of wasted time,
I see discriptions of the fairest wights,
And beautie making beautifull old rime,
In praise of Ladies dead, and lovely Knights, 4
Then in the blazon of sweet beauties best,
Of hand, of foote, of lip, of eye, of brow,
I see their antique Pen would have exprest,
Even such a beauty as you maister now. 8
So all their praises are but prophesies
Of this our time, all you prefiguring,
And for they look'd but with devining eyes,
They had not still enough your worth to sing: 12
 For we which now behold these present dayes,
 Have eyes to wonder, but lack toungs to praise.

---

1 *wasted* past, spent (Cf. *Merchant of Venice* 3.4.12: "companions That do converse and waste the time together") 2 *wights* persons 5 *blazon* record of excellences (from the earlier meaning "coat of arms"; cf. *Twelfth Night* 1.5.312: "Thy tongue, thy face, thy limbs, actions, and spirit, Do give thee five-fold blazon") 8 *maister* possess (Cf. *Merchant of Venice* 5.1.174: "the wealth that the world masters") 10 *you prefiguring* describing you in advance 11 *for* because, since *devining* conjecturing 12 *still* (Tyrwhitt conjectured "skill," accepted by most but not all modern editors)

1 0 7

Not mine owne feares, nor the prophetick soule,
Of the wide world, dreaming on things to come,
Can yet the lease of my true love controule,
Supposde as forfeit to a confin'd doome.   4
The mortall Moone hath her eclipse indur'de,
And the sad Augurs mock their owne presage,
Incertenties now crowne them-selves assur'de,
And peace proclaimes Olives of endlesse age.   8
Now with the drops of this most balmie time,
My love lookes fresh, and death to me subscribes,
Since spight of him Ile live in this poore rime,
While he insults ore dull and speachlesse tribes.   12
  And thou in this shalt finde thy monument,
  When tyrants crests and tombs of brasse are spent.

1-2 *soule, of the wide world* (b) the *anima mundi* (the animating
principle of the world according to some Neoplatonic mystics) 3
lease (b) duration (Cf. *Macbeth* 4.1.99: "Macbeth Shall live the lease
of nature"; possibly, too, we are expected to catch the opposition between *true* and an archaic meaning of *lease,* that of "falsehood") *controule* (a) limit (Cf. *King John* 2.1.444: "such controlling bounds
shall you be") (b) curb, check (OED cites Drayton: "felt the stiff
curb control his angry jaws") 4 *confin'd* limited, bounded (Contrast
Macbeth 4.3.55: "Macbeth will seem as pure as snow . . . compared
with my confineless harms") *doome* (a) destiny (b) doomsday
(c) sentence, legal judgment (*confin'd doome* thus equaling "judgment which limits it") 5 *mortall Moone* (This phrase has been assumed to refer not only to the earth's satellite, mortal in the sense that
it is subject to eclipse, but to some contemporary historical event as
well—either to some crisis in the life of Queen Elizabeth or, as in
Leslie Hotson's view, to the destruction of the Spanish Armada, called
because of its crescent-shaped battle line "a horned Moon of huge and
mighty shippes") 10 *subscribes* submits (Cf. *Taming of the Shrew*
1.1.81: "to your pleasure humbly I subscribe") 14 *spent* gone, con-
sumed

What's in the braine that Inck may character,
Which hath not figur'd to thee my true spirit,
What's new to speake, what now to register,
That may expresse my love, or thy deare merit?   4
Nothing sweet boy, but yet like prayers divine,
I must each day say ore the very same,
Counting no old thing old, thou mine, I thine,
Even as when first I hallowed thy faire name.   8
So that eternall love in loves fresh case,
Waighes not the dust and injury of age,
Nor gives to necessary wrinckles place,
But makes antiquitie for aye his page,   12
    Finding the first conceit of love there bred,
    Where time and outward forme would shew it dead,

---

1 *character* write 2 *figur'd* portrayed, shown (Cf. *Richard III*
1.2.194: "I would I knew thy heart.—'Tis figur'd in my tongue") 5
sweet boy (altered to "sweet love" in the edition of 1640) 9 *fresh
case* (a) new situation (b) young skin (Cf. for a similar pun *Winter's Tale* 4.4.844: "but though my case be a pitiful one, I hope I shall
not be flayed out of it") 10 *waighes* (b) considers 13 *conceit* conception (Cf. *Othello* 3.3.115: "shut up in thy brain Some horrible conceit")

O never say that I was false of heart,
Though absence seem'd my flame to quallifie,
As easie might I from my selfe depart,
As from my soule which in thy brest doth lye: 4
That is my home of love, if I have rang'd,
Like him that travels I returne againe,
Just to the time, not with the time exchang'd,
So that my selfe bring water for my staine,   8
Never beleeve though in my nature raign'd,
All frailties that besiege all kindes of blood,
That it could so preposterouslie be stain'd,
To leave for nothing all thy summe of good: 12
    For nothing this wide Universe I call,
    Save thou my Rose, in it thou art my all.

---

2 *quallifie* diminish (Cf. *Hamlet* 4.7.114: "Love is begun by Time, And . . . Time qualifies the spark and fire of it")   7 *just to the time* punctually   *exchang'd* changed   8 *my selfe* I myself   12 *for nothing* (a) for no reason (Cf. *Comedy of Errors* 4.4.130: "Will you be bound for nothing?")   (b) in order to get nothing

Alas 'tis true, I have gone here and there,
And made my selfe a motley to the view,
Gor'd mine own thoughts, sold cheap what is most deare,
Made old offences of affections new.   4
Most true it is, that I have lookt on truth
Asconce and strangely: But by all above,
These blenches gave my heart an other youth,
And worse essaies prov'd thee my best of love,   8
Now all is done, have what shall have no end,
Mine appetite I never more will grin'de
On newer proofe, to trie an older friend,
A God in love, to whom I am confin'd.   12
    Then give me welcome, next my heaven the best,
    Even to thy pure and most most loving brest.

---

2 *motley* particolored clothing of a jester (perhaps used figuratively here for "jester") *to the view* to the public view (Cf. *Hamlet* 5.2.389: "order that these bodies . . . be placed to the view") 3 *gor'd* (a) injured? (b) furnished with gores? (i.e., triangular pieces of cloth, as in a jester's motley) (c) besmirched? (from the original meaning of the noun "gore"—i.e., filth) 4 *offences* (b) resentments, dislikes (OED cites J. Stubbs, 1580: "To have incurred hir Majesties greate offence") *of* from, out of (But note double grammar of "made offenses out of affections" and "made old offenses-of-affections new") 5 *truth* (b) fidelity 6 *asconce* askance, obliquely *strangely* distantly, as if I were a stranger 7 *blenches* turnings aside, inconstancies (Cf. *Measure for Measure* 4.5.5: "you do blench from this to that") 8 *essaies* trials 11 *proofe* experiment 12 *confin'd* bound

I I I

O for my sake doe you wish fortune chide,
The guiltie goddesse of my harmfull deeds,
That did not better for my life provide,
Then publick meanes which publick manners breeds.   4
Thence comes it that my name receives a brand,
And almost thence my nature is subdu'd
To what it workes in, like the Dyers hand,
Pitty me then, and wish I were renu'de,   8
Whilst like a willing pacient I will drinke,
Potions of Eysell gainst my strong infection,
No bitternesse that I will bitter thinke,
Nor double pennance to correct correction.   12
    Pittie me then deare friend, and I assure yee,
    Even that your pittie is enough to cure mee.

---

1 *wish* with (misprint) *chide* [*with*] reproach (Cf. *King James Bible*, Genesis 31.36: "And Jacob was wroth, and chode with Laban") 5 *brand* stigma 6–7 *subdu'd* to (a) subjugated by (Cf. Hobbes, *Leviathan* [Oakeshott ed.] 2.17.144: "subdueth his enemies to his will") (b) reduced to (Cf. *King Lear* 3.4.72: "Nothing could have subdued Nature to such a lowness") 8 *renu'de* renewed, restored to my true nature 10 *Eysell* vinegar (a common medicine in the sixteenth century) 11 *bitter thinke* consider to be bitter 12 *nor* nor will I think it *to* (b) too? (with *correct* considered as an adjective) *correct* (b) counteract the harmful effects of (OED cites a 1578 herbal: "Yet ought it [Hellebor] not to be given before it be . . . corrected . . . with long pepper") *correction* (a) punishment (b) rebuke (Cf. *King James Bible*, II Timothy 3.16: "profitable . . . for reproof, for correction")

I I 2

Your love and pittie doth th'impression fill,
Which vulgar scandall stampt upon my brow,
For what care I who calles me well or ill,
So you ore-greene my bad, my good alow? 4
You are my All the world, and I must strive,
To know my shames and praises from your tounge,
None else to me, nor I to none alive,
That my steel'd sence or changes right or wrong, 8
In so profound *Abisme* I throw all care
Of others voyces, that my Adders sence,
To cryttick and to flatterer stopped are:
Marke how with my neglect I doe dispence. 1 2
You are so strongly in my purpose bred,
That all the world besides mc thinkes y'are dead.

---

4 *ore-greene* overgreen (i.e., cover over as grass covers dirt) *alow*
(allow) approve of (Cf. *Troilus & Cressida* 3.2.98: "praise us as we
are tasted, allow us as we prove") 7 *none alive* none, alive? 8 *that
. . . wrong* (No entirely satisfactory explanation of this line has yet
been offered, although it is no doubt parallel in sense to lines 10–11.
It is probably seriously corrupt) *steel'd* hardened, unfeeling (Cf.
Measure for Measure 4.2.90: "the steeled gaoler") 9 *Abisme* abysm
10 *Adders sence* (To the Elizabethans, the adder was the proverbial
example of deafness; cf. *2 Henry VI* 3.2.76: "Art thou, like the adder,
waxen deaf?") 12 *neglect* (a) being disregarded (by others) (b)
indifference (to others) *dispence* [*with*] (a) put up with, disregard
(b) excuse (Cf. the ecclesiastical "dispensation." This reading would
require a colon after *dispence* in modern punctuation) 14 *me thinkes
y'are* (Modern editors emend to "methinks are")

I I 3

Since I left you, mine eye is in my minde,
And that which governes me to goe about,
Doth part his function, and is partly blind,
Seemes seeing, but effectually is out: 4
For it no forme delivers to the heart
Of bird, of flowre, or shape which it doth lack,
Of his quick objects hath the minde no part,
Nor his owne vision houlds what it doth catch: 8
For if it see the rud'st or gentlest sight,
The most sweet-favor or deformedst creature,
The mountaine, or the sea, the day, or night:
The Croe, or Dove, it shapes them to your feature.   12
    Incapable of more repleat, with you,
    My most true minde thus maketh mine untrue.

---

2 *governes* guides (OED cites from 1635: "a straying starr . . . governd these wise-men to Christ")   3 *doth part* (a) partly does (Cf. *Othello* 5.2.296: "This wretch hath part confessed his villany") (b) divides (Cf. *King James Bible*, Leviticus 2.6: "Thou shalt part it in pieces")   4 *effectually* in effect (OED cites from 1662: "effectually he was the Pope's nuntio")   6 *lack* (misprint for "latch") catch, perceive (Cf. *Macbeth* 4.3.195: "words . . . howled out . . . Where hearing should not latch them")   7, 8 *his* its (i.e., the eye's)   7 *quick* vivid (OED cites from 1533: "Als quyk as thai war led afore your Ee")   10 *favor* face (Cf. the modern "ill-favored" and 125.5)   12 *feature* form (not of the face but of the whole body; cf. *Hamlet* 3.1.167: "That unmatched form and feature of blown youth")   13 *more repleat, with* more, replete with   *repleat* filled   14 *mine* (Modern editors emend this obvious misprint to "mine eye")

I I 4

Or whether doth my minde being crown'd with you
Drinke up the monarks plague this flattery?
Or whether shall I say mine eie saith true,
And that your love taught it this *Alcumie?*   4
To make of monsters, and things indigest,
Such cherubines as your sweet selfe resemble,
Creating every bad a perfect best
As fast as objects to his beames assemble: 8
Oh tis the first, tis flatry in my seeing,
And my great minde most kingly drinkes it up,
Mine eie well knowes what with his gust is greeing,
And to his pallat doth prepare the cup.   12
  If it be poison'd, tis the lesser sinne,
  That mine eye loves it and doth first beginne.

1, 3 *or whether . . . or whether* (an Elizabethan construction used
for alternatives in a question; modern usage would retain only the
second *or* and eliminate all else)   5 *indigest* formless (Cf. the noun
form in *King John* 5.7.26: "To set a form upon that indigest, Which
he hath left so shapeless")   8 *beames* eyebeams, glances (Cf. *Venus
& Adonis* 487: "Whose beams upon his hairless face are fixed")   *assemble [to]* gather before (Cf. *King James Bible,* I Kings 8: "the men
of Israel assembled themselves unto King Solomon")   11 *gust* taste,
liking (Cf. *Twelfth Night* 1.3.34: "allay the gust he hath in quarrel-
ing")   *greeing* agreeing (Cf. *Two Gentlemen of Verona* 2.4.184:
"Plotted and greed on")   12 *to his pallat* to his taste, to suit his palate

Those lines that I before have writ doe lie,
Even those that said I could not love you deerer,
Yet then my judgement knew no reason why,
My most full flame should afterwards burne cleerer.   4
But reckening time, whose milliond accidents
Creepe in twixt vowes, and change decrees of Kings,
Tan sacred beautie, blunt the sharp'st intents,
Divert strong mindes to th' course of altring things: 8
Alas why fearing of times tiranie,
Might I not then say now I love you best,
When I was certaine ore in-certainty,
Crowning the present, doubting of the rest: 12
    Love is a Babe, then might I not say so
    To give full growth to that which still doth grow.

---

3 *why* (Read without comma) 5 *reckening* taking into consideration (parallel to *fearing of* in line 9; cf. *Purchas His Pilgrimage* [1614] 5.8.486: "If a man do anything worth reckoning") 7 *tan* (b) coarsen as though making into leather 8 *altring* changeful, inconstant 11 *ore* o'er 13 *say so* (i.e., say "Now I love you best" without setting limits on my love in the future) 14 *grow* (Read with question mark following)

116

Let me not to the marriage of true mindes
Admit impediments, love is not love
Which alters when it alteration findes,
Or bends with the remover to remove.   4
O no, it is an ever fixed marke
That lookes on tempests and is never shaken;
It is the star to every wandring barke,
Whose worths unknowne, although his higth be taken. 8
Lov's not Times foole, though rosie lips and cheeks
Within his bending sickles compasse come,
Love alters not with his breefe houres and weekes,
But beares it out even to the edge of doome: 12
    If this be error and upon me proved,
    I never writ, nor no man ever loved.

---

2 *impediments* (Cf. *Book of Common Prayer:* "If either of you do know any impediment why ye may not be lawfully joined together in matrimony") 4 *bends* inclines *remover* restless, changeful person (Cf. Bacon, *Essays,* "Of Fortune": "A hasty fortune maketh an enterpriser and a remover . . . but the exercised fortune maketh the able man") *remove* move, change 5 *marke* an object or light used as a guide by travelers (OED cites Stanyhurst, 1577: "Hulke tower, which is a notable marke for pilots") 8 *higth* (height) (a) altitude (reckoned in degrees above the horizon) (b) exalted status (Cf. *Richard II* 1.1.189: "Shall I . . . with pale beggar-fear impeach my height . . . ?") *taken* computed (Cf. Gosson, *School of Abuse:* "The height of Heaven is taken by the staff") 12 *beares it out* endures 13 *upon me* against me

Accuse me thus, that I have scanted all,
Wherein I should your great deserts repay,
Forgot upon your dearest love to call,
Whereto al bonds do tie me day by day,　　　　4
That I have frequent binne with unknown mindes,
And given to time your owne deare purchas'd right,
That I have hoysted saile to al the windes
Which should transport me farthest from your sight.　　8
Booke both my wilfulnesse and errors downe,
And on just proofe surmise, accumilate,
Bring me within the level of your frowne,
But shoote not at me in your wakened hate:　　　　12
　　Since my appeale saies I did strive to proove
　　The constancy and virtue of your love

----

1 *scanted* neglected (Cf. *King Lear* 1.1.281: "You have obedience scanted") 3 *call* [*upon*] invoke 4 *bonds* (a) emotional ties (b) legal contracts 5 *frequent* intimate (OED cites from 1615: "A . . . barber; with whome he is the more frequent") *unknown* strangers' 6 *given to time* wasted? 9 *booke . . . downe* record 10 *surmise* (Read without comma) (a) suspicion (Cf. *Cymbeline* 3.4.24: "I speak not out of weak surmises, but from proof") (b) legal allegations (An Elizabethan law book quoted by the OED speaks of "cases of secrecy where the plaintiff cannot prove the surmise of his suit") 11 *level* line of fire (used of guns; cf. *All's Well* 2.1.159: "the level of mine aim") 13 *appeale* (in the legal sense) *proove* test (Cf. 26.14)

118

Like as to make our appetites more keene
With eager compounds we our pallat urge,
As to prevent our malladies unseene,
We sicken to shun sicknesse when we purge.   4
Even so being full of your nere cloying sweetnesse,
To bitter sawces did I frame my feeding;
And sicke of wel-fare found a kind of meetnesse,
To be diseas'd ere that there was true needing.   8
Thus pollicie in love t'anticipate
The ills that were, not grew to faults assured,
And brought to medicine a healthfull state
Which rancke of goodnesse would by ill be cured.   12
  But thence I learne and find the lesson true,
  Drugs poyson him that so fell sicke of you.

---

1 *like as* just as   2 *eager* (b) pungent, acrid (OED cites from 1574: "To mingle . . . sweete and toothsome with sower and eigre")   *compounds* mixtures, concoctions   *urge* stimulate, irritate   3 *as* and just as   4 *purge* take a purgative (Cf. Bunyan, *Pilgrim's Progress* 2.86: "he must purge and vomit")   5 *nere cloying* (a) never-cloying (b) near-cloying   6 *frame* direct   7 *wel-fare* (a) welfare (b) well-fare (i.e., healthful food)   *meetnesse* propriety, fitness (with allusion to "meat," food)   8 *to be* in being   *diseas'd* (b) troubled, disturbed (i.e., dis-eased; cf. *Macbeth* 1.3.117: "she will but disease our better mirth")   9 *pollicie* (a) prudence (Cf. 124.9) (b) cunning (Cf. *Coriolanus* 3.2.42: "Honor and policy . . . In the war do grow together")   *in love t'anticipate* in love, to anticipate   10 *were, not grew* were not, grew (Note what such errors imply about the punctuation of the manuscript)   12 *rancke* overfull (OED cites from 1652: "Rank of successe he was so puft with pride")

What potions have I drunke of *Syren* teares
Distil'd from Lymbecks foule as hell within,
Applying feares to hopes, and hopes to feares,
Still loosing when I saw my selfe to win?   4
What wretched errors hath my heart committed,
Whilst it hath thought it selfe so blessed never?
How have mine eies out of their Spheares bene fitted
In the distraction of this madding fever?   8
O benefit of ill, now I find true
That better is, by evil still made better.
And ruin'd love when it is built anew
Growes fairer then at first, more strong, far greater.   12
   So I returne rebukt to my content,
    And gaine by ills thrise more then I have spent.

---

2 *Lymbecks* alembics (distilling vessels used in alchemy; OED cites from 1529: "A lymbeke for stilling of watters")   3 *applying* (frequently used by Shakespeare in speaking of remedies; cf. *Winter's Tale* 3.2.153: "apply to her Some remedies for life")   4 *still* always (Cf. 153.6)   7 *Spheares* (a) sockets (Cf. *Hamlet* 1.5.17: "Make thy two eyes . . . start from their spheres")   (b) proper orbits (as of planets; cf. pun in *Romeo & Juliet* 2.2.15–17: "the fairest stars . . . do entreat her eyes To twinkle in their spheres")   *bene fitted* (Note punning repetition in line 9)   *fitted* forced by fits or paroxysms? (OED finds no example but this)   8 *madding* maddening

That you were once unkind be-friends mee now,
And for that sorrow, which I then didde feele,
Needes must I under my transgression bow,
Unlesse my Nerves were brasse or hammered steele.   4
For if you were by my unkindnesse shaken
As I by yours, y'have past a hell of Time,
And I a tyrant have no leasure taken
To waigh how once I suffered in your crime.   8
O that our night of wo might have remembred
My deepest sence, how hard true sorrow hits,
And soone to you, as you to me then tendred
The humble salve, which wounded bosomes fits!   12
    But that your trespasse now becomes a fee,
    Mine ransoms yours, and yours must ransome mee.

---

2 *for* because of (Cf. 27.14) 4 *Nerves* (b) sinews (Cf. *Cymbeline* 3.3.94: "he sweats, Strains his young nerves") 7 *leasure* opportunity, time (Cf. *1 Henry VI* 1.1.115: "No leisure had he to enrank his men") *have no leasure taken* have not taken the time, the trouble 9 *remembred* reminded (Cf. *Tempest* 1.2.243: "Let me remember thee what thou hast promised") 12 *fits* is fitting for, is good for 13 *but that your trespasse* but that trespass of yours 14 *ransoms* atones for (Cf. 34.14 and *Two Gentlemen of Verona* 5.4.75: "if hearty sorrow Be a sufficient ransom for offence")

Tis better to be vile then vile esteemed,
When not to be, receives reproach of being,
And the just pleasure lost, which is so deemed,
Not by our feeling, but by others seeing.   4
For why should others false adulterat eyes
Give salutation to my sportive blood?
Or on my frailties why are frailer spies;
Which in their wils count bad what I think good?   8
Noe, I am that I am, and they that levell
At my abuses, reckon up their owne,
I may be straight though they them-selves be bevel
By their rancke thoughtes, my deedes must not be shown   12
   Unlesse this generall evill they maintaine,
   All men are bad and in their badnesse raigne.

---

1 *vile* (a) morally depraved (b) worthless (OED cites from 1678: "separate betwixt the Precious and the Vile") 2 *not to be* not being (vile) 3 *just pleasure* (a) virtuous, lawful pleasure (b) pleasure I'm entitled to so (a) just (b) vile (one of several antithetical double meanings in this poem) 5 *adulterat* (a) lewd, adulterous (b) counterfeit, deceptive (Cf. Daniel, *Complaint of Rosamond* 20: "Th'adulterate beauty of a falsed cheek") 6 *give salutation to* welcome, greet *sportive* (a) playful, jesting (b) randy, libidinous (Cf. *Richard III* 1.1.14: "Shaped for sportive tricks") 7 *frailer* frailer men 8 *which* who (Cf. 84.1) *wils* sexual passions (Cf. 135.1) 9 *levell* (a) take aim, point (b) guess (Cf. *Merchant of Venice* 1.2.41: "according to my description, level at my affection") 11 *bevel* crooked 14 *raigne* (reign) live, flourish

1 2 2

Tthy guift,, thy tables, are within my braine
Full characterd with lasting memory,
Which shall above that idle rancke remaine
Beyond all date even to eternity.   4
Or at the least, so long as braine and heart
Have facultie by nature to subsist,
Til each to raz'd oblivion yeeld his part
Of thee, thy record never can be mist: 8
That poore retention could not so much hold,
Nor need I tallies thy deare love to skore,
Therefore to give them from me was I bold,
To trust those tables that receave thee more,   12
   To keepe an adjunckt to remember thee,
   Were to import forgetfulnesse in mee.

---

1 *tables* (a) notebooks, tablets (Cf. *Two Gentlemen of Verona*
2.7.3: "the table wherein all my thoughts Are . . . charactered")
(b) portraits? (Cf. 24.2) 2 *full* fully *characterd* inscribed (Cf.
108.1) 3 *that idle rancke* (a) the common mass of things? (b)
trivial collection of pages? (Neither explanation is really satisfactory;
the line is probably misprinted. Shakespeare seems to have intended to
say that the writings in question would survive longer in his memory than in the tablets he had given away) 4 *date* fixed limit (Cf.
14.14) 7 *raz'd* erased, blank 9 *retention* capacity for keeping (i.e.,
capacity of the tablets to keep intact against oblivion; cf. *Twelfth
Night* 2.4.99: "woman's heart . . . they lack retention") 10 *skore*
to mark down on a bill, to keep account of (Cf. *1 Henry IV* 2.4.29:
"Score a pint of bastard in the Half Moon") 12 *tables* (Cf. *Hamlet*
1.5.98: "From the table of my memory I'll wipe away all trivial fond
records") *receave thee more* take a deeper impression from you (Cf.
Chaucer, *Treatise on Astrolabe* 2.40: "tables . . . resceyve distynctly
the prikkes of my compas," and *Venus & Adonis* 353) 14 *import*
(b) imply

1 2 3

No! Time, thou shalt not bost that I doe change,
Thy pyramyds buylt up with newer might
To me are nothing novell, nothing strange,
They are but dressings of a former sight: 4
Our dates are breefe, and therefor we admire,
What thou dost foyst upon us that is ould,
And rather make them borne to our desire,
Then thinke that we before have heard them tould: 8
Thy registers and thee I both defie,
Not wondring at the present, nor the past,
For thy records, and what we see doth lye,
Made more or les by thy continuall hast: 12
 This I doe vow and this shall ever be,
 I will be true dispight thy syeth and thee.

---

2 *pyramyds* (b) obelisks, spires (probably a topical allusion—Leslie
Hotson thinks to the raising of obelisks in Rome in 1586, others think
to a London pageant of 1603)   4 *dressings* i.e., superficially changed
versions (Cf. 76.11: "So all my best is dressing old words new")   5
dates lifespans (Cf. 18.4)   *admire* (b) wonder at (as if they were
new)   7 *make* consider (Cf. *Taming of the Shrew* 3.2.193: "Make it
no wonder")   8 *tould* (a) spoken of (b) reckoned (as if in an account; cf. 30.10)   12 *hast* haste   14 *syeth* scythe

124

Yf my deare love were but the childe of state,
It might for fortunes basterd be unfathered,
As subject to times love, or to times hate,
Weeds among weeds, or flowers with flowers gatherd.   4
No it was buylded far from accident,
It suffers not in smilinge pomp, nor falls
Under the blow of thralled discontent,
Whereto th'inviting time our fashion calls: 8
It feares not policy that *Heriticke*,
Which workes on leases of short numbred howers,
But all alone stands hugely pollitick,
That it nor growes with heat, nor drownes with showres.   12
    To this I witnes call the foles of time,
    Which die for goodnes, who have liv'd for crime.

-----

1 *love* i.e., love of you   *state* (b) circumstances, the state of things?
(There are no identical uses of the word, but cf. *Julius Caesar* 1.3.69:
"heaven hath . . . [made] them instruments of fear and warning
Unto some monstrous state")   2 *for* as, as if it were   4 *gatherd*
plucked (either as desirable or as disagreeable, and hence destroyed)
8 *whereto* i.e., to which accidents   *time* times (i.e., the present)   *our
fashion* (in apposition to *time*)   9 *policy* (a) prudence (Cf. 118.9)
(b) cunning (especially in political stratagems; see *state* and *pomp*
above, and also 118.9)   12 *that* since, in that (Cf. *Romeo & Juliet*
1.1.222: "only poor That, when she dies, with beauty dies her store")
nor . . . nor neither . . . nor   13 *witnes call* call as witnesses (Cf.
Cymbeline 2.3.156: "If you will make't an action, call witness to't")
foles fools (Cf. 116.9)

Wer't ought to me I bore the canopy,
With my extern the outward honoring,
Or layd great bases for eternity,
Which proves more short then wast or ruining?   4
Have I not seene dwellers on forme and favor
Lose all, and more by paying too much rent
For compound sweet; Forgoing simple savor,
Pittifull thrivors in their gazing spent.   8
Noe, let me be obsequious in thy heart,
And take thou my oblacion, poore but free,
Which is not mixt with seconds, knows no art,
But mutuall render onely me for thee.   12
    Hence, thou subbornd *Informer*, a trew soule
    When most impeacht, stands least in thy controule.

---

1 *wer't ought* would it matter   *bore the canopy* i.e., honored some-one by carrying a ceremonial protection for him   2 *extern* exterior, mere surface (Cf. adjective in *Othello* 1.1.63: "My outward action doth demonstrate . . . in compliment extern")   6 *rent* (Read as though a comma followed)   7 *sweet* (Read without semicolon) sweetness (Cf. 99.15)   9 *obsequious* devoted (Cf. *Merry Wives of Windsor* 4.2.2: "I see you are obsequious in your love")   10 *oblacion* oblation, offering   11 *seconds* inferior matter (OED cites from 1577: "The fragments of the Coame . . . heated and strained againe, doe make a seconde Hony")   12 *render* (a) surrender (OED cites from 1611: "Hee also tooke sundry places of speciall importance, some by render, some by assault")   (b) return (in a legal sense, as when made by a tenant; OED cites from 1647: "render of rent")   14 *impeacht* accused

O thou my lovely Boy who in thy power,
Doest hould times fickle glasse, his sickle, hower:
Who hast by wayning growne, and therein shou'st,
Thy lovers withering, as thy sweet selfe grow'st.   4
If Nature (soveraine misteres over wrack)
As thou goest onwards still will plucke thee backe,
She keepes thee to this purpose, that her skill.
May time disgrace, and wretched mynuit kill.   8
Yet fear her O thou minnion of her pleasure,
She may detaine, but not still keepe her tresure!
Her *Audite* (though delayd) answer'd must be,
And her *Quietus* is to render thee.   12
          (   )
          (   )

---

2 *glasse* (a) hour glass (Cf. *All's Well* 2.1.168: "the pilot's glass
Hath told the thievish minutes") (b) mirror (Cf. 3.1) 2 *his sickle,
hower* (Most modern editors read "his sickle hour") 3 *wayning*
(b) aging (Evidently this pun was common in Elizabethan England;
cf. William Segar, *Honor, Military & Civill* 198: "But spurned in
vain, youth waneth by increasing") *shou'st* showest 5 *misteres* mistress *wrack* ruin, destruction (Cf. the traditional phrase "going to
wrack and ruin") 7 *to* for 8 *mynuit* minute (emended by many
editors to "minutes") 10 *still* always (Cf. *Hamlet* 4.7.116: "nothing
is at a like goodness still") 11 *Audite* audit (Cf. 4.12) *answer'd*
paid (Cf. *1 Henry IV* 1.3.185: "answer all the debt he owes") 12
Quietus discharge of the debt (short for the legal phrase *quietus est*,
"he is quit"; cf. Webster, *Duchess of Malfi* 3.2: "You had the trick
in audit time to be sick Till I had signed your quietus") *render* (a)
surrender (Cf. *Midsummer Night's Dream* 2.1.185: "I'll make her
render up her page to me") (b) pay (Cf. *Titus Andronicus* 1.1.160:
"my tributary tears I render")

In the ould age blacke was not counted faire,
Or if it weare it bore not beauties name:
But now is blacke beauties successive heire,
And Beautie slanderd with a bastard shame, 4
For since each hand hath put on Natures power,
Fairing the foule with Arts faulse borrow'd face,
Sweet beauty hath no name no holy boure,
But is prophan'd, if not lives in disgrace. 8
Therefore my Mistersse eyes are Raven blacke,
Her eyes so suted, and they mourners seeme,
At such who not borne faire no beauty lack,
Slandring Creation with a false esteeme, 12
    Yet so they mourne becomming of their woe,
    That every toung saies beauty should looke so.

---

1 *blacke* (a) brunette (b) ugly (Cf. "Some say he's black, but I say he's bonny" from the traditional song "I Know Where I'm Going"; cf. also 27.12 and 63.13) *faire* (b) blond 2 *weare* were 3 *successive heire* heir next in order of succession to the title (Cf. *2 Henry VI* 3.1.49: "As next the king he was successive heir") 4 *bastard* (b) counterfeit (Cf. 68.3) 5 *each* everybody's *put on* assumed (Cf. *As You Like It* 5.4.188: "hath put on a religious life") 6 *fairing* prettifying *Arts* artifice's (Cf. 139.4) 7 *boure* bower, dwelling 9, 10 *eyes* (Many editors emend one of these to "brows") 10 *suted* (suited) (a) dressed (Cf. *Merchant of Venice* 1.2.79: "How oddly he is suited") (b) in accord, in keeping (Cf. *Merchant of Venice* 3.5.70: "how his words are suited") 13 *becomming of* making beautiful (Cf. 150.5: "Whence hast thou this becomming of things il"; for Elizabethan "of" where we would omit it, see Abbot's *Shakespearian Grammar* 178)

How oft when thou my musike, musike playst,
Upon that blessed wood whose motion sounds
With thy sweet fingers when thou gently swayst,
The wiry concord that mine eare confounds,   4
Do I envie those Jackes that nimble leape,
To kisse the tender inward of thy hand,
Whilst my poore lips which should that harvest reape,
At the woods bouldnes by thee blushing stand.   8
To be so tikled they would change their state,
And situation with those dancing chips,
Ore whome their fingers walke with gentle gate,
Making dead wood more blest then living lips,   12
    Since sausie Jackes so happy are in this,
    Give them their fingers, me thy lips to kisse.

---

2 *wood* i.e., the wood of a virginal   *motion* (b) playing (Cf. *Cymbeline* 4.2.186: "My ingenious instrument . . . what occasion Hath Cadwal now to give it motion?")   (c) mechanism (Cf. Bacon, *New Atlantis* [G. C. M. Smith ed.] 36: "curious clocks; and other like motions of return")   3 *thou . . . swayst* you govern, you manipulate (Cf. *Midsummer Night's Dream* 1.1.193: "You sway the motion of Demetrius' heart")   5 *Jackes* (a) keys? (In the virginal, the jack was a piece of wood fitted with a quill to pluck the strings, but Shakespeare seems to conceive of it as the whole plucking device including the key; OED cites from 1644: "Like the jack of a Virginall, which striketh the sounding cord")   (b) ill-mannered fellows (Cf. *Taming of the Shrew* 2.1.290: "A mad-cap ruffian and a swearing Jack") 11, 14 *their* thy (misprints)

Th'expence of Spirit in a waste of shame
Is lust in action, and till action, lust
Is perjurd, murdrous, blouddy full of blame,
Savage, extreame, rude, cruell, not to trust, 4
Injoyd no sooner but dispised straight,
Past reason hunted, and no sooner had
Past reason hated as a swollowed bayt,
On purpose layd to make the taker mad. 8
Made In pursut and in possession so,
Had, having, and in quest, to have extreame,
A blisse in proofe and provd and very wo,
Before a joy proposd behind a dreame, 12
 All this the world well knowes yet none knowes well,
 To shun the heaven that leads men to this hell.

---

1 *expence* extravagant expenditure, waste *Spirit* (b) vital power (c) bodily fluid (The Elizabethans spoke of three kinds of spirit—natural, animal, and vital. OED cites Elyot, 1539: "Spirit vitall procedeth from the harte, and . . . is sente into all the body") *waste* (b) waist? (Helge Kökeritz compares the pun in Marston, *Malcontent* 2.5.89: " 'T is now about the immodest waste of night") 2 *action* (often used by the Elizabethans in a specifically sexual sense; cf. *Pericles* 4.2.9: "they with continual action are even as good as rotten") 9 *made* (b) mad 10 *quest, to* (Most modern editors read without comma) 11 *in proofe* in realization, experience (Cf. *Much Ado* 4.1.46: "If you, in your own proof, Have . . . made defeat of her virginity") *and very* a very? 12 *proposd* (Most modern editors read as though a comma followed) imagined (Cf. *Henry IV* 5.2.92: "Be now the father and propose a son")

My Mistres eyes are nothing like the Sunne,
Currall is farre more red, then her lips red,
If snow be white, why then her brests are dun:
If haires be wiers, black wiers grow on her head: 4
I have seene Roses damaskt, red and white,
But no such Roses see I in her cheekes,
And in some perfumes is there more delight,
Then in the breath that from my Mistres reekes.   8
I love to heare her speake, yet well I know,
That Musicke hath a farre more pleasing sound:
I graunt I never saw a goddesse goe,
My Mistres when shee walkes treads on the ground.   12
    And yet by heaven I thinke my love as rare,
    As any she beli'd with false compare.

---

2 *currall* coral   4 *wiers* wires   5 *damaskt* dappled with red ("To damask" meant to ornament with a variegated pattern; a damask rose was "of a color betwixt red and white." Shakespeare seems to exploit both meanings)   8 *reekes* is exhaled (Cf. *Love's Labor's Lost* 4.3.140: "sighs reek from you." The modern sense of "smell unpleasant" was not used in Elizabethan English)   11 *goe* walk   14 *compare* literary comparison, metaphor (Cf. 21.5)

Thou art as tiranous, so as thou art,
As those whose beauties proudly make them cruell;
For well thou know'st to my deare doting hart
Thou art the fairest and most precious Jewell.   4
Yet in good faith some say that thee behold,
Thy face hath not the power to make love grone;
To say they erre, I dare not be so bold,
Although I sweare it to my selfe alone.   8
And to be sure that is not false I sweare
A thousand grones but thinking on thy face,
One on anothers necke do witnesse beare
Thy blacke is fairest in my judgements place.   12
    In nothing art thou blacke save in thy deeds,
    And thence this slaunder as I thinke proceeds.

---

1 *so as* just as   3 *deare* (b) loving (Cf. *Two Gentlemen of Verona* 4.3.14: "what dear good will I bear")   9–10 (Modern punctuation would require commas after *and*, *sweare*, and *grones*)   11 *one on anothers necke* one on top of another (Cf. Ascham, *Toxophilus* [Arber ed.] 56: "Heaping oaths upon oaths, one in another's neck")   12 *judgements place* (a) mind (b) tribunal, court of justice (Cf. *sweare* and *witnesse* above, and *Romeo & Juliet* 1.1.109: "old Freetown, our common judgement place")

Thine eies I love, and they as pittying me,
Knowing thy heart torment me with disdaine,
Have put on black, and loving mourners bee,
Looking with pretty ruth upon my paine.   4
And truly not the morning Sun of Heaven
Better becomes the gray cheeks of th' East,
Nor that full Starre that ushers in the Eaven
Doth halfe that glory to the sober West   8
As those two morning eyes become thy face:
O let it then as well beseeme thy heart
To mourne for me since mourning doth thee grace,
And sute thy pitty like in every part.   12
   Then will I sweare beauty her selfe is blacke,
   And all they foule that thy complexion lacke.

---

2 *torment* torments (misprint) 4 *ruth* pity (Cf. modern "ruthless")
7 *Eaven* evening 8 *doth* gives 9 *morning* (b) mourning ("morn-ing" was a variant spelling in Shakespeare's time) 10 *beseeme* be proper for, suit (Cf. *1 Henry VI* 3.1.19: "more than well beseems A man") 12 *sute* (b) clothe (Cf. 127.10) *like* alike 13 *blacke* (Cf. 127.1 and 131.13) 14 *foule* ugly (Cf. *Venus & Adonis* 133: "Were I hard-favored, foul, or wrinkled old")

Beshrew that heart that makes my heart to groane
For that deepe wound it gives my friend and me;
I'st not ynough to torture me alone,
But slave to slavery my sweet'st friend must be.   4
Me from my selfe thy cruell eye hath taken,
And my next selfe thou harder hast ingrossed,
Of him, my selfe, and thee I am forsaken,
A torment thrice three-fold thus to be crossed: 8
Prison my heart in thy steele bosomes warde,
But then my friends heart let my poore heart bale,
Who ere keepes me, let my heart be his garde,
Thou canst not then use rigor in my Jaile.   12
   And yet thou wilt, for I being pent in thee,
   Perforce am thine and all that is in me.

---

1 *beshrew* curse   6 *harder . . . ingrossed* gained more complete possession of (OED cites from 1641: "ingrossed in the possession of some few particular persons")   8 *crossed* (a) thwarted (Cf. 90.2)   (b) crucified, tortured (OED cite from 1550: "The son of man schal be deliverd to be crossed")   9 *warde* prison cell (Cf. *Hamlet* 2.2.56: "many confines, wards, and dungeons")   10 *bale* (a) bail out, stand bail for   (b) confine, guard (rare, but cf. the noun in Spenser, *Faerie Queene* 7.6.49: "entrapped him . . . within their baile")   11 *keepes* (b) holds captive (Cf. Tindale's *Bible*, Acts 28.16: "Paul was . . . alone with one soldier that kept him")   12 *rigor* (used commonly in the phrase "the rigor of the law," as in *2 Henry VI* 1.3.199)

So now I have confest that he is thine,
And I my selfe am morgag'd to thy will,
My selfe Ile forfeit, so that other mine,
Thou wilt restore to be my comfort still: 4
But thou wilt not, nor he will not be free,
For thou art covetous, and he is kinde,
He learnd but suretie-like to write for me,
Under that bond that him as fast doth binde.   8
The statute of thy beauty thou wilt take,
Thou usurer that put'st forth all to use,
And sue a friend, came debter for my sake,
So him I loose through my unkinde abuse.   12
    Him have I lost, thou hast both him and me,
    He paies the whole, and yet am I not free.

---

2 *will* (b) lust (Cf. 135.1) (c) testament 3 *that other mine* i.e., that other self of mine 6 *kinde* loving (Cf. *2 Henry VI* 1.1.19: "this kind kiss") 7 *write* subscribe his name (as cosigner of a promissory note; cf. *2 Henry VI* 4.1.63: "This hand of mine hath writ in thy behalf") 8 *bond* (a) tie (of affection; cf. 87.4) (b) contract (Cf. 87.4) 9 *statute* bond having the debtor's "Body, Land and Goods" as security (Cf. the Jacobean play *Histrio-mastix* 4.1: "Whilst slaves tie fast our lands In statute staple, or these merchants' bands") 10 *use* (a) usury (b) sexual enjoyment (Cf. 2.9) 11 *sue* (a) bring a law suit against (b) woo (Cf. *Love's Labor's Lost* 3.1.191: "I sue! I seek a wife!") *came* (b) who became (Cf. *Hamlet* 5.1.170: "How came he mad?") 12 *loose* (b) lose *unkinde* (b) unnatural (OED cites from 1546: "for burning and scaldyng, and all unkynde heates") *abuse* (a) ill-usage (Cf. *3 Henry VI* 3.3.188: "the abuse done to my niece") (b) deception (i.e., my having been deceived; cf. *Hamlet* 4.7.50: "Or is it some abuse and no such thing?")

Who ever hath her wish, thou hast thy *Will*,
And *Will* too boote, and *Will* in over-plus,
More then enough am I that vexe thee still,
To thy sweet will making addition thus.   4
Wilt thou whose will is large and spatious,
Not once vouchsafe to hide my will in thine,
Shall will in others seeme right gracious,
And in my will no faire acceptance shine: 8
The sea all water, yet receives raine still,
And in aboundance addeth to his store,
So thou beeing rich in *Will* adde to thy *Will*,
One will of mine to make thy large *Will* more.   12
   Let no unkinde, no faire beseechers kill,
   Thinke all but one, and me in that one *Will*.

---

1 *Will* (b) William (c) willfulness, stubbornness (d) sexual appetite, lust (Cf. *Lucrece* 247: " 'Tween frozen conscience and hot burning will")   2 *too boote* to boot, besides   6 *hide my will* (Cf. *All's Well* 4.3.14: "this night he fleshes his will in the spoil of her honor")   8 *acceptance* acceptability (Cf. Marlowe, *Dido, Queen of Carthage* 3.3.926: "to press beyond acceptance to your sight")   13 *no unkinde, no faire* (Most modern editors preserve this wording either by treating *unkinde* as equivalent to "unkindness" or "unkind woman" or else by punctuating thus: "Let no unkind 'no' fair beseechers kill." But the former reading sounds strained and the latter metrically lame)   14 *all but one* all (the beseechers or the Wills) are only one

If thy soule check thee that I come so neere,
Sweare to thy blind soule that I was thy *Will*,
And will thy soule knowes is admitted there,
Thus farre for love, my love-sute sweet fullfill.　　4
Will, will fulfill the treasure of thy love,
I fill it full with wils, and my will one,
In things of great receit with ease we proove,
Among a number one is reckon'd none.　　8
Then in the number let me passe untold,
Though in thy stores account I one must be,
For nothing hold me so it please thee hold,
That nothing me, a some-thing sweet to thee.　　12
　　Make but my name thy love, and love that still,
　　And then thou lovest me for my name is *Will*.

---

1 *check* reprimand (Cf. *King Lear* 2.2.148: "His fault is much, and
. . . his master Will check him for't") *come so neere* (b) speak the
hidden truth, come so close to the heart of the matter (Cf. Lyly,
Gallathea 3.1: "I think we came near you when we said you loved")
(c) affect you so deeply (Cf. *Two Gentlemen of Verona* 4.3.19: "No
grief did ever come so near thy heart") 2 *Will* (Cf. 135) 3 *there*
i.e., to the soul (in the medieval psychology generally followed by
the Elizabethans, intellect and will were the two rational faculties of
the soul) 5 *fulfill* fill up 6 *I* aye *one* (Read as though comma
were period) 7 *receit* size, capacity (OED cites from 1592: "Take a
large house of infinite receipt") 8 *one is reckon'd none* one is
counted as nothing (According to an Elizabethan saying, "One is no
number") 9 *untold* uncounted 10 *thy stores account* inventory of
your possessions 11 *for nothing hold me* consider me worth nothing
hold (Read without comma)

Thou blinde foole love, what doost thou to mine eyes,
That they behold and see not what they see:
They know what beautie is, see where it lyes,
Yet what the best is, take the worst to be.   4
If eyes corrupt by over-partiall lookes,
Be anchord in the baye where all men ride,
Why of eyes falsehood hast thou forged hookes.
Whereto the judgement of my heart is tide?   8
Why should my heart thinke that a severall plot,
Which my heart knowes the wide worlds common place?
Or mine eyes seeing this, say this is not
To put faire truth upon so foule a face,   12
   In things right true my heart and eyes have erred,
   And to this false plague are they now transferred.

---

5 *corrupt* corrupted   7 *of* out of   8 *tide* tied   9 *that* that to be   *sev-erall* private (OED cites from 1656: "A severall not a common field")
10 *common* public (Cf. preceding entry and, for a similar pun, *Love's Labor's Lost* 2.1.223: "My lips are no common, though several they be")   12 *truth* (b) fidelity (Cf. 160.1)

138

When my love sweares that she is made of truth,
I do beleeve her though I know she lyes,
That she might thinke me some untuterd youth,
Unlearned in the worlds false subtilties.   4
Thus vainely thinking that she thinkes me young,
Although she knowes my dayes are past the best,
Simply I credit her false speaking tongue,
On both sides thus is simple truth supprest: 8
But wherefore sayes she not she is unjust?
And wherefore say not I that I am old?
O loves best habit is in seeming trust,
And age in love, loves not t'have yeares told.   12
        Therefore I lye with her, and she with me,
        And in our faults by lyes we flattered be.

A VARIANT of this sonnet appeared in 1599 in *Passionate Pilgrim;* see
page 157.

1 *truth* faithfulness (Cf. 41.12) 2 *beleeve* (Here this clearly means
"pretend to believe," although we know of no other instance of this
usage in Elizabethan English) 7 *simply* (b) as though simple-
minded (OED cites Holland, 1601: "a man wandering simply . . .
in the wildernesse") 9 *unjust* unfaithful (Cf. *3 Henry VI* 5.1.106: "O
passing traitor, perjured and unjust") 11 *habit* (a) manner, de-
meanor (Cf. *Hamlet* 5.2.197: "he . . . only got the tune of the time
and outward habit of encounter") (b) clothing *trust* (b) fidelity
(Cf. *Romeo & Juliet* 3.2.85: "There's no trust, no faith, no honesty in
men") 12 *told* counted up (Cf. 30.10) 13 *lye* (b) cohabit, sleep

O call not me to justifie the wrong,
That thy unkindnesse layes upon my heart,
Wound me not with thine eye but with thy toung,
Use power with power, and slay me not by Art, 4
Tell me thou lov'st else-where; but in my sight,
Deare heart forbeare to glance thine eye aside,
What needst thou wound with cunning when thy might
Is more then my ore-prest defence can bide? 8
Let me excuse thee ah my love well knowes,
Her prettie lookes have beene mine enemies,
And therefore from my face she turnes my foes,
That they else-where might dart their injuries: 12
   Yet do not so, but since I am neere slaine,
   Kill me out-right with lookes, and rid my paine.

---

4 *Art* cunning, artifice (Cf. *Lover's Complaint* 295: "his passion, but an art of craft"; cf. also 127.6) 8 *ore-prest* overpowered, overwhelmingly assailed (Cf. *Coriolanus* 2.2.97: "he bestrid An o'er-pressed Roman") *bide* withstand, abide (Cf. *Romeo & Juliet* 1.1.219: "bide the encounter of assailing eyes") 13 *neere* nearly 14 *rid* do away with (Cf. *Richard II* 5.4.11: "I am the King's friend, and will rid his foe")

140

Be wise as thou art cruell, do not presse
My toung tide patience with too much disdaine:
Least sorrow lend me words and words expresse,
The manner of my pittie wanting paine.   4
If I might teach thee witte better it weare,
Though not to love, yet love to tell me so,
As testie sick-men when their deaths be neere,
No newes but health from their Phisitions know.   8
For if I should dispaire I should grow madde,
And in my madnesse might speake ill of thee,
Now this ill wresting world is growne so bad,
Madde slanderers by madde eares beleeved be.   12
   That I may not be so, nor thou be lyde,
   Beare thine eyes straight, though thy proud heart goe wide.

---

1 *presse* tax, oppress 2 *toung tide* tongue-tied 3 *least* lest 4 *pittie wanting* (a) pity-lacking, unpitied (b) pity-craving 5 *witte* wisdom *weare* were 6 *so* i.e., that you love me 11 *ill wresting* ill-wresting, forcing an evil construction upon what it hears (Cf. *Much Ado* 3.4.33: "an bad thinking do not wrest true speaking") 13 *be lyde* (belied) lied about 14 *goe wide* wander (Cf. Countess of Pembroke's *Psalms* 67: "Thou their guide Go'st never wide From truth")

In faith I doe not love thee with mine eyes,
For they in thee a thousand errors note,
But 'tis my heart that loves what they dispise,
Who in dispight of view is pleasd to dote.   4
Nor are mine eares with thy toungs tune delighted,
Nor tender feeling to base touches prone,
Nor taste, nor smell, desire to be invited
To any sensuall feast with thee alone: 8
But my five wits, nor my five sences can
Diswade one foolish heart from serving thee,
Who leaves unswai'd the likenesse of a man,
Thy proud hearts slave and vassall wretch to be: 12
    Onely my plague thus farre I count my gaine,
    That she that makes me sinne, awards me paine.

---

2 *errors* flaws (OED cites from 1413 a demand that a statue "be fourged right withoute ony errour") 4 *who* which *in dispight of* in spite of *view* appearance, looks (Cf. *Romeo & Juliet* 1.1.175: "Alas that love, so gentle in his view, Should be so tyrannous") 6 *base* ignoble (Cf. *Timon of Athens* 4.3.29: "will make black white, . . . base noble") 9 *but* but neither 11 *who* which *unswai'd* without a ruler, undirected (since the heart has gone; cf. *swayst* at 128.3) 14 *paine* (b) punishment (Cf. "on pain of death," still current, and seen, e.g., in *Romeo & Juliet* 1.1.110)

Love is my sinne, and thy deare vertue hate,
Hate of my sinne, grounded on sinfull loving,
O but with mine, compare thou thine owne state,
And thou shalt finde it merrits not reprooving,   4
Or if it do, not from those lips of thine,
That have prophan'd their scarlet ornaments,
And seald false bonds of love as oft as mine,
Robd others beds revenues of their rents.   8
Be it lawfull I love thee as thou lov'st those,
Whome thine eyes wooe as mine importune thee,
Roote pittie in thy heart that when it growes,
Thy pitty may deserve to pittied bee.   12
   If thou doost seeke to have what thou doost hide,
   By selfe example mai'st thou be denide.

---

4 *it* i.e., my own state   6 *ornaments* (b) furnishings for a church (suggested by *prophan'd;* cf. Malory, *Le Morte Darthur* 17.15: "held a cross and the ornaments of an altar")   7 *bonds* (a) ties (of affection; cf. 134.8)   (b) legal contracts (Cf. 87.4)   8 *revenues* (accented on second syllable) income, dues (Cf. Spenser, *Tears of the Muses* 469: "Their great revenues all in sumptuous pride They spend")   9 *be it lawfull* if it is permissible   13 *hide* refuse to show (i.e., pity)   14 *selfe* your own (Cf. *Macbeth* 5.7.99: "self and violent hands")

1 4 3

Loe as a carefull huswife runnes to catch,
One of her fethered creatures broake away,
Sets downe her babe and makes all swift dispatch
In pursuit of the thing she would have stay: 4
Whilst her neglected child holds her in chace,
Cries to catch her whose busie care is bent,
To follow that which flies before her face:
Not prizing her poore infants discontent;   8
So runst thou after that which flies from thee,
Whilst I thy babe chace thee a farre behind,
But if thou catch thy hope turne back to me:
And play the mothers part kisse me, be kind.   12
   So will I pray that thou maist have thy *Will*,
   If thou turne back and my loude crying still.

---

4 *pursuit* (often accented on first syllable in Elizabethan verse; cf.
Massinger, *Fatal Dowry* 2.2: "Forsake the pursuit of this lady's
honor")   5 *holds her in chace* pursues her (Cf. *Coriolanus* 1.6.19:
"Spies of the Volsces Held me in chase")   10 *a farre* afar, far   13
Will (a) wish, way (b) sexual desire (c) William (for all three
uses, cf. 135 and 136)

144

Two loves I have of comfort and dispaire,
Which like two spirits do sugjest me still,
The better angell is a man right faire:
The worser spirit a woman collour'd il.   4
To win me soone to hell my femall evill,
Tempteth my better angel from my sight,
And would corrupt my saint to be a divel:
Wooing his purity with her fowle pride.   8
And whether that my angel be turn'd finde,
Suspect I may, yet not directly tell,
But being both from me both to each friend,
I gesse one angel in an others hel.   12
    Yet this shal I nere know but live in doubt,
    Till my bad angel fire my good one out.

A VARIANT of this sonnet appeared in 1599 in *Passionate Pilgrim;* see page 157.

2 *sugjest* (suggest) (a) prompt (b) tempt (Cf. *All's Well* 4.5.48: "to suggest thee from thy master") *still* always (Cf. 147.1) 4 *collour'd il* dark 6 *sight* side (misprint; cf. the *Passionate Pilgrim* version referred to above) 8 *pride* (b) sexual excitement (Cf. *Othello* 3.3.405: "as salt as wolves in pride") 9 *finde* fiend 11 *from me* away from me *each* each other 12 *hel* hell (used here as a sexual allusion; cf. Boccaccio, *Decameron*, Day 3, Tale 10) 14 *fire . . . out* drive away with fire (OED cites from 1530: "Come out, or I shall fyre the[e] out." "Fire" itself was frequently used by the Elizabethans in the sense of "passion")

145

Those lips that Loves owne hand did make,
Breath'd forth the sound that said I hate,
To me that languisht for her sake:
But when she saw my wofull state, 4
Straight in her heart did mercie come,
Chiding that tongue that ever sweet,
Was usde in giving gentle dome:
And tought it thus a new to greete: 8
I hate she alterd with an end,
That follow'd it as gentle day,
Doth follow night who like a fiend
From heaven to hell is flowne away. 12
    I hate, from hate away she threw,
    And sav'd my life saying not you.

---

7 *dome* (doom) sentence, legal judgment (Cf. 107.4)   8 *a new* anew
9 *I hate* i.e., "I hate"

Poore soule the center of my sinfull earth,
My sinfull earth these rebbell powres that thee array,
Why dost thou pine within and suffer dearth
Painting thy outward walls so costlie gay?   4
Why so large cost having so short a lease,
Dost thou upon thy fading mansion spend?
Shall wormes inheritors of this excesse
Eate up thy charge? is this thy bodies end?   8
Then soule live thou upon thy servants losse,
And let that pine to aggravat thy store;
Buy tearmes divine in selling houres of drosse:
Within be fed, without be rich no more,   12
  So shalt thou feed on death, that feeds on men,
  And death once dead, ther's no more dying then.

---

2 *my sinfull earth* (This is obviously a misprint. The line requires a
disyllabic foot that will carry through the idea of a personage of high
estate who is treated shabbily by "rebel powers." Some suggested
emendations are "thrall to," "fooled by," "prince of," "starved by,"
"hemmed with," "fenced by," and "pressed by") *powres* (b) faculties of the body (OED cites from 1526: "Memory, reason, & wyll . . .
ben the thre powers of the soule") *array* (a) dress (b) arrange as
if for battle (c) afflict (OED cites from c. 1600: "Vyce . . . Whiche
hathe hym so Encombered and arayed") 8 *charge* expenditure 10
aggravat increase *store* wealth (Cf. 37.8)

147

My love is as a feaver longing still,
For that which longer nurseth the disease,
Feeding on that which doth preserve the ill,
Th'uncertaine sicklie appetite to please: 4
My reason the Phisition to my love,
Angry that his prescriptions are not kept
Hath left me, and I desperate now approove,
Desire is death, which Phisick did except.   8
Past cure I am, now Reason is past care,
And frantick madde with ever-more unrest,
My thoughts and my discourse as mad mens are,
At randon from the truth vainely exprest.   12
   For I have sworne thee faire, and thought thee bright,
   Who art as black as hell, as darke as night.

---

1 *still* always (Cf. *Romeo & Juliet* 5.3.270: "We still have known thee for a holy man") 2 *nurseth* fosters, preserves (Cf. *Lucrece* 141: "to nurse the life With honor") 4 *uncertaine* changeable, fitful (Cf. *Two Gentlemen of Verona* 1.3.85: "the uncertain glory of an April day") 6 *prescriptions* (b) orders *kept* followed 7 *desperate* (b) incurable, hopelessly ill (Cf. *Hamlet* 4.3.9: "diseases desperate grown") *approove* demonstrate, prove that (Cf. *Merchant of Venice* 3.2.79: "some sober brow Will bless it, and approve it with a text") 8 *Phisick* medicine (Cf. 34.9) *except* object to, refuse (Cf. *Richard II* 1.1.72: "royalty, Which fear . . . makes thee to except") 12 *at randon* at random, disjointedly *from* at variance with (Cf. *Julius Caesar* 1.3.35: "clean from the purpose") *vainely* (b) falsely (Cf. *2 Henry IV* 4.5.239: "Jerusalem, Which vainly I supposed the Holy Land")

148

O me! what eyes hath love put in my head,
Which have no correspondence with true sight,
Or if they have, where is my judgment fled,
That censures falsely what they see aright?   4
If that be faire whereon my false eyes dote,
What meanes the world to say it is not so?
If it be not, then love doth well denote,
Loves eye is not so true as all mens: no,   8
How can it? O how can loves eye be true,
That is so vext with watching and with teares?
No marvaile then though I mistake my view,
The sunne it selfe sees not, till heaven cleeres.   12
　　O cunning love, with teares thou keepst me blinde,
　　Least eyes well seeing thy foule faults should finde.

---

4 *censures* judges (Cf. the noun form in *Winter's Tale* 2.1.37: "In my
just censure, in my true opinion")　5 *false* deceptive (Cf. 67.5)　7
denote demonstrate, indicate (Cf. *Merry Wives* 4.6.39: "The better
to denote her to the Doctor")　8 *eye* (b) "aye" (Cf. Heywood,
Royall King 2.4: " 'Me, my lord?' 'Ey you my Lord' ")　*mens: no*
men's "no"　10 *watching* sleeplessness (Cf. *Love's Labor's Lost*
3.1.210: "To sigh for her! to watch for her")　11 *though* if (Cf. *Venus
& Adonis* 390: "no marvel though thy horse be gone")　14 *least* lest
(Cf. 151.4)

149

Canst thou O cruell, say I love thee not,
When I against my selfe with thee pertake:
Doe I not thinke on thee when I forgot
Am of my selfe, all tirant for thy sake?   4
Who hateth thee that I doe call my friend,
On whom froun'st thou that I doe faune upon,
Nay if thou lowrst on me doe I not spend
Revenge upon my selfe with present mone?   8
What merrit do I in my selfe respect,
That is so proude thy service to dispise,
When all my best doth worship thy defect,
Commanded by the motion of thine eyes.   12
   But love hate on for now I know thy minde,
   Those that can see thou lov'st, and I am blind.

---

2 *pertake* (partake) join forces, take part (We know of no other identical usage, but cf. Holinshed's *Chronicles* 3.495: "some fray or tumult might rise amongst his nobles, by quarrelling or partaking," and also "partaker" in OED quotation: "And all his partackers I shall slea") 3–4 *forgot am of* am forgotten by 7 *thou lowrst on* you scowl at *spend* take, expend (Cf. *Midsummer Night's Dream* 3.2.74: "You spend your passion on a misprised mood") 8 *present* immediate (Cf. *Henry VIII* 1.2.211: "Call him to present trial") *mone* grief, suffering (Cf. 30.11) 12 *motion* (b) bidding, commandment (Cf. *King James Bible*, Translator's Preface 5: "with this motion: 'Read this, I pray you'")

Oh from what powre hast thou this powrefull might,
With insufficiency my heart to sway,
To make me give the lie to my true sight,
And swere that brightnesse doth not grace the day?   4
Whence hast thou this becomming of things il,
That in the very refuse of thy deeds,
There is such strength and warrantise of skill,
That in my minde thy worst all best exceeds?   8
Who taught thee how to make me love thee more,
The more I heare and see just cause of hate,
Oh though I love what others doe abhor,
With others thou shouldst not abhor my state.   12
   If thy unworthinesse raisd love in me,
   More worthy I to be belov'd of thee.

---

2 *insufficiency* (b) weakness (Cf. Spenser, *State of Ireland:* "reject them as incapable and insufficient") *sway* control (Cf. 128.3) 3 *give the lie to* accuse of lying 5 *becomming* beauty, ability to beautify (Cf. *Antony & Cleopatra* 1.4.96: "my becomings kill me, when they do not Eye well to you") 7 *warrantise* warranty 12 *abhor* (b) cuckold? (Cf. the pun in *Othello* 4.2.161: "I cannot say 'whore.' It does abhor me")

Love is too young to know what conscience is,
Yet who knowes not conscience is borne of love,
Then gentle cheater urge not my amisse,
Least guilty of my faults thy sweet selfe prove.   4
For thou betraying me, I doe betray
My nobler part to my grose bodies treason,
My soule doth tell my body that he may,
Triumph in love, flesh staies no farther reason,   8
But rysing at thy name doth point out thee,
As his triumphant prize, proud of this pride,
He is contented thy poore drudge to be
To stand in thy affaires, fall by thy side.   12
   No want of conscience hold it that I call,
   Her love, for whose deare love I rise and fall.

---

2 *not* not that   3 *urge not* (a) do not charge (me) with (Cf.
Richard III 3.5.80: "urge his hatefull luxury And bestial appetite") (b)
do not provoke, do not incite (OED cites from 1594: "Forbeare ambitious Prelate to urge my griefe")   *amisse* offense, sin (Cf. 35.7)   4
least lest   5 *for thou betraying* for, since you betray (Cf. participle
in 152.2, and Abbot, *Shakespearian Grammar* 377)   6 *my nobler part*
i.e., my soul   8 *staies* waits for (Cf. *Two Gentlemen of Verona*
2.2.13: "My father stays my coming")   9 *rysing* (Cf. *pride* below)
10 *proud of* (b) swelling with (Cf. current "proud flesh," and *Midsummer Night's Dream* 2.1.91: "Have every pelting river made so
proud")   *pride* (b) sexual excitement (Cf. 144.8)   13 *conscience*
(b) awareness (Cf. *Henry V* 4.1.124)   *call* (Read without comma)

In loving thee thou know'st I am forsworne,
But thou art twice forsworne to me love swearing,
In act thy bed-vow broake and new faith torne,
In vowing new hate after new love bearing: 4
But why of two othes breach doe I accuse thee,
When I breake twenty: I am perjur'd most,
For all my vowes are othes but to misuse thee:
And all my honest faith in thee is lost. 8
For I have sworne deepe othes of thy deepe kindnesse:
Othes of thy love, thy truth, thy constancie,
And to inlighten thee gave eyes to blindnesse,
Or made them swere against the thing they see. 12
   For I have sworne thee faire: more perjurde eye,
   To swere against the truth so foule a lie.

---

1 *am forsworne* have broken an oath (presumably his marriage vows)
3 *act* sexual relations (Cf. *Merchant of Venice* 1.3.84: "When the
work of generation was Between these woolly breeders in the act")
bed-vow marriage vow *broake* broken (Cf. 143.2) *torne* broken
(Cf. *Love's Labor's Lost* 4.3.285: "and our faith not torn") 7 *misuse*
(a) abuse, revile (with *othes* considered as curses; cf. *Taming of the
Shrew* 2.1.160: "with twenty such vile terms As had she studied to
misuse me so") (b) lie about, misrepresent? (so the OED, citing this
as a single instance) (c) deceive (OED cites from 1601: "We are
misused by these spirites both night and day") 11 *inlighten* (a)
make brighter (b) give sight to (Cf. *King James Bible*, I Samuel
14.29: "mine eyes have been enlightened") *gave eyes to* (b) gave
my eyes over to 13 *eye* (with pun on *I*)

153

Cupid laid by his brand and fell a sleepe,
A maide of Dyans this advantage found,
And his love-kindling fire did quickly steepe
In a could vallie-fountaine of that ground: 4
Which borrowd from this holie fire of love,
A datelesse lively heat still to indure,
And grew a seething bath which yet men prove,
Against strang malladies a soveraigne cure: 8
But at my mistres eie loves brand new fired,
The boy for triall needes would touch my brest,
I sick withall the helpe of bath desired,
And thether hied a sad distemperd guest.   12
    But found no cure, the bath for my helpe lies,
    Where Cupid got new fire; my mistres eye.

THIS and the succeeding sonnet are almost certainly derived from a Latin translation of a poem by the Byzantine poet Marianus. The original in the *Greek Anthology* reads: "Heavy with soft sleep, Love slept under the plane trees, with his torch laid aside near the nymphs. Then the nymphs said to one another, 'Why don't we do something? The pity is that when we put out this torch we cannot also quench all the blaze in mortal hearts.' But the torch set the water afire, and now the amorous nymphs must bathe in water hot with the heat of that torch."

1 *brand* torch 2 *Dyans* Diana's *advantage* favorable opportunity (Cf. *Tempest* 3.3.13: "The next advantage Will we take") 6 *datelesse* endless (Cf. 30.6) *still* always (Cf. 119.4) 7 *prove* find to be (Cf. 72.4) 12 *thether . hied* thither hurried *distemperd* (a) sick (Cf. *2 Henry IV* 3.1.41: "a body yet distempered, Which to his former strength may be restored") (b) distracted, disturbed (Cf. *Romeo & Juliet* 2.3.33: "it argues a distempered head So soon to bid good morrow to thy bed")

154

The little Love-God lying once a sleepe,
Laid by his side his heart inflaming brand,
Whilst many Nymphes that vou'd chast life to keep,
Came tripping by, but in her maiden hand,   4
The fayrest votary tooke up that fire,
Which many Legions of true hearts had warm'd,
And so the Generall of hot desire,
Was sleeping by a Virgin hand disarm'd.   8
This brand she quenched in a coole Well by,
Which from loves fire tooke heat perpetuall,
Growing a bath and healthfull remedy,
For men diseasd, but I my Mistrisse thrall,   12
    Came there for cure and this by that I prove,
    Loves fire heates water, water cooles not love.

----

2 *brand* torch (Cf. 153.1) 9 *by* nearby (Cf. *Love's Labor's Lost* 5.2.94: "I stole into a neighbor thicket by") 11 *bath* medicinal bath, mineral spring

Addenda

From: THE PASSIONATE PILGRIME.
By W. Shakespeare . . . 1599.

I (cf. 138)

When my Love sweares that she is made of truth,
I do beleeve her (though I know she lies)
That she might thinke me some untutor'd youth,
Unskilful in the worlds false forgeries.   4
Thus vainly thinking that she thinkes me young,
Although I know my yeares be past the best:
I smiling, credite her false speaking toung,
Outfacing faults in love, with loves ill rest.   8
But wherefore sayes my love that she is young?
And wherefore say not I, that I am old:
O, Loves best habit's in a soothing toung,
And Age in love, loves not to have yeares told.   12
  Therefore I'le lye with Love, and love with me,
  Since that our faultes in love thus smother'd be.

II (cf. 144)

Two loves I have, of Comfort and Despaire,
That like two Spirits, do suggest me still:
My better Angell, is a Man (right faire)
My worser spirite a Woman (colour'd ill.)   4
To win me soone to hell, my Female evill
Tempteth my better Angell from my side:
And would corrupt my Saint to be a Divell,
Wooing his puritie with her faire pride.   8
And whether that my Angell be turnde feend,
Suspect I may (yet not directly tell:)
For being both to me: both, to each friend,
I ghesse one Angell in anothers hell: 12
  The truth I shall not know, but live in dout,
  Till my bad Angell fire my good one out.

II

Essays

Robert Graves and Laura Riding

A Study in Original Punctuation and Spelling

THE OBJECTIONS raised against the 'freakishness' of modernist poetry are usually supported by quotations from poems by Mr. E. E. Cummings and others which are not only difficult in construction and reference but are printed oddly on the page. The reader naturally looks for certain landmarks in a poem before he can begin to enjoy it: as the visitor to Paris naturally sets his mental map of the city by the Eiffel Tower, and if the Eiffel Tower were to collapse, would have difficulty in finding his way about for a few days. Modernist poets have removed the well-known landmarks and the reader is equally at a loss. The reasons for this removal are, apparently, that landmarks encourage the making of paths, that paths grow to roads, that roads soon mean walls and hedges, and that the common traveller who keeps to the roads never sees any new scenery.

> because
> you go away i give roses who
> will advise even yourself, lady
> in the most certainly(of what we
> everywhere do not touch)deep
> things;
> > remembering ever so . . .

This is the beginning of one of Mr. Cummings' poems. The first obvious oddity is the degrading of the personal pronoun 'I' to 'i.' This

SOURCE: Robert Graves, *The Common Asphodel* (London: Hamish Hamilton, 1949), pp. 84–95. Copyright 1949 International Authors, N.V. NOTE: this is an extensively revised version of Robert Graves and Laura Riding, "William Shakespeare and E. E. Cummings," in *A Survey of Modernist Poetry* (London: William Heinemann, Ltd., 1927), pp. 49–82.

has a simple enough history. The 'upper case' was once used for all nouns and proper names and the adjectives formed from them; but since the eighteenth century has been reserved for the Deity; for Royalty (in 'We' and 'Our'); for certain quasi-divine abstractions [84] such as Mystery, Power, Poetry; sometimes for 'She' and 'Thou' and so on, where love gives the pronoun a quasi-divine character. Mr. Cummings protests against the upper case being also allotted to 'I': he affects a humility, a denial of the idea of personal immortality responsible for 'I.' Moreover, 'i' is more casual and detached: it dissociates the author from the speaker of the poem. The use of 'i' is in keeping with his use of 'who,' instead of 'which,' to qualify the roses; the roses become so personal as to deserve the personal rather than the neutral relative. His next idiosyncrasy is his denial of a capital letter to each new line of the poem. Now, if this convention were not so well established, it would seem as odd and as unnecessary as, for instance, quotation marks seem in eighteenth-century books when they enclose each line of a long speech. The modernist rejection of the initial capital letter can be justified on the grounds that it gives the first word of each line, which may be a mere 'and' or 'or,' an unnatural emphasis. If for special reasons the poet wishes to capitalize the first word, the fact that it is capitalized in any case, like all the other initial 'And's' and 'Or's,' makes any such niceness impossible.

Later in the poem a capital letter occurs at the beginning of a new sentence to call attention to the full stop which might otherwise be missed: but the 'because' at the beginning of the poem need not be capitalized since it obviously *is* the beginning. Similarly, the conventional comma after 'lady' is suppressed because the end of the line makes a natural pause without the need of punctuation. Commas are used to mark pauses, not merely as the geographical boundaries of a clause. Mr. Cummings has even inserted one in another poem between the *n* and *g* of the word 'falling' to suggest the slowness of the falling. Colons, semicolons and full stops he uses to mark pauses of varying length. To indicate a still longer pause he leaves a blank line. In the quotation just given, the new line at 'remembering' is to mark a change of tone, though the pause is no longer than a semicolon's worth. He uses parentheses for *sotto voce* pronunciation; or if they occur in the middle of a word, as in:

the taxi-man p(ee)ps his whistle

they denote a certain quality of the letters enclosed—here the sharp whistling sound between the opening and closing (the two *p*'s) of the taxi-man's lips. When this system of notation is carried to a point of great accuracy we find lines like the following: [85]

with-ered unspeaking:tWeNtY, f i n g e r s, large

which, if quoted detached from their context, seem to support any charge of irrational freakishness, but in their context are completely intelligible. Moreover, Mr. Cummings is protecting himself against future liberties that printers and editors may take with his work, by using a personal typographical system which it will be impossible to revise without destroying the poem.

He has perhaps learned a lesson from the fate of Shakespeare's sonnets: not only have his editors changed the spelling and pronunciation, but certain very occasional and obvious printer's errors in the only edition printed in Shakespeare's lifetime have been made the excuse for hundreds of unjustifiable emendations and 'modernizations.' Mr. Cummings and Shakespeare have in common a deadly accuracy. It frightens Mr. Cummings' public and provoked Shakespeare's eighteenth-century editors to meddle with his texts as being too difficult to print as they were written. We shall find that though Shakespeare's poems have a more familiar look than Mr. Cummings' on the page, they are more difficult in thought: Mr. Cummings accurately expresses, in a form peculiar to himself, what is common to everyone; Shakespeare expressed, as accurately but in the common form of his time, what was peculiar to himself.

Here are two versions of a sonnet by Shakespeare: first, the version found in *The Oxford Book of English Verse* and other popular anthologies whose editors may be assumed to have chosen this sonnet from all the rest as being particularly easy to understand; next, the version printed in the 1609 edition of the *Sonnets* and apparently copied from Shakespeare's original manuscript, though Shakespeare is most unlikely to have seen the proofs. The alterations, it will be noticed in a comparison of the two versions, are with a few exceptions chiefly in the punctuation and spelling. By showing what a great difference to the sense of juggling of punctuation marks has made in the original sonnet, we shall perhaps be able to persuade the plain reader to sympathize with what seems typographical perversity in Mr. Cummings. The modernizing of the spelling is not quite so serious a matter, though we shall see that to change a word like *blouddy* to *bloody* makes a difference not only in the atmosphere of the word but in its sound as well.[86]

I

Th' expense of Spirit in a waste of shame
Is lust in action; and till action, lust
Is perjured, murderous, bloody, full of blame,
Savage, extreme, rude, cruel, not to trust;
Enjoy'd no sooner but despisèd straight;
Past reason hunted; and, no sooner had,
Past reason hated, as a swallow'd bait
On purpose laid to make the taker mad:
Mad in pursuit, and in possession so;
Had, having, and in quest to have, extreme;
A bliss in proof, and proved, a very woe;
Before, a joy proposed; behind, a dream.
   All this the world well knows; yet none knows well
   To shun the heaven that leads men to this hell.

II

Th' expence of Spirit in a waste of shame
Is lust in action, and till action, lust
Is periurd, murdrous, blouddy full of blame,
Sauage extreame, rude, cruell, not to trust,
Inioyd no sooner but dispised straight,
Past reason hunted, and no sooner had
Past reason hated as a swollowed bayt,
On purpose layd to make the taker mad.
Made In pursut and in possession so,
Had, hauing, and in quest, to haue extreame,
A blisse in proofe and proud and very wo,
Before a ioy proposd behind a dreame,
   All this the world well knowes yet none knowes well,
   To shun the heauen that leads men to this hell.

First, to compare the spelling. As a matter of course the *u* in *proud* and *heauen* changes to *v;* the Elizabethans had no typographical *v.* There are other words in which the change of spelling does not seem to matter. *Expence, cruell, bayt, layd, pursut, blisse, proofe, wo*—these words taken by themselves are not necessarily affected by modernization, though much of the original atmosphere of the poem is lost by changing them in the gross. Sheer facility in reading a poem is no gain when one tries to discover what the poem looked like to the poet who wrote it. But other changes designed to increase reading facility [87] involve more than changes in spelling. *Periurd* to *perjured,* and *murdrous* to *murderous,* would have meant, to Shakespeare, the addition of another syllable. *Inioyd*, with the same number of syllables as *periurd*, is however printed *Enjoy'd;* while *swollowed*, which must have been meant as a three-syllabled word (Shakespeare used *ed* as a separate syllable very strictly and frequently allowed himself an extra syllable in his iambic foot) is printed *swallow'd*. When we come to *dispised*, we find in the modern version an accent over the last syllable. These liberties do not make the poem any easier; they only make it less accurate. The sound of the poem suffers through re-spelling as well as through alterations in the rhythm made by this use of apostrophes and accents. *Blouddy* was pronounced more like *blue-dy* than *bluddy;* the *ea* of *extreame* and *dreame* sounded like the *ea* in *great;* and *periurd* was probably pronounced more like *peryurd* than *pergeurd*.

But it is the changes in punctuation which do the most damage: not only to the atmosphere of the poem but to its meaning. In the second line a semicolon substituted for a comma after the first *action* gives a longer rest than Shakespeare gave; it also cuts the idea short at *action* instead of keeping *in action* and *till action* together as well as the two *lust*'s. A comma after *blouddy* makes this a separate characterization and thus reduces the weight of the whole phrase as rhythmic relief to the string of adjectives; it probably had the adverbial form of *blouddily*. Next, several semicolons are substituted for commas; these introduce pauses which break up the continuous interpenetration of images. If Shakespeare had intended such pauses he would have used semicolons, as he does elsewhere. Particularly serious is the interpolation of a comma after *no sooner had*, which confines the phrase to the special meaning 'lust no sooner had *past reason* is hated past reason.' Shakespeare did not write in the syntax of prose but in a sensitive poetic flow. The comma might as well have been put between *reason* and *hated;* it would have limited the meaning, but no more than has been done here. On the other hand a comma is omitted where Shakespeare was careful to put one, after *bayt*. With the comma, *On purpose layd*—though it refers to *bayt*—also looks back to the original idea of *lust;* without the comma it merely continues the figure of *bayt*. In the original there is a full stop at *mad*, closing the octave; in the emended version a colon is used, making the next line run on and causing the unpardonable change from *Made* to *Mad*. The capital 'I' of *In* shows how carefully the printer copied the manuscript. Evidently, Shakespeare first wrote the line without *Made*, and then, deciding that such an irregular [88] line was too dramatic, added *Made* without troubling to change the capital 'I' to a small one. In any case *Made* necessarily follows from *make* of the preceding line: 'to make the taker mad, made (mad)'; but it also enlarges the mad-making bayt to the generally extreame-making lust. The change from *Made* to *Mad* limits the final *so* of this line to *Mad* and provokes a change from comma to semicolon—'Mad in pursuit and in possession so (mad)'— whereas *mad* is only vaguely echoed in this line from the preceding one. The meaning of the original line is: 'Made In pursut and in possession as follows,' and also: 'Made In pursut and in possession as has been said.'

The comma between *in quest* and *to have extreame* has been moved forward to separate *have* from *extreame*. This line originally stood for a number of interwoven meanings:

1. The taker of the bait, the man in pursuit and in possession of lust, is made mad: is so made that he experiences both extremes at once. (What these extremes are the lines following show.)

2. The *Had, having and in quest*, might well have been written in parentheses. They explain, by way of interjection, that lust comprises all the stages of lust: the after-lust period (*Had*), the actual experience of lust (*having*), and the anticipation of lust (*in quest*); and that the extremes of lust are felt in all these stages (*to have extreame*—i.e. to have in extreme degree).

3. Further, one stage in lust is like the others, is as extreme as the others. All the distinctions made in the poem between *lust in action* and *till action lust*, between lust *In pursut* and lust *in possession* are made to show that in the end there are no real distinctions. *Had, having and in quest* is the summing up of this fact.

4. *Had* and *having* double the sense of *possession* to match the double sense of *action* implied by *Th' expence of Spirit in a waste of shame*; and *in quest* naturally refers to *In pursut*, which in turn recalls *till action*.

5. Throughout the poem it must be kept in mind that words qualifying the lust-interest refer interchangeably to the man who lusts, the object of lust and lust in the abstract. This interchangeability accounts for the apparently ungrammatical effect of the line.

With the emended punctuation the line has only one narrow sense, and this not precisely Shakespeare's; the semicolon placed after *so* of the preceding line, cuts the close co-operation between them. The shifting of the comma not only removes a pause where Shakespeare put one, and thus changes the rhythm, but the line itself loses point and does not pull its weight. In this punctuation the *whole* line ought [89] to be put into parentheses, as being a mere repetition. The *to have* linked with *in quest* is superfluous; *extreme* set off by itself is merely a descriptive adjective already used. Moreover, when the line is thus isolated between two semicolons, *Had, having,* etc., instead of effecting a harmony between the interchangeable senses, disjoints them and becomes ungrammatical. *Mad in pursuit, and in possession so* refers only to *the taker mad.* The next line, *A blisse in proofe and proud and very wo,* should explain *to have extreame;* it is not merely another parenthetical line as in the emended version. To fulfil the paradox implied in *extreame* it should mean that lust is a bliss during the proof and after the proof, and also *very wo* (truly woe) during and after the proof. The emended line, *A bliss in proof, and proved, a very woe,* which refers only to lust in the abstract, not equally to the man who lusts, means that lust is a bliss during the proof but a woe after the proof—and thus denies what Shakespeare has been at pains to show all along, that lust is all things at all times.

Once the editors began repunctuating the line they had to tamper with the words themselves. A comma after *proof* demanded a comma after *provd.* A comma after *provd* made it necessary to change *and very wo* so that it should apply to *provd* only. Another semicolon which they have put at the end of this line again breaks the continuity of the sense: the succeeding line becomes only another antithesis or rhetorical balance ('a joy in prospect, but a dream in retrospect,' to repeat the sense of 'a bliss during proof but woe after proof'), instead of carrying on the intricate and careful argument that runs without a stop through the whole sestet. The importance of the line is that it takes all the meanings in the poem one stage further. Lust in the extreme goes beyond both bliss and woe: it goes beyond reality. It is no longer lust *Had, having and in quest;* it is lust face to face with *love.* Even when consummated, lust still stands before an unconsummated joy, a proposed joy, and proposed not as a joy possible of consummation but as one only to be known through the dream by which lust leads itself on, the dream behind which this proposed joy, this love, seems to lie. This is the over-riding meaning of the line. It has other meanings, but they all defer to this. For example, it may also be read: 'Before a joy can be proposed, it must first be renounced as a real joy, it must be put behind as a dream'; or: 'Before the man in lust is a prospect of joy, yet he knows by experience that this is only a dream'; or: 'Beforehand he says that he proposed lust to be a joy, afterwards he says that it came as involuntarily as a dream'; or: 'Before (in face of) a joy proposed [90] only as a consequence of a dream, with a dream impelling him from behind.' All these and even more readings of the line are possible and legitimate, and each reading could in turn be made to explain precisely why the taker is made mad, or how lust is *to have extreame*, or why it is both *a blisse* and *very wo.* The punctuated line in the emended version, cut off from what has gone before and from what follows, can mean only: 'In prospect, lust is a joy; in retrospect, a dream.' Though a possible contributory meaning, when made the *only* meaning it presents as the theme of the poem that lust is impossible of satisfaction, whereas the theme, as carried on by the next line, is that lust as lust *is* satisfiable but that satisfied lust is in conflict with itself.

The next line, if unpunctuated except for the comma Shakespeare put at the end, is a general statement of this conflict: the man in lust is torn between lust as he well knows it in common with the world and lust in his personal experience which crazes him to hope for more than lust from lust. The force of the second *well* is to deny the first *well:* no one really knows anything of lust except in personal experience, and only through personal experience can lust be known *well* rather than 'well-known.' But separate the second *well* from the first, as in the emended version, and the direct opposition between *world* and *none*, *well knowes* and *knowes well* is destroyed, as well as the word-play between *well knowes* and *knowes well;* for by the removal of the comma after the second *well*, this becomes an adverb modifying *To shun* in the following line—*well* now means merely 'successfully' in association with *To shun*, instead of 'well enough' in association with *knowes.* This repunctuation also robs *All this* of its significance, since it refers not only to all that has gone before but to the last line too: 'All this the world well knowes yet none knowes well' the moral to be drawn from the character of lust (i.e. to shun the heaven that leads men to this hell). The character and the moral of lust the whole world well knows, but no one knows the character and the moral really well unless he disregards the moral warning and engages in lust: no one knows lust well enough to shun it because, though he knows it is both heavenly and hellish, lust can never be recognized until it has proved itself lust by turning heaven into hell.

The effect of this emended punctuation has been to restrict meanings to special interpretations of special words. Shakespeare's punctuation allows the variety of meanings he actually intends; if we must choose any one meaning, then we owe it to Shakespeare to choose at least one he intended and one embracing as many meanings as possible,[91] that is, the most difficult meaning. It is always the most difficult meaning which is the most nearly final. No prose interpretation of poetry can have complete finality, can be difficult enough. Shakespeare's editors, in trying to clarify him for the plain man, weakened and diluted his poetry and in effect deprived him of clarity. There is only one way to clarify Shakespeare: to print him as he wrote or as near as one can get to this. Making poetry easy for the reader should mean showing clearly how difficult it really is.

Mr. Cummings safeguards himself against emendation by setting down his poems, which are not complex in thought, so that their most difficult sense strikes the reader first. By giving typography an active part to play he makes his poems fixed and accurate in a way which Shakespeare's are not; but in so doing he forfeits the fluidity that Shakespeare kept by not cramping his poems with heavy punctuation and by placing more trust in the reader—a trust that may have been merited in his own day, though betrayed later. It is important to realize that the *Sonnets* were first circulated in manuscript 'among his private friends' and not intended for popular publication; the 1609 edition is now generally regarded as a piracy. The trouble with Mr. Cummings' poems is that they are too clear, once the reader sets himself to work on them. Braced as they are, they do not present the eternal difficulties that make poems immortal; they merely show how difficult it is for Mr. Cummings or for any poet to stabilize a poem once and for all. Punctuation marks in any poem of his are the bolts and pins that make it a foolproof piece of machinery requiring common sense rather than poetic intuition for its working. The outcry against his typography shows that it is as difficult to engage the common sense of the reader as his imagination. A reviewer of Mr. Cummings' recent book *is 5*, writes:

I know artists are always saying that a good painting looks as well upside down as any other way. And it may be true. The question now arises: does the same principle apply to a poem? But it is not necessary to answer the question; if a poem is good, people will gladly stand on their heads to read it. It is conceivable, if not probable, that the favourite poetic form of the future will be a sonnet arranged as a cross-word puzzle. If there were no other way of getting at Shakespeare's sonnets than by solving a cross-word puzzle sequence, I am sure the puzzles would be solved and the sonnets enjoyed. But what about Mr. Cummings? Can his poems surmount such obstacles? Well, perhaps if they cannot survive as poems they can survive as puzzles.[92]

This may be the immediate verdict on Mr. Cummings' typography, but he can be sure of one thing which Shakespeare could not: that three centuries hence his poems if they survive (and worse poets' have) will be the only ones of the early twentieth century reprinted in facsimile, not merely because he will be a literary curiosity but because he has edited his poems with punctuation beyond any possibility of re-editing. The Shakespeare to whose sonnets this reviewer makes a rhetorical appeal is the popular Shakespeare of the anthologies and not the facsimile Shakespeare. How many of our readers have ever before seen the original version quoted here? So few, surely, that it is safe to conclude that no one is willing to stand on his head to understand Shakespeare, that everyone wants a simplified Shakespeare as well as a simplified Cummings. Indeed, very few people can have looked at Shakespeare's sonnets in the original since the eighteenth century, when the popular interest in his high-spirited comedies sent a few dull commentators and book-makers to his poems. In 1766 George Steevens printed the *Sonnets* in the original and without annotations, apparently because he thought they deserved none. Twenty-seven years later he omitted the *Sonnets* from an edition of Shakespeare's works 'because the strongest Act of Parliament that could be framed would fail to compel readers into their service.' Edmund Malone, who undertook in 1780 to justify the *Sonnets* to an apathetic public by simplifying the difficult originals, was considered by Steevens to be 'disgracing his implements of criticism by the objects of their culture.' Steevens' view was the general one. Chalmers reaffirmed it as late as 1810, and if Malone had not defied the general critical opinion of the *Sonnets* by emending the texts and presenting them, well-filleted, to the plain man of the eighteenth century, the plain man of the twentieth would be unaware of their existence. Unlike Mr. Cummings' poems, Shakespeare's *Sonnets* would not even have 'survived as puzzles.'

Thus far does a study of Shakespeare's typography take one: to the difficulties of a poet with readers to whom his meanings are mysteries and for the most part must remain mysteries. A modernist poet like Mr. Cummings handles the problem by trying to get the most out of his readers; Shakespeare handled it by trying to get the most out of his poem. Logically the modernist poet should have many readers, but these with an elementary understanding of his poems; Shakespeare only a few readers, but these with an enlarged understanding of his poems. The reverse, however, is true because the reading public has [93] been so undertrained on a simplified Shakespeare and on anthology verse, that modernist poetry seems as difficult as Shakespeare really ought to seem.

Only a few points of the original sonnet have been left uncovered by our typographical survey, and these occur principally in the first few lines, which suffer from fewer emendations than the rest of the poem. The delicate inter-relation of the words of the two opening lines should not be overlooked: the strong parallelism between *expence* and *waste* and *Spirit* and *shame* expressing at once the terrible quick-change from lust as lust-enjoyed to lust as lust-despised; the double meaning of *waste* as 'expense' and as 'wilderness,' the *waste* place in which the Spirit is *wasted*; the double meaning of *expence* as 'pouring out' and as the 'price paid'; the double meaning of *of shame* as 'shameful,' i.e. 'deplorable' and as *ashamed*, *i.e.* 'self-deploring'; the double meaning of *shame* itself as 'modesty' and 'disgrace'; and the double meaning of *lust in action* as 'lust unsuspected by man in his actions because disguised as shame' (in either sense of the word), and as 'lust in progress' as opposed to 'lust contemplated.' All these alternate meanings interacting on one another, and other possible interpretations of words and phrases besides, make as it were an oracle which can be read in many senses at once, none of the senses, however, being incompatible with any others. The intensified inbreeding of words continues through the rest of the poem. *Periurd* is another example, meaning both 'falsely spoken of' and 'false.' Again, *heaven* and *hell* have the ordinary prose meaning of 'pleasure' and 'pain'; but 'heaven,' for Shakespeare, was the longing for a temperamental stability which at the same time he mistrusted; his 'hell' was akin to Marlowe's hell, which

> . . . hath no limits nor is circumscribed
> In one selfe place, for where we are is hell.

The reader who complains of the obscurity of modernist poets must be reminded of the intimate Shakespearian background with which he needs to be familiar before he can understand Shakespeare. The failure of imagination and knowledge in Shakespeare's editors has reduced his sonnets to the indignity of being easy for everybody. Beddoes, an early nineteenth-century imitator of Shakespeare, said:

About Shakespeare. You might just as well attempt to remodel the seasons and the laws of life and death as to alter one 'jot or tittle' of his eternal [94] thoughts. 'A Star,' you call him. If he was a star all the other stage-scribblers can hardly be considered a constellation of brass buttons.

Few of the modernist poets are Stars, but most of them are very highly polished brass buttons and entitled to protect themselves from the sort of tarnishing which Shakespeare, though a Star, has suffered.

Shakespeare's attitude towards the perversely stupid reorganizing of lines and regrouping of ideas is jocularly shown in the satire in repunctuation given in the prologue of *Piramus and Thisby* in *A Midsummer Night's Dream:*

QUINCE: If we offend, it is with our good will.
                That you should thinke, we come not to offend,
                But with good will. To shew our simple skill,
                That is the true beginning of our end.
                Consider then, we come but in despight.
                We do not come, as minding to content you,
                Our true intent is. All for your delight,
                We are not heere. That you should here repent you,
                The Actors are at hand; and by their show,
                You shall know all, that you are like to know.
THESEUS: This fellow doth not stand vpon points.

            .   .   .   .   .

LYSANDER: His speech was like a tangled chaine: nothing
                impaired, but all disordered . . . [95]

L. C. Knights

Shakespeare's Sonnets

I

THAT THERE IS so little genuine criticism in the terrifying number of books and essays on Shakespeare's Sonnets can only be
partly accounted for by the superior attractiveness of gossip. A more
radical explanation is to be found in certain wide-spread, more or less
unconscious assumptions. In the first place, although consciously we
may not believe that the Sonnets—even the first hundred and twenty-
six—form a continuous and ordered collection, we tend to assume that
the collection is more homogeneous than in fact it is, and we tend,
therefore, to make rather sweeping generalizations about 'The Sonnets'
as a whole.[1] A second assumption was made amusingly explicit in the
words which John Benson, the publisher of the 1640 edition—who
had an eye on changing taste—addressed to the Reader: 'In your
perusall you shall finde them SEREN, cleere and eligantly plaine, such
gentle straines as shall recreate and not perplex your braine, no intricate or cloudy stuffe to puzzell intellect, but perfect eloquence.'
Many of the sonnets were written about the time of *A Midsummer
Night's Dream* and *Romeo and Juliet;* the verse is therefore essentially
unlike the verse of *King Lear*—it is incapable of subtleties; the meaning is on the surface. No doubt this is an exaggeration, but the effects
of an assumption not very dissimilar to this can be seen in such essays
as keep decently clear of William Hughes, the Sea Cook, and the rest,

SOURCE: *Scrutiny*, III (September, 1934), 133–160. Reprinted in *Explorations*
(London: Chatto & Windus, 1946), pp. 40–65.

[1] The tendency is encouraged by the fact that the sonnets are printed in
a numbered sequence, without titles. And remembering the part played by
verbal habit in directing thought, we may consider the effect of the mere
repetition of the phrase, 'The Sonnets.'

and which attempt to approach the sonnets directly, as poetry. George Wyndham, for example, in his essay on 'The Poems of Shakespeare' does not entirely confine himself to pointing out the more picturesque aspects of [133] imagery and the melodic effect of certain lines; but his criticism encourages the belief not only that such things have an intrinsic importance, but that visual imagery, 'the music of vowel and consonant' and so on, have much the same function in the sonnets as they have, say, in Spenser's stanzas on the Bower of Bliss. 'Apart from all else, it is the sheer beauty of diction in Shakespeare's Sonnets which has endeared them to poets.' Maybe (though they were endeared to Keats and Coleridge for other reasons, and Spenser, we remember, is the Poets' Poet); but the sentence illustrates the kind of limitation that the second assumption imposes: criticism is confined to a surface approach; it remains inappropriately and unnecessarily naïve. It is unfortunate that most readers are familiar with the Sonnets only in modern editions in which, as Laura Riding and Robert Graves pointed out, 'the perversely stupid reorganizing of lines and regrouping of ideas'—all in the interests of 'clarity'—is achieved by the simple expedient of altering the original punctuation.[2] In the Arden edition the majority of deviations of this kind are not even recorded in the textual notes. The assumption is thus imposed and perpetuated by the common text.

If we can rid ourselves of these two presuppositions we shall have gone some way towards a revaluation of the Sonnets. 'Shakespeare's Sonnets' is a miscellaneous collection of poems, written at different times, for different purposes, and with very different degrees of poetic intensity. (Gildon's edition had the appropriate title, *Poems on Several Occasions*). The first necessity of criticism is to assess each poem independently, on its merits as poetry, and to abandon all attempts to find an ordered sequence. The second necessity is to know what kind of *development* to look for—which is a different matter.

I may as well say here that I believe all the Sonnets to be comparatively early in date—roughly from 1592 to 1597 or 1598; none of them is likely to have been written after the second part [134] of *King Henry IV*.[3] We have no means of knowing how they came to be

---

[2] See their analysis of Sonnet 129 in *A Survey of Modernist Poetry*, pp. 63–81. No one need suppose that, in complaining of wanton 'emendations,' I am claiming complete infallibility for the Quarto, of which, by the way, there is an admirable facsimile edition published by Noel Douglas at 5/-.

[3] The mortal moon hath her eclipse endur'd' (107)—the only 'external reference' of any difficulty—is more likely to refer to the ending of the

published by Thorpe in 1609 (J. M. Robertson made some attractive guesses), but the evidence suggests that the publication was unauthorized by Shakespeare, that the poems therefore had not been revised for publication, and that the arrangement adopted in the Quarto (except for the grouping of certain Sonnets which obviously go together) has no particular validity; although the printed sequence seems to represent a rough approximation to the time order in which they were composed. The possibility that some of the Sonnets—like *A Lover's Complaint,* which was published with them—are not by Shakespeare, is not likely to be disputed on *a priori* grounds by those who are familiar with the habits of contemporary publishers and the fortunes of authors' manuscripts in the 16th and 17th centuries. (The fate of the MS. of *Astrophel and Stella* is a common instance). One can point to such things as the 17th century poetical miscellanies with their haphazard assignment of authorship; and Cowley's Preface to the 1656 edition of his Poems begins with some interesting remarks in this connection. But since there is no room for argument of this kind I assume a high degree of authenticity.

II

I do not of course propose to employ my slender resources in the long-standing Southampton-Pembroke controversy and its subtle ramifications; but the popular view that the Sonnets are in some way 'autobiographical' demands some notice. The eloquent chapters in which Frank Harris melts out Shakespeare's personal history from the poetic alloy ('The Sonnets give us the story, the whole terrible, sinful, magical story of Shakespeare's passion.') are merely an exotic development of a kind of writing that is common among more eminent critics. 'No capable poet,' says Dr. Bradley, 'much less a Shakespeare, intending to produce a merely "dramatic" series of poems, would dream of inventing [135] *a story like that of the Sonnets,* or, even if he did, of treating it as they treat it.' [4] Now the first point that I wish to make against the common forms of biographical excursion (leaving aside for the moment more important considerations) is that the foundations on which they are built have not, to say the least, been the

Queen's climacterical year (1596) than to her death—as Dr. G. B. Harrison has pointed out.

[4] I have italicized the phrase that forces the dilemma: *either* autobiographical *or* 'merely dramatic' and conventional.

subject of any very discriminating attention. Those who are unwilling to accept the particular validity of Mr. Eliot's remark that 'the more perfect the artist, the more completely separate in him will be the man who suffers and the mind which creates; the more perfectly will the mind digest and transmute the passions which are its material,' backed though it is by the authority of Coleridge (Compare *Biographia Literaria*, XV, 2), have only to turn to the Sonnets of supposedly highest biographical significance and consider them as examples of personal poetry: that is, as expressions by a powerful mind of reactions to a situation in which the man himself is deeply concerned.

Sonnets 33 to 42 are headed by Sir Israel Gollancz, 'Love's First Disillusioning,' the various sub-titles ending with 'Forgiveness.' Sonnet 42 runs:

> That thou hast her it is not all my griefe,
> And yet it may be said I lov'd her deerely,
> That she hath thee is of my wayling cheefe,
> A losse in love that touches me more neerely.

Since the obvious is sometimes necessary, we may say that if Shakespeare had suffered the experience indicated by a prose paraphrase (for some of the biographical school the Sonnets might as well have been in prose) it would have affected him very differently from *this*. The banal movement, the loose texture of the verse, the vague gestures that stand for emotion, are sufficient index that his interests are not very deeply involved. (Contrast the run and ring of the verse, even in minor sonnets, when Shakespeare is absorbed by his subject— 'Devouring time blunt thou the Lyons pawes . . .'). His sole interest is in the display of wit, the working out of the syllogism: [136]

> Loving offendors thus I will excuse yee,
> Thou doost love her, because thou knowst I love her,
> And for my sake even so doth she abuse me,
> Suffering my friend for my sake to approove her,
>
> .   .   .
>
> But here's the joy, my friend and I are one,
> Sweete flattery, then she loves but me alone.

This, I admit, is a particularly glaring example, though it has its parallels amongst the False Friend and Faithless Mistress sonnets of 'Group B' (Numbers 127-152) to which the notes commonly refer us at this point, and the complete insipidity of one 'autobiographical' sonnet is enough to cause some honest doubt. Sonnets 78 to 86, dealing with the rival poets, are superior as poetry, but here also it is plain that Shakespeare derived a good deal of pleasure from the neatness of the argument:

> I grant (sweet love) thy lovely argument
> Deserves the travaile of a worthier pen,
> Yet what of thee thy Poet doth invent,
> He robs thee of, and payes it thee againe.

Wyndham remarked that these nine sonnets are 'playful throughout, suggesting no tragedy'—though 'playful' hardly does them justice. They are rather fine examples of an unusual mode of compliment and complaint, at once courtly and ironic. Those who picture Shakespeare as completely enthralled by his love for a particular friend or patron, and therefore deeply wounded by neglect, can hardly have noticed the tone of critical, and sometimes amused, detachment adopted towards himself ('Cleane starved for a looke'), the rival ('He of tall building and of goodly pride'), and the recipient of his verses ('You to your beautious blessings adde a curse, Being fond on praise, which makes your praises worse').

Of course I do not mean to imply that Shakespeare had never felt love or friendship or exasperation, or that his personal experiences had no effect on his poetry.—One can hardly say of the Sonnets, as Johnson said of Cowley's *Mistress*, that 'the compositions are such as might have been written for penance by [137] a hermit, or for hire by a philosophical rhymer who had only heard of another sex.'—I am merely insisting that those who are attracted by biographical speculation should be quite sure of what Shakespeare is doing, of the direction and quality of his interests, before they make a flat translation into terms of actual life: that is, even the biographers must be literary critics. Some of the most interesting and successful sonnets may well have had their context in a personal relationship; but whenever we analyse their interest (further illustration at this point would involve a good deal of repetition later) we find that it lies, not in the general theme or situation, which is all that is relevant to a biographical interpretation, but in various accretions of thought and feeling, in 'those frequent witty or profound reflections, which the poet's ever active mind has deduced from, or connected with, the imagery and the incidents,' in the exploration of a mood or discrimination of emotion.

If this is so, the attempt to isolate the original stimulus (which in any case *may* have been an imagined situation—'Emotions which the poet has never experienced will serve his turn as well as those familiar to him.') is not only hazardous, it is irrelevant. After all, even if Shakespeare had assured us that the Sonnets were written under the stress of a friendship broken and restored and an intrigue with Mary Fitton, the only importance they could have for us would be as poetry, as something *made out* of experience.

With this criterion of importance we can see in proper perspective a second argument—commonly offered as the only alternative to the biographical theory—that the sonnets are exercises on conventional themes, embellished with conventional ornaments. The argument has a definite place in criticism, and we should be grateful to Sir Sidney Lee for his exhaustive collection of parallels. When we read

> Not marble, nor the guilded monument,
> Of Princes shall out-live this powrefull rime

it is perhaps as well that we should know that the lines have an ancestry reaching back at least as far as Horace; it is as well that we should be familiar with the theme of mutability and the various forms of diluted Platonism that were common when Shakespeare wrote. But a convention is a general thought, a general attitude,[138] or a general mode of presentation, and a discussion of Shakespeare's Sonnets in terms of the 'typical' Elizabethan sonnet sequence tells us no more about them than an account of the Revenge Play tells us about *Hamlet*.

III

The most profitable approach to the Sonnets is, it seems to me, to consider them in relation to the development of Shakespeare's blank verse. There are certain obvious difficulties: the Sonnets take their start from something that can, for convenience, be called the Spenserian mode, whereas the influence of Spenser on the early plays is both slighter and more indirect; and the dramatic verse naturally contains a good many elements that are not to be found in any of the sonnets. But it is only by making what may seem an unnecessarily roundabout approach—even then at the risk of over-simplification—that one can hope to shift the stress to those aspects of the sonnets that it is most profitable to explore.

No account of the development of Shakespeare's blank verse in general terms can be very satisfactory. A comparison will help to point my few necessary generalizations. Richard's lament at Pomfret is a fairly typical example of the early set speeches:

> And here have I the daintiness of ear
> To check time broke in a disorder'd string;
> But for the concord of my state and time
> Had not an ear to hear my true time broke.
> I wasted time, and now doth time waste me;
> For now hath time made me his numbering clock:
> My thoughts are minutes; and with sighs they jar
> Their watches on unto mine eyes, the outward watch,
> Whereto my finger, like a dial's point,
> Is pointing still, in cleansing them from tears.
> Now sir, the sound that tells what hour it is
> Are clamorous groans, which strike upon my heart,
> Which is the bell: so sighs and tears and groans
> Show minutes, times, and hours: but my time
> Runs posting on in Bolingbroke's proud joy,
> While I stand fooling here, his Jack o' the clock.[139]

The only line that could possibly be mistaken for an extract from a later play is the last, in which the concentrated bitterness ('Jack o' the clock' has a wide range of relevant associations, and the tone introduces a significant variation in the rhythm) serves to emphasize the previous diffuseness. It is not merely that the imagery is elaborated out of all proportion to any complexity of thought or feeling, the emotion is suspended whilst the conceit is developed, as it were, in its own right. Similarly the sound and movement of the verse, the alliteration, repetition and assonance, seem to exist as objects of attention in themselves rather than as the medium of a compulsive force working from within. Such emotion as is communicated is both vague and remote.

Set beside this the well known speech of Ulysses:

> Time hath, my lord, a wallet at his back,
> Wherein he puts alms for oblivion,
> A great-siz'd monster of ingratitudes:
> Those scraps are good deeds past; which are devour'd
> As fast as they are made, forgot as soon
> As done: perseverance, dear my lord,
> Keeps honour bright: to have done is to hang
> Quite out of fashion, like a rusty mail
> In monumental mockery. Take the instant way;

> For honour travels in a strait so narrow
> Where one but goes abreast: keep then the path;
> For emulation hath a thousand sons
> That one by one pursue: if you give way,
> Or hedge aside from the direct forthright,
> Like to an enter'd tide they all rush by
> And leave you hindmost.

The verse of course is much more free, and the underlying speech movement gives a far greater range of rhythmic subtlety. The sound is more closely linked with—is, in fact, an intimate part of—the meaning. The imagery changes more swiftly. But these factors are only important as contributing to a major development: the main difference lies in the greater immediacy and concreteness of the verse. In reading the second passage more of the mind is involved, and it is involved in more ways. It does not contemplate a general emotion, it *lives* a particular experience. Crudely,[140] the reader is not told that there is a constant need for action, he experiences a particular urgency.

This account could be substantiated in detail, but for my purpose it may be sufficient to point to a few of the means by which the reader is influenced in this way. Oblivion, at first a kind of negative presence, becomes (via 'monster') an active, devouring force, following hard on the heels of time. ('Forgot,' balancing 'devoured,' keeps the image in a proper degree of subordination). The perseverance which keeps honour bright introduces a sense of effort, as in polishing metal, and (after a particularly effective jibe at inactivity) the effort is felt as motion. Moreover, 'Take the instant way' and 'Keep then the path,' involving muscular tension, suggest the strain of keeping foremost. In the next two lines the roar and clatter of emulation's thousand sons are audible, and immediately we feel the pressure of pursuit ('hedge aside' is no dead metaphor) and—in the movement of the verse, as though a dam had broken—the overwhelming tide of pursuers. The short and exhausted line, 'And leave you hindmost,' is the lull after the wave has passed.

This line of development (continued in the plays of complete maturity) is central. Primarily it is a matter of technique—the words have a higher potency, they release and control a far more complex response than in the earlier plays—but it is much more than that. The kind of immediacy that I have indicated allows the greatest subtlety in particular presentment (The thing 'which shackles accidents, and bolts up change' is *not* the same as 'The deed which puts an end to

human vicissitude'), whilst 'the quick flow and the rapid change of the images,' as Coleridge noted, require a 'perpetual activity of attention on the part of the reader,' generate, we may say, a form of activity in which thought and feeling are fused in a new mode of apprehension. That is, the technical development implies—is dependent on—the development and unification of sensibility. It is this kind of development (in advance of the dramatic verse of the same period in some respects and obviously behind it in others) that we find in the Sonnets, and which makes it imperative that discussion should start from considerations of technique.

Those aspects of technique which can to some extent be isolated as showing 'the first and most obvious excellence . . .[141] the sense of musical delight' have been well illustrated by George Wyndham, but his belief that 'Eloquent Discourse' is 'the staple of the Sonnets and their highest excellence' precludes the more important approach.

After 1579 the most pervasive influence on Elizabethan lyric poetry was that of Spenser. *Astrophel and Stella* may have been the immediate cause of the numerous sonnet cycles, but it was from Spenser that the sonneteers derived most of their common characteristics—the slow movement and melody, the use of imagery predominantly visual and decorative, the romantic glamour, the tendency towards a gently elegiac note. In the Spenserian mode no object is sharply forced upon the consciousness.

> Of mortall life the leafe, the bud, the floure,
> Ne more doth flourish after first decay,
> That earst was sought to decke both bed and bowre,
> Of manie a Ladie, and many a Paramoure:
> Gather therefore the Rose, whilest yet is prime . . .

As music this is perfect and one is forced to admire; but one is only mildly affected by the vision of the passage of time, and even the injunction to pluck the rose has no urgency. Now there is in Shakespeare's Sonnets a quality that, at a first reading, seems very near to this: Sonnets 98 and 102, for example, are successful as fairly direct developments of the Spenserian mode. But if we turn to Sonnet 35 we see the conjunction of that mode with something entirely new.

> No more bee greev'd at that which thou hast done,
> Roses have thornes, and silver fountaines mud,
> Cloudes and eclipses staine both Moone and Sunne,
> And loathsome canker lives in sweetest bud.

All men make faults, and even I in this,
Authorizing thy trespas with compare,
My selfe corrupting salving thy amisse,
Excusing thy sins more then thy sins are:
For to thy sensuall fault I bring in sence,
Thy adverse party is thy Advocate,
And gainst my selfe a lawfull plea commence,
Such civill war is in my love and hate,[142]
That I an accessary needs must be,
To that sweet theefe which sourely robs from me.

The first four lines we may say, both in movement and imagery, are typically Spenserian and straightforward. The fifth line begins by continuing the excuses, 'All men make faults,' but with an abrupt change of rhythm Shakespeare turns the generalization against himself: 'All men make faults, and even I in this,' *i.e.* in wasting my time finding romantic parallels for your sins, as though intellectual analogies ('sence') were relevant to your sensual fault. The painful complexity of feeling (Shakespeare is at the same time tender towards the sinner and infuriated by his own tenderness) is evident in the seventh line which means both, 'I corrupt myself when I find excuses for you' (or 'when I comfort myself in this way'), and, 'I'm afraid I myself make you worse by excusing your faults'; and although there is a fresh change of tone towards the end (The twelfth line is virtually a sigh as he gives up hope of resolving the conflict), the equivocal 'needs must' and the sweet-sour opposition show the continued civil war of the emotions.

Some such comment as this was unavoidable, but it is upon the simplest and most obvious of technical devices that I wish to direct attention. In the first quatrain the play upon the letters *s* and *l* is mainly musical and decorative, but with the change of tone and direction the alliterative *s* becomes a hiss of half-impotent venom:

All men make faults, and even I in this,
Authorizing thy trespas with compare,
My selfe corrupting salving thy amisse,
Excusing thy sins more then thy sins are:
For to thy sensuall fault I bring in sence . . .

The scorn is moderated here, but it is still heard in the slightly rasping note of the last line,

To that sweet theefe which sourely robs from me.

From the fifth line, then, the alliteration is functional: by playing off against the comparative regularity of the rhythm it expresses an important part of the meaning, and helps to carry the experience alive into the mind of the reader. With Spenser or [143] Tennyson in mind we should say that both alliteration and assonance were primarily musical devices, as indeed they are in many of the sonnets:

> Noe longer mourne for me when I am dead,
> Than you shall heare the surly sullen bell
> Give warning to the world that I am fled
> From this vile world with vildest wormes to dwell.

Here, for example, the sound, if not independent of the meaning, usurps a kind of attention that is incompatible with a full and sharp awareness. But that which links the sonnets, in this respect, with the later plays is the use of assonance and alliteration to secure a heightened awareness, an increase of life and power:

> Your love and pity doth the impression fill,
> Which vulgar scandall stampt upon my brow.

> Cheared and checkt even by the self-same skie.

> All this the world well knowes yet none knowes well.

>   So shall I taste
> At first the very worst of fortune's might.

> And made myselfe a motley to the view.

In reading the last line the nose wrinkles in disgust, and we hear the rattle of the fool,—but I hope the reader will be inclined to look up the examples in their context (112, 15, 129, 90, and 110 respectively).

A slight shift of attention brings into focus a second aspect of development connected with the first. If we open any of the great plays almost at random we find effects comparable in kind to this, from *Lear:*

> Crown'd with rank fumiter and furrow-weeds,
> With hor-docks, hemlocks, nettles, cuckoo-flowers,
> Darnel, and all the idle weeds that grow
> In our sustaining corn.

The rank and bristling profusion of the weeds is there, in the clogged movement of the first two lines, whilst the unimpeded [144] sweep of the verse that follows contributes powerfully to the image of never-failing

fertility. In many of the sonnets we can see Shakespeare working towards this use of his medium, learning to use a subtly varied play of
the speech rhythm and movement against the formal pattern of the
verse: [5]

> Ah yet doth beauty like a Dyall hand,
> Steale from his figure, and no pace perceiv'd.

> And on just proofe surmise, accumilate.

> Then hate me when thou wilt, if ever, now,
> Now while the world is bent my deeds to crosse . . .

> That it could so preposterouslie be stain'd . . .

In the steady movement of the first extract, in the slightly impeded
progress of the second, in the impetuous movement of the third, and
the rising incredulity of the fourth, the verse (if I may borrow the
phrase) 'enacts the meaning.' Perhaps one can hardly miss this kind
of effect, but a development connected with it—the use of speech
movement and idiom in the sonnets to obtain a firmer command of
tone (a matter of some importance in determining their meaning)—
seems to have been fairly consistently overlooked. The sonnet form
is a convention in which it is only too easy to adopt a special 'poetic'
attitude, and to the four 'strong promises of the strength of Shakespeare's genius' which Coleridge found in the early poems might well
be added a fifth: the way in which, in his sonnets, he broke away
from the formal and incantatory mode (convention and precedent
being what they were) to make the verse a more flexible and trans-
parent medium. Sonnet 7 has a typically stylized opening:

> Loe in the Orient when the gracious light,
> Lifts up his burning head, each under eye
> Doth homage to his new appearing sight,
> Serving with lookes his sacred majesty.[145]

Contrast, say, Sonnet 82:

> I grant thou wert not married to my Muse,
> And therefore maiest without attaint ore-looke
> The dedicated words which writers use
> Of their faire subject, blessing every booke.

[5] I ought to refer in this connection to F. R. Leavis' essay on Milton
(*Scrutiny*, September, 1933) and the chapter on Hopkins in *New Bearings
in English Poetry*. See also Professor Grierson's Introduction to *Metaphysical Poetry*, pp. xxii-xxv.

In the first line we hear the inflexion of the speaking voice, and it is the conversational movement that contributes the equivocal note of amused irony, directed towards the fulsome dedications and their—inevitably—fair subject. (Compare the 'precious phrase by all the Muses filed' of Sonnet 85). Sometimes a similar effect is used for deliberate contrast, as in

> Thus have I had thee as a dreame doth flatter,
> In sleepe a King, but waking no such matter

where after a line and a half of yearning the offhand colloquialism shows us Shakespeare detached and critical. It is of course only by exploiting speech movement that any kind of delicacy of statement is possible (Reservation is an obvious case, as in 'I found—or thought I found—you did exceed . . .'), but it is the fairly frequent use of various ironic inflexions that it seems particularly important to stress:

> He nor that affable familiar ghost
> Which nightly gulls him with intelligence . . .

> Farewell thou art too deare for my possessing,
> And like enough thou knowst thy estimate . . .

—and there are other examples more or less immediately apparent.[6] [146] To be alive to modulations of this kind is to recognize—which is what one would expect—that the *intelligence* that created, say, *Troilus and Cressida*, is also at work in the sonnets.

I have already suggested that the critics who reconstruct a Shakespeare hopelessly and uncritically subjugated by a particular experience must be quite deaf to variations of tone. It is the same incapacity which causes them to read the sonnets in which the touch is lightest with portentous solemnity and to perform various feats of legerdemain with the meaning. In Sonnet 94 the irony is serious and destructive.

---

[6] Of course the tone is not determined solely by the movement; often, for example, the degree of seriousness with which Shakespeare is writing is indicated by the imagery. Consider the roses of Sonnet 99 which 'fearefully on thornes did stand,' or the poet's thousand groans, 'one on anothers necke,' in Sonnet 131. The advantages of verse based on conversational movement for a comic or satiric effect are plain in Dryden; contrast his account of Shimei with Clough's 'The Latest Decalogue'—'Did wisely from expensive sins refrain' with

> No graven images shall be
> Worshipped, except the currency.

> They that have powre to hurt, and will doe none,
> That doe not do the thing, they most do showe,
> Who moving others, are themselves as stone,
> Unmooved, could, and to temptation slow:
> They rightly do inherit heavens graces,
> And husband natures ritches from expence,
> They are the Lords and owners of their faces,
> Others, but stewards of their excellence:
> The sommers flowre is to the sommer sweet,
> Though to itselfe, it onely live and die,
> But if that flowre with base infection meete,
> The basest weed out-braves his dignity:
>   For sweetest things turne sowrest by their deedes,
>   Lillies that fester, smell far worse then weeds.

This is commonly taken with Sonnet 95 and read as an exhortation to chastity—' 'Tis a sign of greatness to be self-contained' is Gollancz's summary, and J. Q. Adams glosses: 'The friend has fallen into a life of gross sensuality, and the poet finds it necessary to rebuke him in the strongest language.' If nothing else, 'Lillies that fester' (an image suggesting less the excesses of sensuality than 'the distortions of in-grown virginity') might cast some doubts on this simple interpretation. The opening is coldly analytic (I at least am unable to detect any symptoms of moral fervour), and the unprepossessing virtues of those 'who moving others, are themselves as stone' can hardly be held up for admiration; they remind us rather of Angelo, 'whose blood was very snow-broth.' If we remember Shakespeare's condemnation, in the early sonnets, of those who husband their riches instead of [147] act-ing as stewards of their excellence, we shall hardly be able to mistake the second quatrain for unambiguous praise; in any case the image suggested by 'They are the Lords and owners of their faces' is unob-trusively comic, and the comma after 'Others' suggests that Shake-speare is ironically repeating the opinion of the self-righteous. The sonnet may have been intentionally equivocal, but there can be little doubt of Shakespeare's attitude—it is the attitude of *Measure for Measure*—and the poem (though not altogether successful) forms an interesting complement to the more famous Sonnet 129. Perhaps I had better add that I do not regard the earlier sonnet as an encouragement to incontinence.

The vivid and surprising 'Lillies that fester' has been commented upon as typically Shakespearean, and indeed the image (whether bor-

rowed or not) is typical of the way in which contrasted sets of associations are fused in the verse of the later plays. But it is hardly representative of the imagery of the sonnets. In the later plays a wide range
of relevant associations, both of thought and feeling ('relevant' is
clearly a matter for concrete illustration), are compressed into the
single image ('The bank and shoal of time'). Images of sight, touch,
muscular adjustment and so on follow in rapid succession (No cata-
logue of 'visual,' 'tactile,' etc., is sufficient to cover the variety), and
different modes may be combined in our response at any one point.
And there are those unexpected and startling juxtapositions of contrasted images:

> The *crown* o' the earth doth *melt*.

> This sensible warm *motion* to become
> A kneaded *clod*.

Now in the sonnets not all of these characteristic uses of imagery
are developed: it is largely this which justifies us in assigning them a
date earlier than *Troilus and Cressida* or *Measure for Measure*. With
the exception of the striking line, 'Mine appetite I never more will
grind On newer proof,' we can find no parallels to 'Lillies that fester.'
Such lines as

> Gor'd mine own thoughts . . .

and

> To bitter sawces did I frame my feeding [148]

indicate an important line of development, but there is little of the
intensely physical impact that we find in *Macbeth* ('The blanket of
the dark' 'We'd jump the life to come'). Most of the images—even
when finely effective—arouse only one set of vibrations in the mind:

> Full many a glorious morning have I seene,
> Flatter the mountaine tops with soveraine eie

> My nature is subdu'd
> To what it workes in, like the Dyers hand.

If we place 'the dust and injury of age' (108) and '. . . whose mil-
lion'd accidents Creep in 'twixt vows . . .' (115) beside Macbeth's

> Tomorrow, and tomorrow, and tomorrow,
> Creeps in this petty pace from day to day . . .
> And all our yesterdays have lighted fools
> The way to dusty death

and ask ourselves exactly why 'creep' and 'dust' are used in each instance, we shall have a fair measure of the later development.

But even when we have made these qualifications the stress remains
on the positive achievement; there is a clear advance on the early
plays. In the sonnets no image is *merely* decorative, as in Romeo's
'Two of the fairest stars in all heaven . . .' Few are excessively developed, as in the laments of Richard II or even as in the Bastard's
'Commodity, the bias of the world . . .' There is indeed a constant
succession of varied images, which, because they are concrete and
because they are drawn from the world of familiar experience, give
precise expression to emotion:

> Beated and chopt with tand antiquitie.
>
> Incertenties now crowne them-selves assur'de.
>
> But makes antiquitie for aye his page.
>
> And captive-good attending Captaine ill.

What it comes to is this: in the sonnets, as in the later plays, the
imagery gives immediacy and precision, and it demands and fosters
an alert attention. But the range of emotions liberated by any [149]
one image is narrower, though not always less intense. We have not
yet reached the stage in which 'the *maximum* amount of apparent
incongruity is resolved simultaneously.' [7] That is, the creating mind
has not yet achieved that co-ordination of widely diverse (and, in the
ordinary mind, often conflicting) experiences, which is expressed in
the imagery no less than in the total structure of the great tragedies.
Put in this way the conclusion may seem obvious, but it is a point to
which I shall have to return when I deal with Shakespeare's treatment
of the Time theme in the sonnets.

A complete account of technical development in the sonnets would
include a detailed discussion of ambiguity—a technical device (if we
may call it that) of which, since the publication of Mr. Empson's
Seven Types and the Riding and Graves analysis of Sonnet 129, one
can hardly fail to be aware; though the word seems to have caused
some unnecessary critical shyness. But the argument would raise
fundamental issues with which I do not feel competent to deal, and
all that I have to offer—after a very brief indication of the way in
which the language of the sonnets is 'charged' by means of overlaying
meanings—is some caution.

[7] The phrase is Edgell Rickword's.

There is a clear difference between the kind of compression that we find in 'The steepe up heavenly hill' (7), 'The world without end houre' (57), or 'Th'imprison'd absence of your libertie' (58), and in such lines as 'So thou, thy selfe out-going in thy noon' (7), or 'That I have frequent binne with unknown mindes' (117). The first three are forms of elliptical construction requiring no unusual agility in the mind accustomed to English idiom. In the last two the context demands that we shall keep two or more meanings in mind simultaneously: 'thy selfe outgoing' means both 'over-reaching yourself' and 'you yourself going further on'; 'unknown minds' are 'strangers,' 'nonentities,' and perhaps 'such minds as I am ashamed to mention' (the Arden edition gives precedents for all these interpretations). In the same way as two or more meanings are fused in one word, different constructions may be run together, as in

> None else to me, nor I to none alive,
> That my steel'd sence or changes right or wrong.   (112) [150]

or they may be overlaid:

> My selfe corrupting salving thy amisse   (35)

There can, I think, be no doubt that Shakespeare deliberately (though 'deliberately' may be too strong a word) avails himself of the resources of the language in this way; I have chosen what seem to be the most incontrovertible examples, and they are clearly in line with his later development. In Sonnet 40 and one or two others we have something very like conscious experimenting with simple forms of ambiguous statement.

Now the important point is this: that when ambiguity occurs in successful verse it is valuable in much the same way as successful imagery is valuable, as representing a heightened, more inclusive and more unified form of consciousness. One need hardly say that the mere presence of ambiguities is not necessarily an indication of poetic value—they may equally represent unresolved contradictions in the poet's mind—or that the estimate of success is a more delicate matter (concerned with the whole poetic effect) than the working-out of alternative meanings. There is no need for me to praise Mr. Empson, though I may say that he is the only critic I know of who has detected the equivocal attitude which Shakespeare sometimes expresses towards his subject, and that some of his analyses (of Sonnet 58, for example) seem to me immediately convincing. But in perhaps the majority of cases (I am confining my attention entirely to the pages he devotes to the Sonnets [8]) his lists of meanings seem to me to be obtained by focussing upon a part of the poem (almost one might say by forgetting the poem) and considering the various grammatical possibilities of the part so isolated. His analysis of Sonnet 83, for example (pp. 168–175), is valuable as suggesting the conscious and subliminal meanings that may well have been in Shakespeare's mind at the time of writing, but only a few of them are there, in the poem. It is very unfair to make this charge without substantiating it in detail, but to do so would add many pages to the already excessive length of this essay; I can only hope that the reader will look up the analysis for himself,—and my account of Sonnet 123, below, is relevant here. Mr. Eliot has [151] remarked that the sonnets are 'full of some stuff that the writer could not drag to light, contemplate, or manipulate into art.' [9] The sentence might be taken by the biographers to refer to an especially painful personal experience lying behind the sonnets. But it suggests more profitable speculation if we interpret it that Shakespeare had not yet fully mastered the technique of complex expression.

IV

These imperfect considerations of technique will perhaps have been sufficient to establish the main point, that in the sonnets Shakespeare is (within the limitations of the sonnet form) working towards the maturity of expression of the great plays. But having said this we need to remind ourselves of two things. (The prevailing conception of technique as having something to do with the place of the caesura and hypermetric feet may justify the repetition.) The first is that the kind of technical development that we have been discussing is in itself an attempt to become more fully conscious (just as Spenser's technique is a method of exclusion), an attempt to secure more delicate discrimination and adjustment. The second is that technique does not function in a vacuum, it can only develop as the servant of an inner impulse. I shall conclude this essay by pointing to (I have no space for more than that) one or two of the major interests that lie behind the sonnets.

I have already said that I do not think 'The Sonnets' in any sense an ordered collection; they vary from the most trivial of occasional

[8] *Seven Types of Ambiguity*, pp. 65–73 and pp. 168–175.
[9] *The Sacred Wood*, p. 100.

verses to poems in which a whole range of important emotions is involved, and in the latter we find in embryo many of the themes of the later plays; there is variety enough to make discussion difficult. But it seems to me that two interests predominate, making themselves felt, often, beneath the ostensible subject: they cannot be altogether disentangled from each other or from other interests, and they are not quite the same in kind; but the artificial grouping seems unavoidable. One is the exploration, discrimination and judgment of modes of being—attention [152] consciously directed towards the kind of integration of personality that is implied by the development of technique. The second is an overwhelming concern with Time.

The first of these is not only expressed directly. Sonnet 30 is one of the sonnets concerned with 'Friendship in Absence':

> When to the Sessions of sweet silent thought,
> I summon up remembrance of things past,
> I sigh the lack of many a thing I sought,
> And with old woes new waile my deare times waste;
> Then can I drowne an eye (un-us'd to flow)
> For precious friends hid in deaths dateles night,
> And weepe afresh loves long since canceld woe,
> And mone th' expence of many a vannisht sight.
>
> .   .   .
>
> But if the while I thinke on thee (deare friend)
> All losses are restord, and sorrowes end.

The sonnet seems to be an early one, but even here beneath the main current of elegiac emotion (The tribute to friendship is gracefully conventional) there is a counter current of irony directed by the poet towards himself. In the eighth line Shakespeare is conscious that the present moan, like the sighs [sights] previously expended, involves a fresh expense ('Every sigh shortens life'), so that the line means, 'I waste my time and energy regretting the time and energy wasted in regrets'; and the slight over-emphasis of the third quatrain adds to the irony. In other words Shakespeare is aware of what he is doing (after all, 'sessions' implies judgment), and therefore achieves a more stable equilibrium. This is a minor example, but the implicit self-criticism is pervasive (Compare the previous sonnet: 'Yet in these thoughts myself almost despising'); and—although the poem quoted is far enough from anything by Donne or Marvell—the constant reference of the immediate emotion to a mature scale of values reminds us that Shakespeare—Nature's Darling—is not far removed from the Tradition of Wit.

In many of the sonnets ostensibly concerned with a personal relationship we find there is something of far greater interest to [153] Shakespeare than the compliments, complaints and pleas that provide the occasion of writing. Sonnet 110 is in the form of a plea for the restoration of friendship:

> Alas 'tis true, I have gone here and there,
> And made my selfe a motley to the view,
> Gor'd mine owne thoughts, sold cheap what is most dear,
> Made old offences of affections new.
> Most true it is, that I have lookt on truth
> Asconce and strangely: But by all above,
> These blenches gave my heart an other youth,
> And worse essaies prov'd thee my best of love,
> Now all is done, have what shall no end,
> Mine appetite I never more will grin'de
> On newer proofe, to trie an older friend,
> A God in love, to whom I am confin'd.
>   Then give me welcome, next my heaven the best,
>   Even to thy pure and most most loving brest.

There can be no doubt that here the most powerful lines are those recording self-disgust,[10] and that there is a drop in intensity when Shakespeare turns to address the friend directly, as in the final couplet. The sonnet is important as a direct approach to sincerity—it records the examination and integration of character. Indeed in many of the sonnets in which the friend is given something more than perfunctory recognition it is hard to resist the conclusion that Shakespeare is addressing his own conscience.

> You are my All the world, and I must strive,
> To know my shames and praises from your tounge,
> None else to me, nor I to none alive,
> That my steel'd sence or changes right or wrong,
> In so profound Abisme I throw all care
> Of others voyces, that my Adders sence,
> To cryttick and to flatterer stopped are . . .

---

[10] To take the first three lines as referring merely to the profession of actor and playwright is too narrow an interpretation; the reference seems to be to the way in which a sensitive intelligence has displayed its wares of wit and observation in common intercourse.

—'Like the deaf adder that stoppeth her ear; which will not hearken to the voice of charmers, charming never so wisely.' The reference is important; in the sonnets Shakespeare is working out [154] a morality based on his own finest perceptions and deepest impulses.[11] Sonnet 121 is explicit:

> Tis better to be vile then vile esteemed,
> When not to be, receives reproach of being,
> And the just pleasure lost, which is so deemed,
> Not by our feeling, but by others seeing.
> For why should others false adulterat eyes
> Give salutation to my sportive blood?
> Or on my frailties why are frailer spies;
> Which in their wils count bad what I think good?
> Noe, I am that I am, and they that levell
> At my abuses, reckon up their owne,
> I may be straight though they them-selves be bevel
> By their rancke thoughtes, my deedes must not be shown
>   Unlesse this generall evill they maintaine,
>   All men are bad and in their badnesse raigne.

This has caused a good deal of perplexity and I offer no apology for giving my own interpretation: 'As things are, it is more expedient to be really vile than vile in the opinion of the world, since not to be so is no safeguard against the reproach of vileness ['Reproach of being' also suggests: 'I am reproached for being what I am.'], and just pleasure has to be forfeited not because I feel it as wrong but because it appears wrong in the sight of others.' The next two lines are straight-forward—'give salutation' means 'have effect on'—then: 'Why should my (real or apparent) frailties be judged by those who have a greater share of human imperfections, particularly since the scheme of morality [155] imposed by their wills (or by convention) is opposed to mine? I am myself, not to be judged by them, and the way in which they condemn my offences provides a measure of their own deviations. [Also, 'Those that count my sins, let them reckon up their own!'] I may be following a right line of development, even if they are not, and my deeds are not to be judged by their rank thoughts ['They themselves are "bevelled" by their rank thoughts']—unless of course they think that human nature is fundamentally bad.' I have

[11] 'But we have to know ourselves pretty thoroughly before we can break the automatism of ideals and conventions . . . Only through fine delicate knowledge can we recognize and release our impulses.'—*Fantasia of the Unconscious*, p. 60.

ignored various secondary meanings in order to make the main sense explicit. The sonnet is a protest against the rigidly imposed moral scheme that the majority see fit to accept, a protest on behalf of a morality based on the nature of the writer. But that morality can only be discussed in terms that the poetry supplies.

An essay might well be written on the Time theme in Shakespeare. Starting from an examination of *King Henry IV*, *Troilus and Cressida* and the Sonnets, it would illuminate some important aspects of Shakespeare's genius and of the Elizabethan mind. But before discussing Shakespeare's handling of this theme some distinctions must be made.

In the sonnets Shakespeare's interest in the passage of time and the allied themes of death and mutability is sufficiently obvious. Not only does it provide the main theme of many of the more important sonnets, it continually encroaches on other interests and overshadows them. And there is a clear difference in intensity, tone and treatment between Shakespeare's 'Time' sonnets and other Elizabethan poems dealing with 'Time's thievish progress to eternity'; between

> When I consider everything that growes
> Holds in perfection but a little moment   (15)

or

> Like as the waves make towards the pibled shore . . .   (60)

and such typically Elizabethan things as

> In time the strong and stately turrets fall,
> In time the rose and silver lilies die,
> In time the monarchs captive are, and thrall,
> In time the sea and rivers are made dry [156]

or

> Soon doth it fade that makes the fairest flourish,
> Short is the glory of the blushing rose

or anything to be found in Spenser's Mutability Cantos.

Now 'the problem of Time' is a metaphysical problem, and in various forms it is a preoccupation of many of the Metaphysical Poets. Moreover between Shakespeare's mature verse and Donne's there are similarities which it is important to recognize—the immediacy, the images generating intense mental activity ('the intellect at the tip of the senses'), the exploiting of speech rhythm and idiom, and so on: a good deal of Mr. Eliot's account of Metaphysical Poetry applies equally—as he points out—to the blank verse of Shakespeare and other late Elizabethans. This being so, it is all the more important to stress that in the sonnets 'the problem of Time' is not a metaphysical problem at all,—and the discussion of Platonic Forms and Ideal Beauty is irrelevant. Wherever we look Shakespeare is concerned merely with the *effects* of time on animate and inanimate beings, on persons and personal relationships. As a poet, he reports and evaluates experiences, but he does not attempt to *explain* them, nor do they arouse speculation in his mind. So, too, the plays explain nothing; they are experiences to be lived. Indeed if Time had presented itself to Shakespeare as a metaphysical problem it could not have been dealt with in the verse of the sonnets. Mr. James Smith has made a necessary distinction.[12] He points out that 'verse properly called metaphysical is that to which the impulse is given by an overwhelming concern with metaphysical problems; with problems either deriving from, or closely resembling in the nature of their difficulty, the problem of the Many and the One,' and that in Metaphysical Poetry it is the conflict arising out of the perception of such problems that is resolved by means of the metaphysical conceit, in which there is both unity and 'high strain or tension, due to the sharpness with which its elements are opposed.' Shakespeare's imagery in the sonnets, as I have pointed out, rarely involves a high degree of tension; and when, in the later plays, we find images which not only possess richness of association but embrace conflicting elements, those elements are [157] invariably drawn from experience and sensation, never from speculative thought: they make finer experience available for others, but they offer no resolution of metaphysical problems. The Shakespearean pathos is stoical and pagan.

The temptation to look for the development of a metaphysical mode in the sonnets is not perhaps very common. A second temptation has not proved so easy to resist, and most accounts of the sonnets point to certain of them as showing 'Love's Triumph over Time,' without bothering to explain what this may mean. Certainly, if we isolate those sonnets in which a reaction to the passage of time and the inevitability of death provides the main emotional drive it is permissible to look for a coherently developing attitude culminating in a solution which shall be at least emotionally satisfying. There is an obvious advance in maturity, an increasing delicacy in exposition, but unless we are prepared to accept assertion as poetry (that is, bare statement deliberately willed, instead of the communication in all its depth, fulness and com-

[12] 'The Metaphysical Note in Poetry' in *Determinations*.

plexity, of an experience that has been lived) we shall not find that solution in the sonnets. An example may make my meaning clearer. Sonnet 123 is commonly taken to show that 'Love conquers Time':

> No! Time, thou shalt not bost that I doe change,
> Thy pyramyds buylt up with newer might
> To me are nothing novell, nothing strange,
> They are but dressings of a former sight:
> Our dates are breefe, and therefor we admire,
> What thou dost foyst upon us that is ould,
> And rather make them borne to our desire,
> Then thinke that we before have heard them tould:
> Thy registers and thee I both defie,
> Not wondring at the present, nor the past,
> For thy records, and what we see doth lye,
> Made more or les by thy continuall hast:
> > This I doe vow and this shall ever be,
> > I will be true dispight thy syeth and thee.

It is upon the ambiguity of the first two quatrains that I wish to direct attention. *Sense 1:* 'Time cannot make his boast that [158] I change with his passage. The admired wonders of modern architecture are not novelties to me (since my conscious self is, in a sense, outside time); I have seen them all before, and I know that the modern examples are only variations on the old. Man's life is short; therefore he tends to wonder at things foisted upon him by Time as novelties, which are really old, preferring to believe them newly created for his satisfaction [born to our desire] than to see them truly as repetitions of the old.' *Sense 2* (Wyndham's interpretation): 'Time cannot boast that I change. The pyramids—built with a skill that was new compared with my age-old self [with newer might to me]—were, I saw, no novelties even in ancient Egypt, but merely dressings of a former sight. Man's life is short; therefore he tends to wonder at the antiquities foisted upon him by Time, preferring to accept as absolute the limitations imposed by birth and death [to make them (dates) the bourn to his desire] than to think that the years of his life have been counted [told] before.' A rough paraphrase of the last six lines is: 'I refuse to accept as ultimate truth either history (recording that time has passed) or the present passage of time; neither novelty nor antiquity move me; the evidence of universal change given by history and the present time is false: only in appearance are past and present governed by time. I vow that I will be myself (and—perhaps—true to some person) in spite of death and time.'

The purpose of the sonnet is clear: to affirm the continuous identity of the self in spite of the passage of time. But, though a remarkable achievement, its failure is indicated by the unresolved ambiguity. That *Sense 1* is intended seems clear from line 10—'Not wondering at the present, nor the past'—as well as from the Elizabethan use of the word 'pyramids'; and even if we do away with the maladroit pun on 'borne' by interpreting it as 'bourn' in *Sense 1* as well as in *Sense 2* (and I find it impossible to exclude the meaning 'born to our desire') we are left with 'that is old' fitting awkwardly into the first interpretation. Moreover—and perhaps it is more important to notice this than the conflicting meanings which somehow refuse to resolve themselves into unity—the poem *asserts* rather than expresses a resolved state of mind: 'Thou shalt not boast,' 'I defy,' 'This I do vow,' 'I will be true.'

In the manner of its assertion the sonnet is in line with the more famous Sonnet 116 ('Love's not time's fool')—a [159] poem of which the difficulties have never, I think, been squarely faced—and with those sonnets promising some form of immortality. And, we may remark in conclusion, in all the sonnets of this last type, it is the contemplation of change, not the boasting and defiance, that produces the finest poetry; they draw their value entirely from the evocation of that which is said to be defied or triumphed over. In the plays—from *Henry IV* to *The Tempest*—in which the theme of Time occurs, there is no defiance; the conflict is resolved by the more or less explicit acceptance of mutability. I should like to give this remark precision in terms of literary criticism by examining the second part of *King Henry IV*, a play of which the prelude is spoken by the dying Hotspur:

> But thought's the slave of life, and life time's fool . . .

But perhaps enough has been said to show that, in this respect as in all others, the sonnets yield their proper significance only when seen in the context of Shakespeare's development as a dramatist.[160]

John Crowe Ransom

Shakespeare at Sonnets

O NE MAY BE WELL DISPOSED to the New Deal, and not relish the attitude of giving comfort to the enemy by criticizing Mr. Roosevelt publicly, yet in a qualified company do it freely. The same thing applies in the matter of the poet Shakespeare. It is out of respect to the intelligence of the editors and readers of a serious literary publication that I will not hold back from throwing a few stones at Shakespeare, aiming them as accurately as I can at the vulnerable parts. I have no fear that any group of intellectual critics may succeed beyond their intentions in demolishing Shakespeare, so that he will suffer extinction and be read no more, and I am well aware that if this should happen the public attendance upon poetry in our language would be reduced one-half. For Shakespeare is an institution as well established as the industrial revolution, or the Protestant churches. In the midst of the bombardment he will smile, and smile, and be a villain.

In this paper I must limit attention to the Sonnets, and within this field to a few features only. In a way the Sonnets should prove the most interesting of all this poet's works—unless the reader's interest in the poetry is tangled hopelessly with his interest [270] in drama, the form which dominates most of Shakespeare's verse. For here I must propose a certain distinction, and it will be arbitrary in the sense that I will not argue it. Let us distinguish drama as one literary form, and lyric or pure poetry as another. In poetic drama, a hybrid, it is the dramatic form which rules. The poetry is the auxiliar. At any moment it is relative to the action, and to that extent determinate, not free. In the plays Shakespeare furnishes a multitude of characters with always-

SOURCE: "Shakespeare at Sonnets" (copyright 1938 Louisiana State University) is reprinted with the permission of Charles Scribner's Sons from *The World's Body* by John Crowe Ransom.

appropriate speeches—with speeches big and royal, tender and pitying, conspiratorial, even philosophizing speeches and soliloquies, indeed speeches of almost any sort, and thoroughly poeticized—but probably none of them will quite do as a round and separate poem. None is really so intended.

The standard of poetic range and complication which is practical for a successful producing playwright cannot be so high as that adhered to by some formal poet who cares nothing about the affections of the people, and knows that his art for a long time, certainly since Caxton set up for business, has been of a mental age far beyond its original oral condition. I will come to my point at once. It is not likely that John Donne could have written Shakespeare's plays, but on the other hand it seems impossible that Shakespeare could have got into the plays the equivalent of Donne's lyrics.

The virtue of formal lyrics, or "minor poems," is one that no other literary type can manifest: they are [271] the only complete and self-determined poetry. There the poetic object is elected by a free choice from all objects in the world, and this object, deliberately elected and carefully worked up by the adult poet, becomes his microcosm. With a serious poet each minor poem may be the symbol of a major decision. It is as ranging and comprehensive an action as the mind has ever tried.

Shakespeare left monument enough behind him, but no face of it is of that precise significance which is attested by a large and assorted volume of minor poems. The truth is that Shakespeare, as compared with writers like Sidney and Spenser, had rare luck as a literary man, and I do not mean to say this out of any regard to whether he was or was not a superior man naturally. It would be impossible to tell how much our poet was determined by the fact that he was not an aristocrat, did not go to the university and develop his technical skill all at once, got into the rather low profession of acting, grew up with the drama, and never had to undergo the torment of that terrible problem: the problem of poetic strategy; or what to do with an intensive literary training. Yet Shakespeare did indulge in one diversion from his natural and happy career as a dramatist. He composed a laborious sonnet sequence. And in the degree that the sonnets are not tied down to "story," to the simple dramatizing of the stages in a human relation, they give us a Shakespeare on the same terms [272] as those on which we are used to having our other poets.

II

I begin with a most obvious feature: generally they are ill constructed.

They use the common English metrical pattern, and the metrical work is always admirable, but the logical pattern more often than not fails to fit it. If it be said that you do not need to have a correspondence between a poet's metrical pattern and his logical one, I am forced to observe that Shakespeare thought there was a propriety in it; often he must have gone to the pains of securing it, since it is there and, considering the extreme difficulty of the logical structure in the English sonnet, could not have got in by a happy accident. The metrical pattern of any sonnet is directive. If the English sonnet exhibits the rhyme-scheme ABAB CDCD EFEF GG, it imposes upon the poet the following requirement: that he write three co-ordinate quatrains and then a couplet which will relate to the series collectively.

About a third of the sonnets of Shakespeare are fairly unexceptionable in having just such a logical structure. About half of them might be said to be tolerably workmanlike in this respect; and about half of them are seriously defective.

Already the poet Spenser had calculated very well what sort of thing could be done successfully in this [273] logical pattern. It was something like the following (*Amoretti*, LVI):

> Fayre be ye sure, but cruell and unkind,
> As is a Tygre, that with greedinesse
> Hunts after bloud; when he by chance doth find
> A feeble beast, doth foully him oppresse.
>
> Fayre be ye sure, but proud and pitilesse,
> As is a storm, that all things doth prostrate;
> Finding a tree alone all comfortlesse,
> Beats on it strongly, it to ruinate.
>
> Fayre be ye sure, but hard and obstinate,
> As is a rocke amidst the raging floods;
> Gaynst which, a ship, of succour desolate,
> Doth suffer wreck both of her selfe and goods.
>
> That ship, that tree, and that same beast, am I,
> Whom ye do wreck, do ruine, and destroy.

Now Spenser's metrical scheme has a special and unnecessary complication, it exhibits rhyme-linkage; the second quatrain begins by echoing the last rhyme of the first quatrain, and the third by echoing the last rhyme of the second. It makes no difference logically. The three quatrains are equal yet sharply distinct. Possibly the linking was Spenser's way of showing off his virtuosity at rhyming, and possibly also he used it as a mnemonic device, to say, The new quatrain must be just like the old one, a logical co-ordinate, but wait till we come to the couplet, which will not be linked and must not be co-ordinate. At [274] any rate, his quatrains nearly always are true co-ordinates. In his architectural design he is superior, I believe, to any other writer of the four-part or English sonnet.

And this means that he carefully attended to the sort of object which might permit this three-and-one division. In the given example each quatrain is a simile which he applies to the lady, and the couplet is a summary comment which is brief, but adequate because the similes are simple and of the same kind. It is not every matter, or logical object, which allows this; and, particularly, the couplet does not give enough room for the comment unless the burden of the quatrains has been severely restricted. If the poet is too full of urgent thoughts, he had better use the two-part or Italian form, which is very much more flexible. The English form, with the more elaborate and repetitive pattern, implies the simpler substance; in this it would be like other complicated forms, such as the ballade or sestina.

But structurally good also is the following Shakespearean sonnet, the one numbered 87:

> Farewell! thou art too dear for my possessing,
> And like enough thou know'st thy estimate;
> The charter of thy worth gives thee releasing;
> My bonds in thee are all determinate.
>
> For how do I hold thee but by thy granting?
> And for that riches where is my deserving?
> The cause of this fair gift in me is wanting,
> And so my patent back again is swerving.[275]
>
> Thyself thou gav'st, thy own worth then not knowing,
> Or me, to whom thou gav'st it, else mistaking;
> So thy great gift, upon misprision growing,
> Comes home again, on better judgment making.

Thus have I had thee, as a dream doth flatter,
In sleep a king, but waking no such matter.

This sonnet is daring and clever. It is legalistic, therefore closely limited in its range, yet the three quatrains all manage to say the same thing differently, and the couplet translates the legal figure back into the terms of a lover's passion.

It is only a large minority of Shakespeare's sonnets in which we can find this perfect adaptation of the logic to the metre. In the others we can find the standard metrical organization, and then some arbitrary logical organization which clashes with it. At least twice we find only fourteen-line poems, with no logical organization at all except that they have little couplet conclusions: in 66, "Tir'd with all these, for restful death I cry," and in 129, "The expense of spirit in a waste of shame." Occasionally, as in 63, "Against my love shall be, as I am now," the sonnet divides frankly into octave and sextet, so far as the logic goes, though it does not follow that an honest printer has set it up just so. Many modern sonnet-writers, such as my friend, Mr. David Morton, are careful to have their sonnets set up as two-part structures though their rhyme-scheme is four-part. I am afraid some critics will always be wondering [276] whether the poets are unequal, or simply insensitive, to the logical demands made by the English form. I scarcely think that Shakespeare's practice sanctified a procedure.

Possibly the commonest irregularity of logical arrangement with Shakespeare is in sonnets of the following type (64):

When I have seen by Time's fell hand defac'd
The rich proud cost of outworn buried age;
When sometime lofty towers I see down-raz'd,
And brass eternal slave to mortal rage;

When I have seen the hungry ocean gain
Advantage on the kingdom of the shore,
And the firm soil win of the watery main,
Increasing store with loss and loss with store;

When I have seen such interchange of state,
Or state itself confounded to decay,
Ruin hath taught me thus to ruminate,
That Time will come and take my love away.

This thought is as a death, which cannot choose,
But weep to have that which it fears to lose.

Here the three quatrains look co-ordinate, but only the first two really are so. The third begins with the same form as the others, but presently shows that it is only summary of their content, and then actually begins to introduce the matter which will be the concern of the couplet. We must believe that Shakespeare found the couplet too small to hold its matter,[277] so that at about line ten he had to begin anticipating it. But, as I said, this sonnet represents a pattern fairly common with him, and it is possible to argue that he developed it consciously as a neat variant on the ordinary English structure; just as Milton developed a variant from the Italian structure, by concluding the logical octet a little before or a little after the rhyme-ending of the eighth line.

Probably Shakespeare's usual structural difficulty consists about equally in having to pad out his quatrains, if three good co-ordinates do not offer themselves, and in having to squeeze the couplet too flat, or else extend its argument upward into the proper territory of the quatrains. But when both these things happen at once, the obvious remark is that the poet should have reverted to the Italian sonnet.

Structurally, Shakespeare is a careless workman. But probably, with respect to our attention to structure, we are careless readers.

III

Poetry is an expressive art, we say, and perhaps presently we are explaining that what it expresses is its poet; a dangerous locution, because the public value of the poem would seem to lie theoretically in the competence with which it expresses its object. There is no reason why it should not offer an absolute knowledge of this object, so far as the adjective is ever applicable to a human knowledge, including a scientific knowledge, and a knowledge however "objective." [278] Nevertheless one knowledge will differ from another knowledge in glory, that is, in the purity of intention, and sometimes it is scarcely a knowledge at all; it is rather a self-expression. There is probably a poetry of the feelings just as much as there is a poetry of knowledge; for we may hardly deny to a word its common usage, and poetry is an experience so various as to be entertained by everybody. But the poetry of the feelings is not the one that the critic is compelled to prefer, especially if he can say that it taints us with subjectivism, sentimentality, and self-indulgence. This is the poetry, I think, which we sometimes dispose of a little distastefully as "romantic." It does not pursue its object with much zeal, and it is so common that it involves in a general disrepute all poets, the innocent as well as the guilty, by comparison with those importunate pursuers, the scientists—who will not exactly be expected to fail to make the most of the comparison.

This sort of poetry, I am afraid, is as natural to Shakespeare as language is, and he is a great master in it. In 33 we read:

> Full many a glorious morning have I seen
> Flatter the mountain-tops with sovereign eye,
> Kissing with golden face the meadows green,
> Gilding pale streams with heavenly alchemy.

It is pure Shakespeare, it sounds like nobody else; and in it the failure of objectivity, or perhaps "realism" we might prefer to call it, is plain about as soon [279] as we look closely. What the poet intends is simply to have something in the way of a fine-morning quatrain, with an all-ruling fair-weather sun to be the symbol of his false friend, as the sonnet goes on to disclose. But this sun is weakly imagined; rather, it may be said to be only felt, a loose cluster of images as obscure as they are pleasant, furnished by the half-conscious memories attending the pretty words. (In strict logic: I suppose this sun's eye flatters the mountain-tops in that his look makes them shine; but at once he is kissing the meadows, which is unseemly for a face that contains a sovereign eye; then in the character of an alchemist he is transmuting streams. A mixed and self-defeating figure, and a romantic effect unusually loose; but it does not seem to matter.)

So this is poetry; a poetry that has in mind the subjective satisfactions of the poet, and of reputed millions of readers after him. The cognitive impulse of the participating millions has to be of low grade, yet there is an object, and it is rich and suggestive even while it is vague and cloudy. This is what we might call an associationist poetry. The pretty words have pleasing if indefinite associations; and they are fairly harmonious, that is, the associations tend rather to cohere than to repel each other. And if they do not cohere into a logical or definitive object, at any rate—this is the subtlety of the romantic style—they are arranged externally with great care into a characteristic musical phrase, or at least a metrical one, which [280] is really (by comparison) objective and absolute. Metric saves this kind of poetry, and its function could not be shown to better advantage than here; a meretricious function, as it lends its objectivity to an act in which the subject does not really propose to lose himself in the object. In other words, it persuades us, unless we are professionally critical, that this is a poetry of wonderful precision, when logically it is a poetry of wonderful imprecision, and the only precision it has is metrical, therefore adventitious. It is not without significance that the age gave to this poet his adjective: sweet. It would be hard to estimate the extent of the influence which Shakespeare's way of writing poetry has exerted upon subsequent English poetry. But Exhibit A would be the actual poems, and Exhibit B, scarcely less significant, would be the critical dictum upon which almost innumerable writers seem to be in perfect agreement, that science if it likes may try to know its object, but that the business of poetry is to express its author's feelings. The Restoration and Eighteenth Century in their poetry resisted Shakespeare's example of sweetness, but the Nineteenth Century did not, and when we are grieving because modern poetry has learned how to furnish such exquisite indulgences to the feelings and yet at the same time so little food for the intellect, there is no reason why we should not remember who is its most illustrious ancestor.

The image is often conventional, or "literary," [281] which means that it is not really shaped by a genuine observation. In 53:

> Describe Adonis, and the counterfeit
> Is poorly imitated after you;
> On Helen's cheek all art of beauty set,
> And you in Grecian tires are painted new.

Asseverations like this are the right of a literary lover, but they do more credit to his piety than to his wit. (The mediæval lover had a code which obliged him to say, My lady is more beautiful than yours, though I have not seen yours.) The urgency is that of a subject to express his own feelings, not that of an object so individual as to demand expression. But the phrasing is grave and musical; there is great care behind it to get words with the right general associations, and to make the melody; phrase, in this subjective sense, and regarded as the trick of the poet as workman, receives commonly the particularity that might have gone into the object.

Mr. Santayana says something like this when he remarks, with his usual wisdom, that Shakespeare's poetry is an art like landscaping; for it is pervasive, and tones down every object exposed to it, and is not like architecture, which articulates its objects right to the last constituent stone. Carrying out our figure, Shakespeare's poetry would not be so much the wall, or the temple, as the ivy that clings to it sentimentally, and sometimes may very well even obscure it.

Violence of syntax and of idiom is supposed to express [282] strength
of feeling. In the sonnets are many violences. For instance, in 25,

<blockquote>The painful warrior famoused for fight,</blockquote>

and in 64,

<blockquote>The rich proud cost of outworn buried age.</blockquote>

In the first of these Shakespeare makes a verb of an adjective, but his
coinage could not give it a currency, for it is not that kind of adjective. He also makes a qualitative noun of *fight*, which is less exception-
able, though its present currency seems to lie within the American
sporting jargon. Both these forced meanings follow surprisingly upon
painful, which is exact and even Miltonic. The other bristles with
logical difficulties. They attach to the meaning of *cost*, and of the adjective series *rich* and *proud*, and of *outworn* and *buried*. Malone
worried over the line and proposed *rich-proud*, but it still strongly
resists paraphrase. These phrases will illustrate what is common in
romantic poetry: a very great "obscurity," unknown to some "intel-
lectualist" poetry which popularly rates as difficult.

I quote also, and I think not vindictively, from 12:

<blockquote>
When I do count the clock that tells the time,
And see the brave day sunk in hideous night,
When I behold the violet past prime,
And sable curls, all silver'd o'er with white. . . .
</blockquote>

The third line of this quatrain interests me as a critic. Shakespeare
ordinarily plays safe by electing good [283] substantial conventional
objects to carry his feelings, but here his judgment should have come
to his aid. The violet, in its exalted context, looks to me like a poet's
ridiculus mus, for no instance of floral mortality could well be more
insignificant. This little mouse had the merit of being named with
three syllables, and a two-minute imaginary tour in the garden does
not seem to disclose another one of like syllabic dimensions who
would do any better. Shakespeare did not bother; he trusted in the
music, and the power of the pleasant associations, to make the line
impervious to logical criticism. He trusted also, and not without reason, for the point will generally be conceded by critics who are grateful for any excellence in their difficult art, in the comfortable faith
that a poetical passage is unlike a chain in that its true strength is
that of its strongest part.

On the other hand, there are certainly sonnets of Shakespeare's in this romantic vein which are without absurdities, structural defects, and great violences, and which are also compact, that is, without excessive dispersion in the matter of the figures; and they are doubtless the best sonnets of the kind there could possibly be. It would be presumptuous to deny this general type of poetry, or Shakespeare's occasional mastery of it.

Those perfect sonnets are not many. It is not a wild generalization, when we look at the sonnets, to say that Shakespeare was not habitually a perfectionist; [284] he was not as Ben Jonson, or Marvell, or Milton, and he was not as Pope.

IV

The sonnets are mixed in effect. Not only the sequence as a whole but the individual sonnet is uneven in execution. But what to the critic is still more interesting than the up and the down in one style is the alternation of two very different styles: the one we have been considering, and the one which we are accustomed to define (following Doctor Johnson) as metaphysical. What is the metaphysical poetry doing there? Apparently at about the time of *Hamlet*, and perhaps recognizably in the plays but much more deliberately and on a more extended scale in the sonnets, Shakespeare goes metaphysical. Not consistently, of course.

So far as I know, Shakespeare has not ordinarily been credited with being one of the metaphysicals, nor have specimen sonnets been included in lists or anthologies of metaphysical poems. But many sonnets certainly belong there; early examples of that style. If it was not then widely practised, had no name, and could hardly yet have been recognized as a distinct style, then I would suppose that the sonnets as a performance represent Shakespeare seeking such effects as John Donne, a public if still unpublished wonder, by some curious method was achieving. But there was also, on a smaller scale, the example of a genuine pioneer in this field in the person of Sidney, if Shakespeare [285] cared to look there; see his *Astrophel and Stella*, xcIv, "Grief, find the words, for thou hast made my brain."

Certainly Shakespeare's 87, "Farewell! thou art too dear for my possessing," already quoted as an instance of good structure, is in the style. For its substance is furnished by developing the human relation (that of the renouncing lover) through a figure of speech; a legal one, in which an unequal bond is cancelled for cause. Three times, in as many quatrains, the lover makes an exploration within the field of the figure. The occasions are fairly distinct, though I should think their specifications are hardly respective enough to have satisfied Donne. But the thing which surprises us is to find no evidence anywhere that Shakespeare's imagination is equal to the peculiar and systematic exercises which Donne imposed habitually upon his. None, and it should not really surprise us, if we remember that Donne's skill is of the highest technical expertness in English poetry, and that Shakespeare had no university discipline, and developed poetically along lines of least resistance.

He is upon occasions metaphysical enough, but not so metaphysical as Donne; nor as later poets, Donne's followers, who were just as bold in intention as their master, though not usually so happy in act.

The impulse to metaphysical poetry, I shall assume, consists in committing the feelings in the case—those of unrequited love for example—to their determination within the elected figure. But Shakespeare [286] was rarely willing to abandon his feelings to this fate, which is another way of saying that he would not quite risk the consequences of his own imagination. He censored these consequences, to give them sweetness, to give them even dignity; he would go a little way with one figure, usually a reputable one, then anticipate the consequences, or the best of them, and take up another figure.

The simplest way to define Shakespeare's metaphysical accomplishment would be by comparison with Donne's, which is standard. I have often tried to find the parallel cases where the two poets developed the same figure of speech. But I have always been forced to conclude that these poets do not even in outline or skeleton treat quite the same things; Shakespeare's things being professionally conventional, and Donne's being generally original. The nearest I can come to this sort of illustration is by comparing Sonnet 55 with that Valediction of Donne's which has the subtitle: *of the booke*. It is a "strong" sonnet, not quite intelligent enough to be metaphysical It begins,

> Not marble, nor the gilded monuments
> Of princes shall outlive this powerful rime,

yet what it develops is not the circumstantial immortality of the rime, and of the beloved inhabiting it, but the mortality of the common marbles and monuments, an old story with Shakespeare, and as to the immortality makes this single effort:

'Gainst death and all-oblivious enmity
Shall you pace forth.[287]

The only specific thing here is something about a gait.

The immortality of the rime, and of the beloved preserved in it (like a beautiful fly stuck in amber? let poets tell) is as classical, or typical, as anything in European sonnetry; but its specific development is not. It remained for Donne, and hardly anybody or nobody else, really on its own merits to develop it, or an easy variation from it, and that not in a sonnet. In the Valediction he bids his lady, when he is going on an absence from her, to study his manuscripts, "those Myriades of letters," and writes the annals of their love for the sake of posterity. I quote the third stanza, with a little editing of the punctuation:

This Booke, as long-liv'd as the elements,
Or as the world's forme, this all-graved tome
In cypher writ, or new made Idiome
(We for love's clergie only are instruments),—
When this booke is made thus,
Should again the ravenous
Vandals and Gauls inundate us,
Learning were safe; in this our universe
Schooles might learn Sciences, Spheares Musick,
　　　Angels Verse.

One understands that he really means what he says: a book. In the three stanzas following he shows respectively what the Divines, the Lawyers, and the Statesmen will learn from this book, and in a final stanza returns to relate to a lover's absence the labor of compiling it. Donne would have performed well with an English sonnet-structure, where he might have gone on three separate little adventures into his [288] image; there are three here, though the stanza is bigger, and perhaps therefore easier, than quatrain. (Structurally, there is no firmer architect of lyric anywhere in English than Donne.) The trick consists, apparently, in guiding the imagination to the right places and then letting it go. To make this controlled yet exuberant use of the imagination is an intellectual feat; though it would not follow that there is no other recipe which will confer upon verse its intellectual distinction.

Metaphysical poetry has received in our time a new analytic attention, and for example from Professor Grierson. (Less formally if not less influentially from Mr. T. S. Eliot.) The revival of interest in this poetry evidently suits the taste of our post-romantic generation. And Professor Grierson says in many places that what Donne does is to combine intellect and passion. But no poet would find that a practicable formula; and we may well shiver with apprehension lest theory, or the æsthetic of poetry, waver and relax and perish under such a definition. The primary business of theorists is to direct their analyses of poetry to what is objective in it, or cognitive, and they will always be safe in assuming if they like that behind any external body of knowledge there will have been feeling enough, possibly amounting to passion, to have attended the subject through his whole exercise. Indeed, the feeling must have been entirely proportionate to the exercise. It is right to attribute the feelings to Donne's lover, in the poem, but our assurance [289] is inferential; the intellectual effects appear as the fruits of the feelings. Ferdinand's feelings for Miranda, said Prospero to himself, are measurable better by the wood he will chop for her than by the passion, or even the iambic melody, of his protestations.

But may I talk a little about feelings? I have often wanted to. It is conceivable that Ferdinand might have expressed his in a garland of metaphysical poems, and that Prospero might have been fully competent to judge of the comparative values in this art, and therefore that the poems might have served alone as a sufficient index, obviating the wood-pile. They would have been just as objective an evidence. For what are feelings? I am sure I do not know, but I will suppose for the present they are calls to action, and always want to realize their destiny, which is to turn into actions and vanish. I will suppose also, and this is from experience, that we find ourselves sometimes possessed of powerful feelings and yet cannot quite tell what actions they want of us; or find ourselves even learning to enjoy the pangs of feelings, in the conceited consciousness they are our very own, and therefore reluctant to resolve them in action, and taking a perverse pleasure in stirring them up, like a harrowing of hell; for we are marvellously indeterminate in our inner economy. That is what comes fundamentally, I think, from our egoism, a strange and peculiarly human faculty. For I do not think animals distinguish their feelings at one end of a scale from their actions at the other end, since Nature as plain [290] biologist would hardly seem to require it. But we distinguish; clearly we are able to stop at the feeling-end, or to perform half-way actions that will partly relieve the feelings and partly permit them still to luxuriate, but less painfully.

Lovers (and other persons too) often have feelings which cannot take, and do not seek, their natural outlet in physical actions. The feelings may be too complex anyhow, and too persistent, to be satisfied with simple actions, they overrun the mark; or perhaps the lovers have to go upon an absence, and the feelings get dammed up. Then they find appropriate actions through imagination, in intellectual constructions. These lovers at their best are poets. These poets at their best perform complete actions, very likely by means of metaphysical poems. So, on the one hand, there is an associationist poetry, a half-way action providing many charming resting-places for the feelings to agitate themselves; and, on the other hand, there is a metaphysical poetry, which elects its line of action and goes straight through to the completion of the cycle and extinction of the feelings.

This gives us associationist poetry *versus*, I think, behavioristic. For our discussion seems to have turned psychological. If romantic poets are not fully aware of what they are doing, metaphysical poets are self-conscious and deliberate, and in fact they are very like technical psychologists. They start with feelings, they objectify these imaginatively into external actions. They think that poetry, just as behavioristic psychologists [291] think that psychology, can make nothing out of feelings as they stand.

V

And now a little moralization.

A metaphysical poem is an intellectual labor, and all the intellect may be active in it, but it is under the presidency of imagination. And here comes a difficulty. Feelings are not satisfied by a ridiculous and impossible action, for they themselves are painfully real. But what is imagination? A faculty of excessive versatility: equally ready to take the photograph of objective reality, or to reproduce it from memory, or to create it originally in a painting; and if the last, the detail is perceptual but not actually perceived. This is the great trouble. The deterrent to our reception of metaphysical effects is distrust; we do not believe in the validity of the imaginative organ. It is for us a powerfully inherited distrust, going back to the tyranny of that modernism, technically to be defined as scientific positivism, which killed the religious credulity of Europe, beginning in the Renaissance; it was going strongly by Shakespeare's time, and was quite sufficient to damn the foolish magic which Spenser, by mistaken strategy, had lifted from mediæval poetry and stuffed into his *Faerie Queene*. We cannot escape it. A nice exhibit of our scruple is to be found later in Coleridge's rejection of fancy as the irresponsible bastard variety of the image-forming faculty, though [292] necessarily he discovered insuperable difficulties in drawing the exact line round it. And altogether proper must we think anybody's insistence that imagination must be representative, or realistic, in order that poetry may speak the truth. It seems too early in our history, or else intelligence is simply too weak, to arrive at any but dogmatic judgments respecting a nest of exquisite problems with which sensitive moderns are too well acquainted: how far a "metaphysical" particularity which goes beyond actual observation is valid; how far the body of modern science, symbol of what is valid and eternal, is itself built upon this sort of particularity; whether any particularity is still eligible in religion, which deals with supernaturals that always escape observation; and, at the same time, whether natural bodies do not imply supernatural ones, and whether there can be supernatural ones which propose to have no particularity at all. We can only observe that the moment looks favorable to an improvement in the public status of imaginative works.

But Professor Grierson makes an acute observation when he notes the almost solid Catholic front (Anglo-Catholic and Roman) upon which we are fairly astonished to find the seventeenth-century metaphysical poets arrayed. (This test might eliminate Shakespeare, if we applied it too strictly, for he does not group with them in a public or official sense.) It is hardly a mere coincidence. Catholicism is not afraid of particularizing the God, evidently believing that you cannot have "God in general," you must have [293] Him in particular if at all. But Protestantism is afraid. It is subject to a fatal scruple of conscience. On its behalf it should be said that for modern men Protestantism is probably a necessity; it represents the scepticism which is incidental to sincere epistemological studies, and at a certain point of scientific advancement is inevitable. But this scepticism once started finds no end, and promises to conclude by destroying what is most peculiarly human in our habit of mind; indeed, it seems to proceed on a psychological assumption suitable to the animal societies, that superfluous feelings are not significant, and that it is simple, and desirable, to suppress them.

Doctor Johnson had a dry Protestant temper, and also something of the Catholic inheritance which he may have thought of as an old-fashioned decency. Oscillating fairly between these two prejudices, he was a just if never profound critic. He admired while he deprecated and repudiated the metaphysical poets. But in 1747 he prepared for Garrick's reading a Prologue upon the opening of Drury Lane Theatre, and began it as follows:

> When Learning's triumph o'er her barbarous foes
> First reared the stage, immortal Shakespeare rose;
> Each change of many-colored life he drew,
> Exhausted worlds, and then imagined new;
> Existence saw him spurn her bounded reign,
> And panting Time toiled after him in vain.
> His pow'rful strokes presiding Truth impressed,
> And unresisted Passion stormed the breast.[294]

A defender of metaphysical poetry might suggest that in these eight lines the poet cites about that number of separate figures, and takes the profit of them, when there could be no profit to be taken except on the understanding that they were as mines, that might be or had been worked by real metaphysical imaginations. This poet offers no bodily manifestations of Learning triumphing o'er her foes, and then rearing the stage, which she could never have accomplished without being involved with shapes, agents, and events that were capable of images; or of Shakespeare rising, exhausting old worlds, imagining new ones, spurning the bounds of Existence; or of Time panting in his pursuit; or of Truth presiding over something, and impressing Shakespeare's strokes; or of Passion in some military manner storming the breast. It is necessary after all to raise the question of intellectual integrity against Doctor Johnson, as against many a Protestant at one time or another. If he rejects the metaphysicals he should reject also their fruits. These verses come out of the handsome enlightenment which lives substantially but without knowing on the scraps of a past from which it thinks it is emancipated.

VI

But Shakespeare honestly realizes the metaphysical image, and I shall cite, with some remark, the sonnets in which he seems to me to have the most conspicuous success.

I begin with 30, "When to the sessions of sweet [295] silent thought"; it is smart work, but only half the sharpness belongs to the strict object; the rest is accidental or mechanical, because it is oral or verbal; it is word-play, and word-play, including punning, belongs to the loose poetry of association. Technically perfect and altogether admirable in its careful modulation is 57, "Being your slave, what should I do but tend"; and so faithfully does it stick to the object, which is the behavior suitable to the slave kept waiting, that not till the couplet is there any direct expression of the feelings of the actual outraged lover.

Sonnet 60, "Like as the waves make toward the pebbled shore," is ambitious and imperfect. The first quatrain says that our minutes are always toiling forward, like waves. The second quatrain introduces a different and pretentious image of this tendency, and shows its fatal consequence:

> Nativity, once in the main of light,
> Crawls to maturity, wherewith being crown'd,
> Crooked eclipses 'gainst his glory fight,
> And Time that gave doth now his gift confound.

The lines will be impressive to that kind of receptivity whose critical defences are helpless against great words in musical phrases. Nativity means the new-born infant, but maturity seems only an object in his path, or at the goal of his path, evidently a crown which he puts on. Thereupon the astrological influences turn against nativity, and Time enters the story to destroy his own gift; this must be the crown that nativity has picked up. We are confused about all these entities.[296] In the third quatrain Shakespeare declines to a trite topic, the destructiveness of Time, and represents him successively as transfixing the flourish set on youth (however he may do that), delving the parallels in beauty's brow (as a small demon with a digging instrument?), feeding on the rareties of nature's truth (as gluttonous monster), and mowing everything with his scythe (as grim reaper). A field of imagery in which the explorer has performed too prodigiously, and lost his chart.

And now 73, with its opening quatrain:

> That time of year thou mayst in me behold
> When yellow leaves, or none, or few, do hang
> Upon those boughs which shake against the cold,
> Bare ruin'd choirs, where late the sweet birds sang.

The structure is good, the three quatrains offering distinct yet equivalent figures for the time of life of the unsuccessful and to-be-pitied lover. But the first quatrain is the boldest, and the effect of the whole is slightly anti-climactic. Within this quatrain I think I detect a thing which often characterizes Shakespeare's work within the metaphysical style: he is unwilling to renounce the benefit of his earlier style, which consisted in the breadth of the associations; that is, he will not quite risk the power of a single figure but compounds the figures. I refer to the two images about the boughs. It is one thing to have the boughs shaking against the cold, and in that capacity they carry very well the fact of the old rejected lover; it is another thing to represent them as ruined choirs [297] where the birds no longer sing. The latter is a just representation of the lover too, and indeed a subtler and richer one, but the two images cannot, in logical rigor, co-exist. Therefore I deprecate *shake against the cold*. And I believe everybody will deprecate *sweet*. This term is not an objective image at all, but a term to be located at the subjective pole of the experience; it expects to satisfy a feeling by naming it (that is, by just having it) and is a pure sentimentalism.

No. 87, "Farewell! thou art too dear for my possessing," which we have already seen and remarked, needs only the further comment that it is rare and charming among sonnets for the almost complete prevalence of the feminine rhyme.

I cite 94, "They that have power to hurt and will do none"; it has proved obscure to commentators, but I think it is clear if taken in context, as an imaginary argument against the friend's relation with the woman, or with any woman, exactly opposite to the argument of the sonnets which open the sequence. And 97, "How like a winter hath my absence been," where the logical structure has some nicety though the detail is rather large of scale.

I am interested in 107, which begins,

> Not mine own fears, nor the prophetic soul
> Of the wide world dreaming on things to come.

The argument is that the auguries of disaster and death to his love need not be trusted; it concludes disappointingly in an old vein, that at any rate this love [298] will endure in the poet's rhyme. I am particularly bothered by the image of the world's prophetic soul; as who is not? The world-soul is a technical concept, I suppose, in the sense that it was of use to Paracelsus and to other theosophists, who knew what they wanted to make of it. It indicates a very fine image for some metaphysical poet who will handle it technically; for Donne or another university poet. It is not fit for amateurs. The question is whether Shakespeare's theological touch here is not amateurish; elsewhere it sometimes is, as in Hamlet's famous soliloquy beginning, "To be or not to be." It is my impression that our poet is faking, or shall we say improvising; the *wide*, denoting extension, seems to destroy the world's aspect as soul, the *dreaming* is too pretty a form for the prophetic action.

There is evenness in 109, "O! never say that I was false of heart." In 121, " 'Tis better to be vile than vile esteem'd," the language of the opening quatrain sounds close and technical enough for a passage of Donne's, but the argument is rather obscure; the later quatrains seem to shift the argument. No. 125, "Were 't aught to me I bore the canopy," is admirable though not unitary enough to be very metaphysical. And finally there is 146, "Poor Soul, the centre of my sinful earth," the most Platonic or "spiritual" sonnet in the entire sequence, a noble revulsion in the progress of the poet's feelings, and the poet might well have employed it to conclude the unhappy history, leaving quite off the eight miscellaneous and [299] indeterminate ones that follow. Perhaps he would have done so if he and not the printer had directed the publication.

VII

I conclude with a note, which is in answer to an editorial query, and may serve as anticipating what will probably be a dissatisfaction on the part of some readers over my estimate of Shakespeare as a metaphysical poet.

Is not Shakespeare a very bold and successful contriver of metaphysical effects in his later plays? For the sonnets come before the final period of play-wrighting, and it is our common impression that this poet's powers developed steadily to their final climax.

It has been remarked above that drama is no place to look for complete little poems; that metaphysical lyrics in particular, like Donne's, would be destructive of any drama into which they might be admitted. Shakespeare's characters have to speak to the point, that is, to an immediate situation within the action of the play. But sometimes a character will get into general difficulties, and have profound if not quite directed feelings of despair; or into a state of happiness, and feel a diffuse joy; and such a character may be allowed to soliloquize (a very suspicious action dramatically, which shows Shakespeare trying to burst the bonds of drama in favor of a freer poetry); and why should not the result be a sizable passage of true metaphysical poetry? [300]

The odds on its being so are here at their greatest. But I should think the passage will be too intellectual to give the oral effect necessary for an audience; for that matter, cannot be spontaneous enough even to suit a reader's sense of dramatic propriety. I look through a few of the soliloquies and seem to find my point confirmed. Macbeth's speech upon hearing of the Queen's death (in v, v) is cited for my benefit, but here is the speech:

> To-morrow, and to-morrow, and to-morrow,
> Creeps in this petty pace from day to day,
> To the last syllable of recorded time;
> And all our yesterdays have lighted fools
> The way to dusty death. Out, out, brief candle!
> Life's but a walking shadow, a poor player
> That struts and frets his hour upon the stage,
> And then is heard no more; it is a tale
> Told by an idiot, full of sound and fury,
> Signifying nothing.

It is a very fine speech. But instead of presenting a figure systematically it presents a procession or flight of figures. The tomorrows creep along till they have crept far enough, and bring up against— what? A syllable; remarkable barrier. After the tomorrows, in the whirling sub-logical mind of this harried speaker, the yesterdays, by the suggestion which prompts antithesis; and, at a venture, he remarks that what they did was to light fools to their death. (I do not know why dusty death; it is an odd but winning detail.) But speaking now of lights, out with this one,[301] a mere candle! Lights also imply shadows, and suggest that life is a walking shadow. Then the lights lead to the torches of the theatre, and the walking shadow becomes a strutting player, who after an hour will be heard no more. Finally, since one thing leads to another, we may as well make life into the thing the player says, the story, whose sound and fury have no meaning. The connections between part and part in this speech are psychological, and looser than logical, though psychological will always include logical, and indeed act as their matrix. And the point is that mere psychological connections are very good for dramatic but not for metaphysical effects. Dramatically, this speech may be both natural and powerful; so I am told. Metaphysically, it is nothing.

Once more: Shakespeare could put a character into a situation that called for a desperate speech, and give him one. But he could not seat this character at the table to compose a finished poem, and then let him stand up and deliver it.

If this is the way of the drama at its most favorable moments, there is still less chance of its achieving metaphysical effects in the usual give and take of dialogue. I think of the brilliant figures crowding a late work like *Antony and Cleopatra*, and note, at random, the passage where Antony is having his account with Cleopatra after the defeat at Actium (iii, ix):

> Now I must
> To the young man send humble treaties, dodge
> And palter in the shifts of lowness. . . .[302]

Antony is a figurative man, and full of feelings. The sending of humble treaties is not enough to express them, therefore he elects to dodge, and also to palter, and he will be in shifts of—of what? Lowness will do. And this vigorous jumping from one thing to another registers Antony very well, and may claim its theoretical justification under dramatic method. But in the coherent poetry of Donne and the metaphysicals there is nothing like it; no more than there is anything there like the peculiar jumpiness and straining of a modern such as, let us say, Mr. Joseph Auslander.

It is not likely that the plays of Shakespeare, even the later ones, can furnish better metaphysical effects than the sonnets do, which deliberately intend them, and in intending them do not have to worry about the peremptory and prior claims of drama.[303]

Arthur Mizener

The Structure of Figurative Language in Shakespeare's Sonnets

In *The World's Body* Mr. John Crowe Ransom has an essay that is pretty severe on Shakespeare's sonnets; Mr. Ransom's strategy is to set Shakespeare up as a metaphysical poet and then to assail his metaphysical weaknesses. The late Shakespeare—the Shakespeare of *Measure for Measure, Antony and Cleopatra,* and the romances—had a good deal more in common with Donne than may sometimes be recognized, but even this Shakespeare was not, I believe, a metaphysical poet in Mr. Ransom's sense of the term. But whether Mr. Ransom is right or wrong, he has done the sonnets a good turn by raising in a serious way, for the first time since the eighteenth century, the problem of their figurative language.

In those distant days, some severe strictures were passed on this aspect of Shakespeare. Dr. Johnson remarked that "a quibble was to him the fatal Cleopatra for which he lost the world and was content to lose it"; Warburton laboriously explained that "he took up (as he was hurried on by the torrent of his matter) with the first words that lay in his way; and if, amongst these, there were two mixed modes that had a principal idea in common, it was enough for him"; Steevens roundly declared that "such labored perplexities of language, and such studied deformities of style, prevail throughout these sonnets" that he saw no reason to print them in 1793, since "the strongest act of parliament that could be framed would fail to compel readers into their service." These eighteenth-century critics were never answered. The usual remarks about this aspect of the sonnets ("An average Shake-

source: Published originally in *Southern Review,* V (Spring, 1940), 730–747. Revised in 1962 for this collection. Students should accordingly use the pagination of this book for documentation.

speare sonnet comes dancing in, as it were, with the effortless grace of a bird, etc.") are not answers but ways of filling an embarrassing pause.

Mr. Ransom, however, is not Steevens or another of those outspoken and outmoded eighteenth-century gentlemen, but a contemporary critic, less outspoken and as a consequence in some ways more devastating, and very far indeed from being outmoded. One can of course say that if we distill off the poetry of Shakespeare's sonnets, leaving in the flask only the bare "idea," that "idea" will be found not only familiar but, indeed, trite. Even the most ardent advocate of this view, however, usually gives his case away before he is through with some reference to the mystery of Shakespeare's language. Nor does this view meet Mr. Ransom's argument. The only way that argument can be met is by a description of the structure of the sonnets' figurative language which accounts for that structure without damning Shakespeare as, at his best, a metaphysical poet who lacks the courage of his convictions, and, at his worst, a manufacturer of trifles. If Shakespeare's sonnets are really metaphysical, then they are bad in the way and to the extent Mr. Ransom says they are.

Mr. Ransom's argument is that good poetry is always airtight extensively (to borrow a term from Mr. Allen Tate). He is willing to allow it to function intensively only within the limits set by a vehicle that is described with logical consistency. A poet, that is, must never be more in earnest about the tenor of his metaphor than about the vehicle, must never be willing to sacrifice the strict logic of his vehicle in order to imply something further about the tenor. This is a seductive definition of good poetry but an arbitrary one, which, if strictly applied, excludes from the category of good poetry all non-metaphysical poetry. In the present state of our knowledge of the way language works, this consideration alone is enough to cast serious doubt on such a definition. It produces, in addition, some curious results. For instance, Mr. Ransom says of the opening quatrain of sonnet 73 ("That time of year thou may'st in me behold") that the metaphor here is compounded and that "the two images cannot, in logical rigor, co-exist." It is true that *choirs* can be looked on as a metaphorical extension of *boughs*,[1] but it is only by a pun that this extension can be

---

[1] By taking the boughs as the choirs and the trees as the cathedral. But "in logical rigor" Mr. Ransom's definition will not permit this ingenuity of Steevens; no metaphor is strictly logical—certainly this one is not—and the metaphorical extension of a metaphor's vehicle is therefore illegal.

maintained in the phrase "sweet birds" and Mr. Ransom cannot allow puns. Not even a pun, moreover, will bring "shake against the cold" within the limits of the figure, since by no stretch of the imagination can ruined cathedrals be thought of as shaking against the cold.

But it is plain before one reaches the end of this analysis that the success of Shakespeare's compound metaphor does not depend on the strict logic of its vehicle. His purpose is apparently to relate to his time of life, by some other means than the strictly logical elaboration of vehicle, both the boughs which shake against the cold and the bare ruined choirs. The age of Shakespeare's love, which is his life, is like the autumnal decline of nature, and thus natural, inevitable and, perhaps, only the prelude to a winter sleep rather than death; it is at the same time like the destruction of an artificial and man-made thing by man's willful violence, and thus not inevitable, save as evil is inevitable, but regrettable as is the destruction of a building beautiful, not only in itself but as a symbolic act. The fusion of these two meanings brought about by the compound metaphor is richer and finer than the sum of them which would be all the poem could offer if the two metaphors did not coexist.

The fusion is brought about by Shakespeare's slurring up from *boughs* to *choirs* and then down again. He gets up to choirs with the adjectival sequence "bare ruin'd"; "bare" modifies, primarily, *boughs*, and it is only through the diplomatic mediation of "ruin'd," primarily the modifier of *choirs*, that "bare" becomes intimate with *choirs*. He gets down again to *boughs* with the pun on "sweet birds"; in the phrase's secondary, euphemistic sense these are the choristers, but in its primary sense they are the quondam occupants of the now shaking boughs. The fact that this fusion gives the vehicle, not logic, but an ingeniously devised air of being logical really deceives no one (least of all, I suspect, Mr. Ransom) into supposing that Shakespeare's lines do rely for their power on the rigorous logical coherence of the metaphor's vehicle. Mr. Ransom's real point is not that he believes Shakespeare *did* intend them to, but that he believes Shakespeare *ought* to have intended them to.

Shakespeare's method is, then, fundamentally different from the metaphysical method: where Donne, for example, surprises you with an apparently illogical vehicle which can be understood only if its logic is followed, Shakespeare surprises you with an apparently logical vehicle which is understandable only if taken figuratively.

The position taken by critics like Mr. Ransom thus forces them to write down as a blunder one of the most essential features of Shake-speare's kind of poetry. A critic is of course free to dislike Shake-speare's kind of poetry, and I imagine Mr. Ransom does not mean to express admiration when he describes Shakespeare's poetry as the kind "which we sometimes dispose of a little distastefully as 'romantic.'" Probably a great many more people than profess to would dislike it were they not bullied by Shakespeare's name into accepting it. But the critic has not the right to treat this poetry as if it were of another kind, as Mr. Ransom does in discussing what he calls Shakespeare's "metaphysical" sonnets.

The characteristic feature of Shakespeare's kind of poetry at its best is a soft focus; a metaphysical poem is in perfect focus, perhaps more than perfect focus (like those paintings in which every detail is drawn with microscopic perfection). In a good metaphysical poem each figurative detail may be examined in isolation and the poem as a whole presents itself to us as a neatly integrated hierarchy of such details. Mr. Ransom suggests that the metaphysical poet shows a special kind of courage in committing his feelings in this way "to their determination within the elected figure"; probably no one will question this claim, or the implication that the special intensity of good metaphysical poetry derives from this self-imposed restriction. But the metaphysical poet shows also a special kind of perversity. He achieves a logical form at the expense of richness and verisimilitude; for the more ingeniously he elaborates his elected figure, the more apparent will it be that it is either distorting or excluding the nonlogical aspects of his awareness of the object.

Mr. Ransom, however, believes that the business of the poem is to express not the poet but the object, and draws a distinction between the poetry of knowledge and the poetry of feelings. This is a useful distinction, particularly in dealing with nineteenth-century poetry of the kind from which Mr. Ransom is such an expert in selecting horrible examples; but it does not go all the way. For whether or not the object has an existence independent of our awareness of it is for poetry an academic question; so far as poetry is concerned its existence is our awareness of it. That awareness may be more or less disciplined by what it thinks things actually are, more or less in control of its tendency to see them as it wishes them to be. But in either case, it remains an awareness. This awareness is what the poem presents; it never presents actual objects (even if poets could somehow present collages or *objets trouvés*, the very process of selection itself would color the objects in such a way as to destroy their objectivity: objects are never just found; someone finds them). Expressing an object, giving to it, in Mr. Ransom's phrase, "public value," consists in "publishing" our awareness of it; and feelings are no less feelings for being a publishable, a communicable, part of that awareness. Mr. Ransom's very proper distaste for a poetry which presents a gross awareness, one which includes undistinguished or ill-distinguished feelings about the object, seems to have led him to try to eliminate the concept "feeling" from his definition of the best poetry. But to say that the best poetry expresses the object is to use a figure of speech which only apparently allows you to escape the fact that "speech as behavior is a wonderfully complex blend of two pattern systems, the symbolic and the expressive, neither of which could have developed to its present perfection without the interference of the other." [2]

Since poetry is not the world's body but a verbal construct between which and the world-as-object the poet's awareness mediates, there are bound to be disadvantages to any kind of poetry which requires a definite distortion of that awareness for its intensity. It is this price which Shakespeare's poetry does not have to pay. There is, certainly, much to be said against his kind of poetry too. It is, for one thing, always wantoning on the verge of anarchy; and I think Mr. Ransom is right as to the unhappy effect of Shakespeare's example on such poets as Matthew Arnold, who brought himself to announce of Shakespeare's receding hairline that an assorted collection of painful sensations "find their sole speech in that victorious brow." But whatever may be said against it, much, too, must be said in favor of a poetic method which made possible the richness and verisimilitude of the best of Shakespeare's sonnets.

II

The only way to particularize this description of Shakespeare's method is to examine one of the sonnets in some detail. I have chosen for this purpose 124 (I have modernized the spelling but kept the punctuation of the 1609 edition):

> If my dear love were but the child of state,
> It might for fortune's bastard be unfathered,
> As subject to time's love, or to time's hate,
> Weeds among weeds, or flowers with flowers gathered.   4

[2] Edward Sapir, "Language," *The Encyclopedia of the Social Sciences.*

No it was builded far from accident,
It suffers not in smiling pomp, nor falls
Under the blow of thralled discontent,
Whereto the inviting time our fashion calls: 8
It fears not policy that heretic,
Which works on leases of short numbered hours,
But all alone stands hugely politic,
That it nor grows with heat, nor drowns with showers.   12
    To this I witness call the fools of time,
    Which die for goodness, who have lived for crime.

This sonnet has at least two advantages in this connection: it is obviously a serious effort and it is not likely therefore that its consequences are unintentional; and it has that "excessive dispersion in the
matter of figures" which seems to be characteristic of Shakespeare at
his most serious and has annoyed others besides Mr. Ransom.

"If my dear love were but the child of state." The difficulty here is
with *state*, which has a very complex meaning. It covers, in its general
sense, the condition of those who live in this world and in time; in its
specific senses, it includes most of the particular aspects of life which
are touched on in the rest of the sonnet. I begin with the general sense.
If Shakespeare's love were the product of, had been generated by, the
combination of circumstances and attributes belonging to the young
man addressed and to the age, it might, as a subject of the kingdom
of time and consequently "subject to" the whimsical decrees of
Time's perverse rule,[3] at any time be "unfathered." The more specific
sense of *state*—the metaphorical father of which Shakespeare's love
would risk being deprived—touched on in the rest of the sonnets are:
(1) Fortune, the deity who rules worldly affairs; (2) status; (3)
wealth; (4) natural endowment (talent, beauty); (5) authority,
pomp, display, the more obvious of the secondary characteristics of
state in the previous senses; (6) the body politic; (7) statesman-
ship, "policy," the kind of maneuvering by which all earthly results,
good or bad, are achieved. Of this complex father Shakespeare's love,
were it the child of state, would run the constant risk of being deprived, either as the bastard of state in sense (1) or in order to make

---

[3] The figure at this point is tending, on the one hand, toward a comparison
to the court of an omnipotent prince, perverse, moody, shrewd, as Queen
Elizabeth was; it is tending, on the other hand, toward the essentially medieval idea of Fortune, who rules everything on this side of the moon, and
whose rule is wholly without order or meaning.

way for some other bastard of state as Fortune. In either case, Shakespeare's love, as a child of state, would be a bastard.[4]

Nothing, I think, could show more clearly than these three lines the difference between Shakespeare's figurative language and that of a metaphysical poem. For no single one of the meanings of *state* will these lines work out completely, nor will the language allow any one of the several emergent figures to usurp our attention; it thus becomes impossible to read the lines at all without making an effort to keep all the meanings of *state*, all the emergent figures, in view at once. That is, the purpose is to make the reader see them all, simultaneously, in soft focus; and the method is to give the reader just enough of each figure for this purpose. The figure of state as Fortune, for example, emerges just far enough to make it possible for the reader to see what this figure would have come to had it been worked out completely; and the figure of state as the body politic within which Shakespeare's love would be subject to Time just far enough to suggest what that figure would have come to. And so of the rest. If any one of these emergent figures had been realized in full, all the rest would necessarily have been excluded. They must then have been developed separately, and Shakespeare would have written a poem in which each of these figures appeared seriatim, perhaps a figure to a stanza, as in Donne's "Valediction; of the booke," which Mr. Ransom offers as an illustration of metaphysical structure.[5]

It is difficult to say how daring a venture "Weeds among weeds, or flowers with flowers gathered" is; it all depends on how familiar in

---

[4] There seems to have been a close connection in Shakespeare's mind between bastardy and Machiavellian, policy-breeding, anarchic cynicism, as if this cynicism presented itself to his mind as the bastard of Time. See, for example, Edmund and Thersites ("I am a bastard begot, bastard instructed, bastard in mind, bastard in valor, in everything illegitimate"), or the cynicism of that strangely unfathered child of state, Hamlet.

[5] There is an interesting parallel between Donne's poem and the present sonnet which not only demonstrates the commonness of the "ideas" treated in both poems but also allows the very different methods of the two poems to be compared. Donne starts his sixth stanza as if he were going to take the other side of the argument from Shakespeare. Statesmen, he says, can learn much useful "policy" by studying the annals of his love, since in both love and statecraft "they doe excell/Who the present governe well,/Whose weaknesse none doth, or dares tell"; but then, just as Shakespeare implies that the "policy" of love is of a very different order from that of statesmen (see page 232), so Donne adds that any statesman who fancies he finds love's methods like his is comparable to the alchemist who believes he finds authority for his art in the Bible.

Shakespeare's day were the associations of weeds and flowers he is using here. It is easy enough to show that they were familiar to Shakespeare, but I suspect they were also peculiar to him. Fortunately the line is carefully paralleled with l. 12; indeed, the primary sense-connection of l. 12 is to l. 4. From this parallel I think l. 4 gains enough support so that it will serve simply in its general sense: if Shakespeare's love were the child of state, so long as Fortune favored it, its every aspect would be a flower gathered with all the other flowers blossoming in the sunshine of Time's love; if Fortune ceased to favor it, its every aspect would be a weed, gathered with all the other weeds which rot noisomely in the damp of Time's hate. *Gather'd* carries out the personifications of the first three lines, and hints at a new one, Father Time (cp., the scythe in the final line of 123); the flowers and weeds represent the specific consequences of Time's love and Time's hate.

But the particular value of this line as a summing up of the whole quatrain depends on our familiarity with Shakespeare's usual use of weeds and flowers; and it is not quite fair therefore to say that this value is communicated as well as expressed. In Shakespeare the contrast between weeds and flowers is most frequently applied to court life, society, problems of state, this-worldly affairs; figures of this kind are frequent in the history plays and in *Hamlet*. Weeds, particularly in their rankness (vigorousness, grossness, rancidity, indecency), are among the strongest of Shakespeare's images for evil.[6] Thus the gardener in *Richard II* ends his elaborate comparison of his garden to a commonwealth by saying:

> I will go root away
> The noisome weeds, which without profit suck
> The soil's fertility from wholesome flowers.[7]

[6] Caroline F. E. Spurgeon, *Shakespeare's Imagery*, pp. 154-55, 220-23.

[7] There is the implication here and throughout *Richard II* that a proper gardener can put things right. The gardener himself specifically adds that "The weeds . . . are pluck'd up root and all by Bolingbroke," and it is only at the end and only from Richard that we hear:

> Nor I nor any man that but man is
> With nothing shall be pleas'd till he be eas'd
> With being nothing.

It is a very different matter in *Hamlet*—and in the present sonnet—where all the authority of Hamlet is behind the belief in the incurable weediness of this world and where the mere easement of death has become the only "felicity." Hamlet's authority is not of course complete, but the king is a distinctly lighter weight in the scale against him than Bolingbroke is against Richard.

Hamlet finds the world

> an unweeded garden,
> That grows to seed; things rank and gross in nature
> Possess it merely.

This sense of evil is primarily a result of his mother's sins; these are for Hamlet both weeds on which she is in danger of spreading compost "to make them ranker" and an "ulcerous place," the rank corruption of which may infect all within unseen. But Hamlet's sense of evil is not limited to its immediate cause; it is *all* the uses of this world which seem to him weary, stale, flat, and unprofitable, just as in the present sonnet Shakespeare distrusts Time's love as much as its hate. The "facts" of both the play and the sonnet are the vehicle for a feeling about the world as a whole. It is the essence of Shakespeare's success with this kind of figurative language that he never loses the individual "facts" in the perilously extended feeling.

With the association of rank weeds and spiritual corruption goes quite naturally the association of physical and spiritual decay which appears in Hamlet's "ulcerous place" figure. The ease with which Shakespeare bridged what may seem to the reader the considerable gap between the imagery of flowers and weeds and the imagery of disease can be demonstrated from a simple narrative passage in *Macbeth*:

> CATHNESS: Well, march we on,
> To give obedience where 'tis truly ow'd:
> Meet we the medicine of the sickly weal;
> And with him pour we, in our country's purge,
> Each drop of us.
> LENOX: Or so much as it needs
> To dew the sovereign flower, and drown the weeds.

Here, quite characteristically, their blood, in Cathness's speech a medicine with which to purge the sick society, becomes the dew which makes the sovereign flower grow and drowns the weed. And, precisely as in the present sonnet, the fact that the ultimate referent of weeds is a group of human beings leads Shakespeare to use a verb (*drown*) which is more immediately applicable to persons than to weeds.[8]

[8] In the present sonnet, of course, Shakespeare is dealing directly with the mystery of loyalty and sovereignty which gave such limited perfection as it possessed to government, whereas in *Macbeth* that mystery is incarnate in the royal family and its loyal followers. Hence, in *Macbeth* the sovereign

The physical decay of this imagery may be either that of disease or that of death. It is the special horror of this aspect of life that the sun's breeding maggots in a dead dog and the son's breeding sinners in that living variety of good kissing carrion, Ophelia, are scarcely distinguishable. Both kinds of physical decay appear frequently in connection with the evils of human life, especially the evils of power and passion. Hamlet's mind is haunted by the smell of rotting flesh as well as by the imposthume that inward breaks. The king will be able to nose the corpse of Polonius as he goes up the stairs into the lobby; and Hamlet's final comment on the humiliating futility of Yorick's life is: "and smelt so? Pah!" But perhaps the most perfect collocation of all these images and their association is the close of sonnet 94:

> The summer's flower is to the summer sweet,
> Though to itself, it only live and die,
> But if that flower with base infection meet,
> The basest weed outbraves his dignity,
>> For sweetest things turn sourest by their deeds:
>> Lilies that fester, smell far worse than weeds.

Rain is closely connected with these images of corruption, too, for though it causes flowers as well as weeds to grow (but "sweet flowers are slow and weeds make haste"), it is also the cause of weeds' and flesh's rotting and stinking. The first gravedigger, after observing that "we have many pocky corpses now-a-days, that will scarcely hold the laying in," remarks that a tanner's corpse will last the longest because " 'a will keep out water a great while, and your water is a sore decayer of your whoreson dead body." And it is the rankness of nettles which lends the terrible dramatic irony to Cressida's reply to Pandarus.

> PANDARUS: I'll be sworn 'tis true: he will weep you,
> and 'twere a man born in April
> CRESSIDA: And I'll spring up in his tears, an 'twere a
> nettle against May.

It is these associations of weeds and flowers (and of heat and showers too) which give such great force to l. 4.

flower is ultimate earthly good, whereas, in the sonnet, it is only smiling Fortune. The overriding metaphor in *Macbeth* is such as to eliminate those impediments to the marriage of true minds the tragic reality of which so haunts Hamlet, Troilus, Othello, Lear, and the present sonnet. But apart from this distinction, the use of weeds and flowers is the same in *Macbeth* and the sonnet.

III

With the second quatrain Shakespeare starts another of his great metaphors for the destructive power of time, that of a building: "No it was builded far from accident" (where "waterdrops have worn the stones of Troy,/And blind oblivion swallow'd cities up,/And mighty states characterless are grated/To dusty nothing"). This metaphor is then compounded in much the same way that the opening metaphor of sonnet 73 is; that is, the building is personified: "It suffers not in smiling pomp, nor falls/Under the blow of thralled discontent." The figurative significances which may be derived from this compounded metaphor, taken in connection with the two metaphors of the first quatrain, are so many and so shaded into each other that a listing of them is neither possible nor desirable. The effect here, as in the first quatrain, depends on our being conscious of as many of these figurative significances as possible without bringing any of them exclusively into focus. They resist any effort to separate them one from the other; if the reader nevertheless insists on trying to force the lines to work for any one meaning alone, they will appear hopelessly defective. If this were not the case, they would be unable to function for all their meanings simultaneously.

The disadvantages of trying to bring any one implication of this complex of interacting metaphors into sharp focus are manifold. If the reader will oversimplify the problem by ignoring the metaphor of a building which intervenes between Shakespeare's love and the personification which suffers in smiling pomp and falls under the blow of thralled discontent, he will discover that there is a variation of meaning in these lines for every variation of meaning to be found in the first quatrain as a result of the multiple signification of *state*. But if he tries to bring each of these possible meanings of the second quatrain successively into focus he will find not only that the lines will not support any one of them alone, but that each of them tends to shade off into every other, till the possibility of bringing any one into focus becomes remote. There are certainly very real differences between *state* as status, as wealth, and as physical beauty, and it is certain, too, that one can associate a different kind of pomp and a different kind of discontent with each of them. But if the reader attempts to elaborate in detail each of these combinations, he finds in the first place that *suffer* and *fall* range from merely awkward to downright impossible, and in the second that the pomp of the young man's status and the pomp of his wealth begin to fade into each other, that the thralled discontent of status unrecognized, of talent unrealized, of policy unsuccessful begin to merge; and so it is with the rest of these distinctions which are perfectly satisfactory in a general focus.

But the reader cannot afford to ignore the fact that the *it* of l. 6 refers quite as clearly to that which was builded far from accident as to "my dear love." For unless he realize that ll. 6–7 retain the metaphor of the building he will miss the delicacy with which Shakespeare carries out the irony, obvious enough, in a general way, in the implications of the negatives. (*Unless* the young gentleman possesses all this state and is at least conceivably within danger of being victimized by it, and *unless* Shakespeare is capable of being hurt by such a development, it would never occur to Shakespeare to protest that his love is not the child of state.) Shakespeare does not say that the young man is tossed from success to failure and from discontent to satisfaction on the whirligig of time and that, in spite of this, Shakespeare's love remains unchanging. What he does say is that his love is like a building, a building which may be thought of most significantly as not like a courtier riding such a whirligig. The delicacy of the irony thus depends on the fact that this comparison is ostensibly chosen as the perfect description of the building and on the implication that Shakespeare would be surprised and dismayed were he to discover the young man taking it as a reference to himself. Shakespeare, that is, ostensibly and indeed ostentatiously disowns any responsibility for the coincidence of the young man's state and this figurative courtier's.

The insistence of Shakespeare's sonnet on generalizing the focus of the reader's attention will be quite clear, I think, if he will work out the simplest meaning for ll. 6–7 at each of the three levels, without considering either the remoter figurative significances, or the interaction of the various levels of meaning, or the interrelations of these lines with other lines. A courtier may be said to go about smiling and pompous in the conceit of his success; he may not be said to "suffer smiling and pompous." He may be described as wholly enslaved by discontent but only by some stretching of the figure as falling under the blow of his discontent. A building may be described as rich and elegant; it can scarcely be said to "suffer rich and elegant." It may fall under the blows of rebelling slaves; one blow, however, seems a little inadequate.[9] Finally, Shakespeare's love, not having been generated

[9] My implication of dislike for richness and success and of sympathy for

by anything that dwells in Time's kingdom, is beyond the power of either Time's love or Time's hate, both of which are spoken of in l. 6 as disastrous (the first causing suffering and the second discontent). The language of ll. 6–7 is directed just sufficiently toward each of these meanings to make it impossible for the reader to ignore any one of them. In no instance is it directed toward any one of them sufficiently to make it possible for the reader to contemplate that meaning to the exclusion of the others. The reader is thus forced to try to contemplate them all simultaneously. This procedure obviously permits an immense concentration of meaning within the particular passage. It has the further effect of almost forcing the poet to use the multitude of interrelations between the various passages which suggest themselves. This is, of course, the great danger of Shakespeare's kind of poetry. It is a danger over which Shakespeare at his best always triumphed but which has pretty consistently defeated his imitators.

"Whereto the inviting time our fashion calls." To such an existence this encouraging age calls us to fashion our lives as nobles, our relatively more permanent structures (both physical and social), our lives. (There is an ominous quality in "inviting" not represented by "encouraging." Perhaps, therefore, a less literal paraphrase would be more accurate; for example, "a way of life in which this easy age encourages us." But the point here is to bring out the metaphorical richness of the line.) But there is another important meaning here. It is impossible to keep this *time* from establishing relations with the *time* that loves and hates in l. 3; thus Time in its local and temporary manifestation, this age, calls on our fashion to become subject to King Time and thus calls on us to expose ourselves to its love and hate (smiling pomp and thralled discontent being the results of accepting).

IV

In the final quatrain Shakespeare draws together all his metaphorical themes. His love "fears not policy" since it is no child of state but was born in another kingdom than that of Time, in which policy

the discontented is, I think, in the lines. Notice that l. 8 tends to attach itself exclusively to "thralled discontent." This implication places Shakespeare, for all his brave show of living in the light, not of this world but of eternity, among the discontented and even, perhaps, among the approvers of violence. This implication may be a deliberate preparation for the irony of the final couplet.

operates.[10] Policy is a heretic by the familiar trick of transferring the vocabulary of the Christian worship of God to the lover's worship of the loved one. But it is also a heretic ("an indifferentist in religion, a worldly-wise man") because it is a child of state, worshipping the god of Time rather than the God of eternity. *Policy* is then said to be able to work only within the limits of human foresight, which is a space of short numbered hours compared to the eternity in terms of which those work who are subjects of God's kingdom. The line in question (10) is another one of those which says several things and works out without defect for none of them alone. That is, policy, personified as a heretic, may be said to work, but scarcely on a lease of any kind; on the other hand this same policy may *have* a lease on life of short numbered hours. A building in Time's world will presumably be held on a short lease, the duration of which is carefully measured; it can hardly, however, be described as *working* on that lease.

"But all alone stands hugely politic." With a slight stretching of "hugely politic" this line will work for the two immediate meanings involved, those of the previous line. That is, Shakespeare's love, as a building, stands all alone, perhaps like New Place with its orchards and gardens rather than like one of those speculative structures in London, crowded between other buildings, which were giving the authorities so much to worry about. It stands "far from accident," incredibly old and wise. (This is the stretching of "hugely politic." The Elizabethans used *politic* in this good sense regularly; as in the phrase "theyr polytycke wyt and learnyng in Physicke." [N.E.D.]) representing, as it were, the good old certainties of faith rather than the newfangled values of shrewdness and calculation. Shakespeare's love, as person, stands apart from the human world of petty policy, de-

[10] "Policy" here is a kind of metonym. That is, the figurative courtier of ll. 6–7 is a politic fellow. The substitution has the advantage of allowing the meaning of ll. 9–11 to extend beyond the courtier to the general philosophic attitude of shrewd, ambitious, and worldly people. The linking of this line to the figurative courtier of ll. 6–7 thus makes it an extension of the statement that Shakespeare's love, since it is not a child of state, is like a building built far from the kingdom of accident and chance and thus not subject to the alternate pomp and discontent of all which is subject to Time: not only does this love know nothing of the maneuvering of courtiers; it knows nothing of worldly policy in any form. It may be worth noting, as a part of the link, the very specific sense of "an indifferentist in religion, a worldly-wise man" which was given the noun *politic* in Shakespeare's day: "A carnal fellow, a mere politic." (N.E.D.)

pendent on no earthly devices, politic only in the infinite's craft, learned not in Machiavelli's but in God's book.

Thus Shakespeare's love is unlike the blooming favorites of Time's love and the rank and weedy creatures of Time's hate; it is unlike the worldly courtier who flourishes in the sun of prosperity ("For if the sun breed maggots in a dead dog . . . Let her not walk i' th' sun") and goes down in the floods of adversity ("Pulled the poor wretch from her melodious lay/To muddy death"); [11] it is unlike the house built upon the sand which shows in pomp in the sun and sinks to ruin in storms. "It nor grows with heat, nor drowns with showers."

Shakespeare calls to witness the truth of this statement those people who are made fools of by Time. In general in Shakespeare everyone is in one way or another made a fool of by Time, those who know enough try to escape its tyranny most tragically of all. For these discover, as Troilus did, that their fears are only too well grounded:

> What will it be
> When that the watery palate tastes indeed
> Love's thrice repured nectar! Death, I fear me,
> Sounding destruction, or some joy too fine,
> Too subtle potent, tun'd too sharp in sweetness
> For the capacity of my ruder powers:
> I fear it much; . . .

Troilus, Hamlet, Isabella, all in their ways tried to escape from the life of this world, and all discovered that they could not escape the human

---

[11] The richness of Shakespeare's flood imagery has been emphasized by Mr. G. Wilson Knight, but the significance of his sun and light imagery seems to have been unduly neglected. Richard uses it in describing his earthly glory and ends with talk of the "brittle glory [which] shineth in this face" and of melting "before the sun of Bolingbroke." Hal, warning the audience that presently he will emerge as the perfect king, says that "herein will I imitate the sun. . . ." Juliet associates the "garish sun" with ordinary, worldly, daily living; it is the light by which Capulet and the nurse live; but the face of Juliet's heaven is made bright by the starlight of her love. For Hamlet Juliet's sun is not merely garish but a breeder of maggots, as Richard's garden is for him weedy not merely through carelessness but by nature, incurably. Angelo combines the sun imagery with that of flowers and weeds: "but it is I/That, lying by the violet in the sun,/Do as the carrion does, not as the flower,/Corrupt with virtuous season." This whole complex of weeds, flowers, carrion, sun and rain, seems, as the Variorum points out, to be derived ultimately from a speech in *Edward III*, but the beautiful and complex use of it in the plays and sonnets is Shakespeare's own.

consequences of the fact that they were living in it. "Does your worship mean to geld and splay all the youth of the city?" [12]

I think these facts are necessary to an understanding of the amazing inclusiveness of Shakespeare's description of the fools of time. At the most obvious level this line (14) makes a distinction between martyrs and worldly-wise men. (*Crime*, not ordinarily a very strong word among the Elizabethans, is here roughly equivalent to "worldly success.") For though *who* certainly modifies *which*, the change of relatives tends to divide those which die for goodness from those who have lived for crime. And this division is reenforced by the ambiguity of *goodness*, which may mean what Shakespeare takes to be good or what the criminals take to be good. Those who die for goodness in this second, ironic sense may, like "Pitiful thrivers in their gazing spent" (cp. the second quatrain of Sonnet 125), die physically for the sake of the "compound sweet" which they, "dwellers on form and favour," have devoted their worldly lives to seeking; it may be that they also die eternally, are damned, for lack of goodness in the serious sense and for living sinful lives. Those who die for goodness in the serious sense, who are martyrs, may die physically, because, like Richard, they failed to give enough attention to the worldly-wise man's kind of good, after living lives which, even at their best, were not without sin ("in the course of justice, none of us/Should see salvation") and, at their troubled worst, offended against more than one of the world's canons, to say nothing of the Everlasting's. [13]

The most astonishing consequence of this line is its inclusion among the fools of Time of the speaker of this sonnet, so that by a terrifying twist of irony Shakespeare offers his own failure—the unavoidable fact that for all he has been saying about it, his love cannot escape the ✳

---

[12] The thought is developed as early as *Richard II*; cp., 5.5. 45–49, where Richard, having mentally escaped from his prison into the timeless world of ideals, is reminded by the imperfect beat of the music that he still lives in this world:

> And here have I the daintiness of ear
> To check time broke in a disordered string;
> But for the concord of my state and time
> Had not an ear to hear my true time broke.
> I wasted time, and now doth time waste me. . . .

A moment later Richard, who has lived for crime, dies for goodness.

[13] I omit the significances which may be derived from taking *die* less literally (i.e., desire deeply) which several editors have noticed, perhaps because they are so prominent in sonnet 125; they are remoter in this sonnet and my paraphrase is already overburdened.

consequences of his being human and not divine—as part of the evidence for the truth of his contention that his love is not "the child of state."

V

The pattern which one of Shakespeare's sonnets aims to establish in the reader's mind is not the pattern of logic aimed at by the metaphysical poem; his typical sonnet is rather a formal effort to create in the reader's mind a pattern, externally controlled, very like the pattern of the mind when it contemplates, with full attention but for no immediately practical purpose, an object in nature. Such a pattern is not built simply of logical relations nor does it consist simply of what is in perfect focus; it is built of all the kinds of relations known to the mind, as a result of its verbal conditioning or for other reasons, which can be invoked verbally. The building of a verbal construct calculated to invoke such a pattern requires the use of every resource language as a social instrument possesses, and it involves a structure of figurative language which at least approaches, in its own verbal terms, the richness, the density, the logical incompleteness of the mind.

No one can say how much the effect which a poem may fairly be said to produce can in the ordinary sense have been intended by the poet; apparently a good deal it does is not consciously intended. But unless the best of Shakespeare's sonnets are to be passed off as miraculous accidents, it is difficult to see what grounds there are for supposing that they are the result of following the path of least resistance in contrast to Donne's poems, which Mr. Ransom quite justly claims must be the result of stern intellectual labors. If the structure of figurative language in Shakespeare's sonnets is not an accident, and if its consequences are calculated, in so far as the consequences of any poem may be said to be calculated, then it seems more than probable that their making involved at least as great an effort of the intellect and imagination as the making of Donne's poems.

Mr. Ransom has it that in a formal lyric "the poetic object is elected by a free choice from all objects in the world, and this object, deliberately elected and worked up by the adult poet, becomes his microcosm. . . . It is as ranging and comprehensive an action as the mind has ever tried." It seems to me that Shakespeare's serious sonnets fail, as they do sometimes fail, not because they do not live up to this admirable description of the formal lyric but because they have tried to live up to it altogether too well.

Edward Hubler

Form and Matter

THE NOTION OF SHAKESPEARE as the natural poet, the artist of
direct self-expression, is now an old one. It has survived many
literary fashions and many revolutions in thinking about nature. To
the young Milton, Shakespeare was "fancy's child" and his poetic effects were both "wild" and "native." At about the time that Milton
was referring to Shakespeare in this way, John Benson found the
sonnets, in his 1640 edition of them, "serene, cleere, and eligantly
plaine"; and ever since then there have been critics to praise them for
their naturalness and simplicity, although they are, in all truth, difficult enough. If the matter is considered relatively—the sonnets in relation to other contemporary sonnets, and the verses in general in relation to, say, Milton's—there is some justification for the opinion.
Some of the sonnets are simple, and sometimes Shakespeare's dramatic
writing is simpler than that of any other poet who has achieved comparable effects. No other English dramatist in a similar context has
dared to be as simple as he is in the "Good-night, sweet prince"
speech toward the close of *Hamlet*. He had learned to write, and, in
Miss Stein's phrase, it had become a "natural thing to do. But there
are others who learn how, they learn to read and write, but they
read and write as if they knew how." [1] It is well said. Although he had
a talent for the natural and simple, the power of simple expression
was not his from the beginning; it grew with his art and is only one
aspect of it, but the one which, how often and how wrongly! is taken
for the whole. In the commonly held view simplicity equals sincerity,
and, conversely, complexity is artificial. The praiseworthy thing is the

SOURCE: *The Sense of Shakespeare's Sonnets* (Princeton: Princeton University Press, 1952), pp. 11–37. Copyright, 1952, by Princeton University
Press.

[1] Gertrude Stein, *Four in America*, Yale University Press, New Haven,
1947, p. 120.

simple thing. "An artist," writes Hesketh Pearson in a [11] discussion of the sonnets, "does not fool about with words when expressing his true emotion." [2] Pearson's study of Shakespeare is a deservedly popular book, popular enough to have been distributed to the armed forces during the Second World War.

The view of the sonnets which has dominated learned criticism for the past fifty years is at first glance a different matter. It was given currency by the late Sir Sidney Lee, who, toward the end of the last century, was engaged in demonstrating Shakespeare's indebtedness to his predecessors and contemporaries. Lee, having pointed out with notable clarity and learning the existence of certain sonnet conventions, concluded that the sonnets were conventional and little more, for he tended, like Pearson, to value only the spontaneous. In one of his sonnets Shakespeare had written,

> When I have seen the hungry ocean gain
> Advantage on the kingdom of the shore,

and Lee, noticing that Shakespeare had come across the idea in Golding, supposed that Shakespeare's statement was without meaning.[3] We need not look into the logic of this; still less should we wonder if Shakespeare really had seen the phenomenon. The point is that for Sir Sidney repetition constituted convention, convention was empty, and the sonnets therefore appeared to be insincere. In this view of poetry a poem's value is finally determined by reference to documents other than the poem itself, and this is very much like Pearson's second measure of value. He tells us that we can recognize the sincerity of certain passages in Shakespeare by, first, their simplicity, and, second, "because they tell us what we already knew about him." [4] In both the learned and the [12] popular view there is, then, a limitation on the function of poetry which Shakespeare was not willing to admit. A reading of the sonnets makes it quite clear that Shakespeare believed, or wanted the reader to believe, that they were a true expression of his individuality. "Every word doth almost tell my name," he wrote in one of them, "Showing their birth and where they did proceed." Shakespeare has a good many remarks on his particular purpose in writing the sonnets, and on poetic theory in general, and I think that the student should not reject them without due consideration.

[2] Hesketh Pearson, *A Life of Shakespeare*, Penguin Books, 1942, p. 27.
[3] Sir Sidney Lee, *A Life of William Shakespeare*, The Macmillan Company, New York, 1931 (14th ed.), p. 32.
[4] *op. cit.*, p. 30.

I hope that it will not be idle to consider them in relation to Shakespeare's poetic practice.

The most cursory reading of Shakespeare will make it clear that he liked to play with words, sometimes with wretched effect; and it ought to be equally plain that no man without an interest in words and word patterns ever became a poet. Shakespeare's native interest in words was encouraged by the tradition of his time which considered the art of writing to be based on a body of precepts and saw no reason to think of craftsmanship as an affectation. Craftsmanship was then known to be what it is—the means by which the thing is said. Now it happens that it is in the nature of conscious artists to be seduced at times into an overemphasis of their craft, and this matters very little to an age which takes an interest in technique. In such times there is an allowance, and quite without condescension, for the performer's pride in skill. The composers of concertos used to allow the performer to provide his own cadenza, to do, in effect, what he could, and simply in order to show what he could do. There was a tendency in Shakespeare's time, and earlier, to admire the formal dexterity of ingenious word play, and this is nowhere better illustrated than in the sonnet tradition. Petrarch, whose exquisite taste saved him from the greatest excesses, was a master at it. One of his sonnets is an elaboration of an image comparing his lady to the sun. She is the [13] sun; her person, her face, her eyes, her hair are suns. If the sun rises before her, he shines brightly; but when she arises, he is dimmed. Petrarch loved to play upon the similarity of his lady's name (Laura) to *l'aura* (the breeze) and *laurea* (the laurel) and to resolve words similar to her name (*laureta*, for example) into its syllables and expand them in terms of praise. All this can be boring enough in Petrarch; in his imitators it often becomes a dreary elaboration of empty virtuosity.

Shakespeare, too, sometimes let his virtuosity get the better of him, as certain spectacular failures in the sonnets to the young man testify:

> To me, fair friend, you never can be old,
> For as you were when first your eye I ey'd. . . .[5]

The modern reader wonders how Shakespeare brought himself to do it. Such passages occur too often to be oversights, and what we know of Shakespeare's poetic practice does not allow us to think that he disliked them. The banished Romeo grieves that he must go to Mantua while every other person and every thing may stay in Verona with

[5] Sonnet 104.

Juliet: "This flies may do, but I from this must fly." Considered simply as form, the line is superb—ten monosyllables arranged almost in their prose order, yet managing to involve two antitheses: the pun and the double use of "this." Shakespeare places "but I" in the middle of the line, leaving on either side phrases of exactly the same duration. The words, as it is customary to remark of the lights in Times Square, would be beautiful if only we did not know what they meant. It should be remembered that such passages are most frequent and most flagrant in the poetry written when Shakespeare was learning his craft and taking pride in what he learned. It should be observed, too, that it is his admiration of the phrase, and [14] not his concern for the metrical form, the scene, or the genre, which sometimes dominates his judgment.

Shakespeare's weakness, since it was of his age, passed almost unnoticed. There was, of course, some adverse criticism. The players, speaking of the ease with which Shakespeare composed, had said that he scarce blotted a line. "Would he had blotted a thousand," was Ben Jonson's response. This seems to be fair enough, but when Jonson proceeds to specific comment we notice that his criticism is not directed at Shakespeare's weakness. He objects to Shakespeare's making Caesar say that he "never did wrong, but with just cause." Although this is a better and wiser line than the one Shakespeare later substituted for it, Jonson nevertheless finds it ridiculous—not formally, mind you, but as an idea. Jonson's objection seems to assume that there is always a right way and that a just action never involves injustice. It is an extraordinary assumption for a man of Jonson's intellect, but, in a way, it is characteristic of him. It indicates his comparative singleness of vision, which, in turn, does much to account for the greater virulence of his comedy and his inability to conceive a living tragedy. Jonson's thought is often clearer than Shakespeare's, his poetry less textured—and precisely because of the greater simplicity of what he had to express. With him there was not the same danger of loss in pruning a phrase. He was not much interested in tangential and associated meanings. To Shakespeare, intensely aware of the many-sidedness of meaning, the play on words was a ready instrument.

In our time we seem to have agreed that the pun is worthless. It is now good form to greet a pun with groans, and not even the punster is offended. There seems to be an assumption that the pun, resulting from the accidental resemblances of words, can have nothing essential about it and is incapable of expressing value. Yet the pun persists in spite of our conviction of its frivolity. Punsters apologize, but they go on [15] punning; and a man is allowed to pun if he deprecates the enjoyment. In Shakespeare's time the pun was a rhetorical figure, and the rhetoricians considered it solemnly, dividing it into four categories and dignifying each with a long name. In those days word play was not necessarily frivolous, and our loss of the point of view which lent puns dignity is not clear gain. A poet is made as well as born, and in the sixteenth century the making was a conscious process. The fledgling poet learned what could be done with words by studying the figures of speech. The man of our time tends to notice only the figures which do not succeed, which are not figures of thought as well as figures of speech. He cries out against the excesses and fails to notice the others, the near relations. Would he call the use of *bier* and *beard* in the following passage a pun?

> When lofty trees I see barren of leaves
> Which erst from heat did canopy the herd,
> And summer's green all girded up in sheaves,
> Born on the bier with white and bristly beard. . . .[6]

If it is a pun, do we wish it otherwise? And why not? And what are we to think of the schematic placing of *unfair* and *fairly* in the fourth line following?

> Those hours that with gentle work did frame
> The lovely gaze where every eye doth dwell,
> Will play the tyrants to the very same,
> And that unfair which fairly doth excell. . . .[7]

The line can be paraphrased, "and make unbeautiful that which now excels in beauty," but the paraphrase for all its clarity is prose. Is there any gain in the repetition of the syllable and the emphasis on the related and unrelated parts of the words? The truth is that Shakespeare's interest in [16] words produced some of his best as well as some of his worst effects.

There are two sonnets, numbers one hundred thirty-five and one hundred thirty-six, which are elaborate four-way puns on his name, Will, which, then as now, also meant *volition* and *obstinacy*. In his day it had the additional meaning of lust. The first begins,

> Whoever hath her wish, thou hast thy *Will*,
> And *Will* to boot, and *Will* in overplus. . . .

[6] Sonnet 12.   [7] Sonnet 5.

Although it would be possible to write a paraphrase giving the multiple meanings of each repetition, no one should be asked to read it. Readers attracted by the ingenuity will find, on piecing out the poems, that they are successful works of a kind no longer admired. They make sense, and their sense is appropriate to the context in which they are found; but they no longer impress. They are bravura pieces in an outmoded manner, and they do not pretend to be anything more. They are, moreover, the only such pieces Shakespeare ever wrote.

Since he was a poet, he inevitably admired formal graces; and since he was very human, he sometimes indulged his admiration; but his admiration never altered his conviction that matter should take precedence over form. He seems to have been primarily attracted to a given form by its potential utility, by its appropriateness to his purpose and talent. It was his way to take a known form and wrest it to his uses, transforming it, sometimes, into an instrument of an effectiveness its inventor could not have foreseen. Then when he had humbled it to his uses, it was his way to move on to something else. His technical practice throughout his career bears witness to this basic attitude, and his use of the sonnet form he adopted is a case in point. Although in two-thirds of his sonnets he placed the main pause after the twelfth line, it comes after the eighth line in twenty-seven [17] of them, and is irregular in the remaining few. Sonnet number ninety-nine has fifteen lines, sonnet one hundred twenty-six has twelve, and is written in couplets. Number one hundred forty-five is in tetrameter verse, and all the rimes in sonnet twenty are double.

Shakespeare's sonnet form had been invented early in the century by Henry Howard, Earl of Surrey. Its fourteen lines were divided into three quatrains and a concluding couplet. In Shakespeare's characteristic use of it, the quatrains state a subject and the couplet sums it up, most often through the application of the subject to a specific situation. In the first quatrain of the familiar seventy-third sonnet, the poet compares himself to autumn leaves; in the second, to twilight; and in the third, to dying embers. From the gathering together of these images, and the poet's application of them to himself, there emerges the idea of approaching death. Then comes the couplet directed to the friend to whom the poem is addressed and stating the idea to be derived from the situation set forth in the quatrains.

> That time of year thou mayst in me behold
> When yellow leaves, or none, or few do hang
> Upon those boughs which shake against the cold,

Bare, ruin'd choirs where late the sweet birds sang;
In me thou see'st the twilight of such day
As after sunset fadeth in the west,
Which by and by black night doth take away,
Death's second self, that seals up all in rest;
In me thou see'st the glowing of such fire
That on the ashes of his youth doth lie,
As the death-bed whereon it must expire,
Consum'd with that which it was nourish'd by;
    This thou perceiv'st which makes thy love more strong
    To love that well which thou must leave ere long.

There is a pause after each quatrain, the greatest coming [18] after the third. It was his customary usage. There are seven rimes: *abab cdcd efef gg*. Shakespeare might have chosen the Italian sonnet with its five rimes, arranged *abba abba* in the octave, and its variety of rime schemes (*cde cde*, for instance) in the sestet. But the fewer rimes of the Italian sonnet make it a more difficult form, and the absence of the couplet makes it less suited to the explicitness Shakespeare favored. The Italian sonnet was magnificently used by Milton (a more fastidious craftsman than Shakespeare), who returned to it throughout his long career as a poet, leaving on his death only eighteen sonnets in English. Apart from the sonnets in his plays, Shakespeare wrote one hundred and fifty-four, ranging in excellence from the best lyrics in the language to quite poor stuff. Given his talent, it was impossible for him to write a worthless poem, but sometimes in the sonnets it is a near thing. One gathers that he worked at a sonnet for a while, and, if it proved recalcitrant, wrote another, not always throwing the first one away. It is notable that the English poets distinguished for their craftsmanship have almost always preferred the Italian sonnet form.

The sonnet, of whatever form, has an affinity for intensity, and the best sonnets, of whatever time and place, are those devoted to the development of a single mood, the elaboration of a single image, or the expression of a single thought. The long line (five feet in English, six in French) is admirably suited to dignified and serious expression, and the number of lines is appropriate to the sonnet's singleness of purpose. A poem intending to be both unified and intense must be long enough to permit development and short enough to allow the reader a retention of everything his eye takes in, from the first to the last words. For this purpose fourteen lines were found to be right. A few more or less would have done, but half as many would have been too few, and half again the number would have been too many. When the sonnet form was in the process of creation, sonnets [19] were written in varying lengths; but the form crystallized at fourteen lines for the reasons given. Within this form it is necessary to make everything contribute to the proposed effect, for the tightness throws into relief everything which does not contribute, or does so only obliquely. The sonneteer intent on unity must either increase the matter to fit the form or fuse both with all the skill in his power. If he permits himself to stretch the matter, there can be no intensity; and, in any case, verbal expansion was not Shakespeare's way. He had no need to pad his lines; the talent for the right word was in his flesh like blood. Although the need for a rime sometimes forces him into brief verbosity, he has nothing at all like "Ten times in the revolving year plus three," a line of our century which stretches the idea of thirteen times a year to pentameter length. But at times he would not trouble to develop his thematic structure to a coincidence with the sonnet form, or to articulate the parts.

In the sonnets of characteristically Shakespearean structure, the first aspect of the idea carries through the quatrains, leaving as the technical problem of greatest difficulty the articulation of the couplet. The proportion of failures in meeting this problem is smaller in those sonnets in which the main pause comes after the eighth line, or thereabouts, leaving in the remainder of the poem (equivalent to the sestet in the Italian sonnet) enough scope to avoid the oversententious and sometimes casual tone into which the brevity of the couplet sometimes trapped him. One of these sonnets, number thirty-five, is a case in point. It is one of Shakespeare's lesser poems, yet in his treatment of the couplet he achieves a greater coherence than is usual with sonnets of like calibre written in his accustomed form. His success with modestly ambitious poems in which the main pause comes after the eighth line is not without exception, but it is normal enough to be worth notice. His technical practice in the sonnets is of a piece with that of his plays. It is sometimes perfect,[20] often brilliant, too often impatient and content to let well enough alone.

In the sonnets he states his admiration for the craftsmanship of the rival poet, but the importance he accords to it does not permit him to admire the poems, for he always grants priority to substance. There is nothing in his works indicating anything but dislike for the "fools . . . that for a tricksy word defy the matter." [8] He praises plain

[8] *The Merchant of Venice*, 3.5.74.

praised plain speaking

speaking and sends satiric shafts at the spinners of "taffeta phrases, silken terms precise" that blow one "full of maggot ostentation."[9] The attitude is everywhere expressed—in the young courtier who so outraged Hotspur, and in Osric, whom Hamlet found not worth his scorn. Shakespeare was a professional writer, but he was not a man of letters; his love of literature did not lead him to tolerate the "literary." He never accepted the idea of style as an end in itself. We are sometimes told that his plays disclose a low view of the writing profession, but I think it is rather that his comic genius kept him aware of the eccentricities of his craft. Hotspur's contempt for "mincing poetry" discloses the common attitude of the man of affairs; it also discloses Shakespeare's awareness of the too frequent justification of it. Some poetry *is* mincing, and some writers are fools, as Shakespeare well knew. From time to time he falls into the "literary," but these descents are failures of taste and, usually, of youth. His conviction was always against the subordination of the thought to the word.

In the sonnets addressed to the young man he contrasts his own expressions of devotion with the "strained touches rhetoric can lend"[10] to the works of other poets, assuring the reader that the old strain needs no variation and declining to employ the latest literary mannerisms.[11] He tells the reader [21] that he wants the sonnets to represent him as he is, and that he believes they do.[12] On another occasion he remarks that the sonnet is sent "to witness duty, not to show my wit."[13] The assurance must be taken with the realization that there is no necessary contradiction between showing both duty and wit in the same poem, for it is obvious that in poetry a condition of complete artlessness is impossible. The appearance of artlessness is another matter. And surely the normally complex reader can be moved by a poem and admire its art at the same time. There can be no question of content *or* art; there must be both; it is a matter of proportion and purpose. The truth is that quite often the sonnets do not show the craftsmanship they should, that the reader sometimes finds the lack of variation all too apparent and is too often confronted with statement that is only partially realized as poetry. The matter of some of the sonnets would be more available if they had more art.

The poet's problem was to formalize and verbalize his thought. It is, of course, only an egregious obstinacy which would refuse to suppose that sometimes it was not the other way about, that at times the

---

[9] *Love's Labours Lost*, 5.2.409.   [10] Sonnet 82.   [11] Sonnet 76.
[12] Sonnet 76.   [13] Sonnet 26.

phrase came first, demanding to be used. But it could not have been generally so. With him *invention*, as with the Elizabethans as a whole, had the primary meaning of finding, not the means of expression, but subject matter for composition; and the sonnets which discuss invention assure us that the subject matter (the friend and the poet's relation to him) is *given*. That is never questioned. What troubles Shakespeare is his inability to handle the subject matter. He insists on the inadequacy of "my pupil pen," a phrase which recalls the references to "my unpolished lines" and "my untutored lines" in the dedications to *Venus and Adonis* and *The Rape of Lucrece*. Although the attitude they express is opposed to Shakespeare's promises of immortality, one would have to have a very wooden notion [22] of mankind to suppose them meaningless. With the greater number of persons confidence is not unwavering, especially professional confidence at the beginning of their careers, and the lives of poets for whom documentation is adequate show periodic resurgences of doubt to be a common experience. Such is the case in the sonnets, but we should notice that it is not a simple alternation of confidence and fear. The poet's sense of inadequacy is set forth in relation to particular matters: he is not equal to his theme, or he is not of the calibre of the other poet, or both. In sonnet number seventy-nine he says that the greatness of this theme deserves the "travail of a worthier pen," and in the succeeding poem he calls the rival poet a "better spirit" and refers to "my saucy bark, inferior far to his."

It is customary to say that the praise of the other poet is grudgingly given, and it is clearly far from wholehearted. Yet there are aspects of the other man's writing which won Shakespeare's admiration. What he disliked about the rival poet was the character of the man. In the eighty-sixth sonnet there is the well-known and enigmatic passage about the "affable familiar ghost" which "nightly gulls" the other poet with intelligence. We cannot know to what rumored events the phrase refers, and we may dispute the meaning of some of the words, but it is clear that Shakespeare suggests something specious about the content of the rival's poems. We gather from many references that Shakespeare considered him an opportunist who praised the young man for reasons other than those of honest friendship. To this pretension, he says, even the graces of the subject can bring only a superficial virtue; they can "but mend the style." [14] The context of the verses about the rival poet is complicated, and their force is far from single, yet the

[14] Sonnet 78.

element of deference, varied in expression and stated at times with bitterness, is present,[23] called forth by the other poet's style—"the proud full sail of his great verse." [15] What Shakespeare praises in the other poet is technical proficiency. What he deplores in his own work is the lack of it.

Since the identity of the other poet is unknown, we cannot weigh the truth of Shakespeare's estimate of him, but it is obvious that his opinions of his own work are on the whole just. In the sonnets the lowest level of excellence is low indeed, but the subject matter of the worst verses is usually that for which in other poems he has been able to find adequate expression. Clearly the normal difficulty is not one of substance; it is the failure to mold the subject matter into a coherent poem. Sometimes he begins a sonnet in an excellent vein and ends it wretchedly. Number one hundred eleven is a case in point. Up to the couplet a poem of considerable stature, it is boundlessly interesting as a statement of a recurrent attitude toward his life in the theatre. With the couplet there is a change in tone and a shocking decrease in magnitude. The idea in the couplet is of course pertinent to what goes before, if only because an assurance of friendship is always proper to a series of poems addressed to a friend; but in this case the assurance come with such a diminution of force that one wonders why it was allowed to stand.

> O, for my sake do you with Fortune chide,
> The guilty goddess of my harmful deeds,
> That did not better for my life provide
> Than public means which public manners breeds.
> Thence comes it that my name receives a brand,
> And almost thence my nature is subdu'd
> To what it works in, like the dyer's hand.
> Pity me, then, and wish I were renew'd;
> Whilst, like a willing patient, I will drink [24]
> Potions of eisel 'gainst my strong infection;
> No bitterness that I will bitter think,
> Nor double penance, to correct correction.
>   Pity me then, dear friend, and I assure ye
>   Even that your pity is enough to cure me.

The artistic failure of the couplet is so accentuated by the double rime that one wonders if at the time of composition the ingenuity of the rime seemed to justify the couplet.

[15] Sonnet 86.

Perhaps we can learn more of Shakespeare's poetic practice if we
turn to a structural pattern with which he always succeeded. No sonnet beginning with "When" is an undistinguished poem. Naturally
there is nothing magical in the word. It is simply that "when" introduces a subordinate clause which must, perhaps after more subordinate
matter, lead to a main clause, thus creating an arrangement of logically
ordered elements in an emphatic sequence. When the arrangement can
be readily made to coincide with the sonnet length, the structure
avoids Shakespeare's most characteristic faults as a sonneteer—the
tacked-on couplet and the broken back. He is almost certain to succeed when the parts of the sonnet stand in a "When I, Then I, Then I,
So" relationship, or in some variant of it. It was an excellent pattern
for a poet impatient with technical problems. But if the pattern did
not reach to the end of the sonnet, or if there was no "so" or "for"
notion to follow the logical sequence, the couplet, as in the fifteenth
sonnet, stood in danger of seeming to be tacked on. Too often the
development of the idea ends with the quatrains, and the couplet fails
to share the power in which the quatrains were conceived. In such
instances the couplet is poetically, but not intellectually, false. It seems,
to use Shakespeare's words, to have been begotten in "the ventricle
of memory . . . and delivered upon the mellowing of occasion." [25]

> Not marble nor the gilded monuments
> Of princes shall outlive this powerful rime,
> But you shall shine more bright in these contents
> Than unswept stone besmear'd with sluttish time.
> When wasteful war shall statues overturn,
> And broils root out the work of masonry,
> Nor Mars his sword nor war's quick fire shall burn
> The living record of your memory.
> 'Gainst death and all-oblivious enmity
> Shall you pace forth; your praise shall still find room,
> Even in the eyes of all posterity
> That wear this world out to the ending doom.
>   So, till the judgement that yourself arise,
>   You live in this, and dwell in lovers' eyes.[16]

A deservedly famous poem, it ends in a couplet of diminished force,
but not because of what the couplet *says*. The promise of immortality
so pallidly stated in the couplet is expressed with vigorous conviction
in the preceding lines, with which, spiritually, the poem ends. The

[16] Sonnet 55.

quatrains had used up the poet's emotion, leaving no power for a repetition of only formal necessity. The couplet serves chiefly to fill out the form and betray critics who, noticing the relaxed feeling, assume hastily that the theme is alien to Shakespeare's sensibility; but this cannot possibly have been the case, for the idea had been congenial enough only a few lines earlier. In general the couplet is used most expertly when its idea follows in logical sequence from the thematic structure of what has gone before, or when its function is a clear and positive summing up or application of the preceding matter, as in the seventy-third and the one hundred and sixteenth sonnets.

Tucker Brooke observed [17] that the couplet sometimes "introduces [26] a surprise or negation which suddenly swings the reader into a point of view antithetical to that developed in the quatrains." It may be of some significance that of the thirteen sonnets [18] using the couplet in this way only one, number thirty, is among the best known, and it, perhaps, hardly deserves the distinction that has been accorded it. Presumably it has won its place in the public's esteem through the beauty of its opening lines:

> When to the sessions of sweet silent thought
> I summon up remembrance of things past . . . ,

for much of what follows is overweighted with decoration. The alliteration of "And with old woes new wail my dear times waste" is not as drearily flamboyant as Poe's "weary way-worn wanderer," but it is a close call. In this sonnet the casualness of the couplet is saved from emphasis by the relaxed lines which lead up to it. But generally Shakespeare's failures with the couplet are owing to a danger inherent in the sonnet form which he chose and to his impatience with formal problems.

There are other failures arising from sources quite beyond the poet's control, just as there are graces which providence seems to have conferred uniquely on him. Both of them can be readily noticed in the sonnets written on the subject of absence.[19] None of these sonnets is among Shakespeare's most distinguished poems. Too often they seem to have been written only to witness duty, and at their worst they are his nearest approach to frigidity. The least interesting are those

---

[17] Tucker Brooke, *Shakespeare's Sonnets*, Oxford University Press, London-New York, 1936, p. 4.

[18] Sonnets 19, 30, 34, 42, 60, 84, 86, 91, 92, 131, 133, 139, 141.

[19] The sonnets clearly written in absence are: 27, 28, 36, 37, 38, 39, 43, 44, 45, 46, 47, 48, 49, 50, 51, 56, 57, 58, 59, 97, 98, 113, 114.

most wholly devoted to absence, and the cause of their lack of distinction is apparent. It was the habit of his time to think of friendship's community of interest in terms of identity (one soul in two bodies), a metaphorical extravagance [27] for which he has been censured, but which is absurd or meaningless only to those of a literal turn of mind, or to those who would reserve it for the poetry of romantic love. In Shakespeare's time it was an accepted manner of speaking about a psychological fact, as Euripides wrote about Aphrodite without, presumably, believing in her physical reality. For Shakespeare it was, as an ideological structure must always be for a poet, a formalized extension of his own perception.

In his selection of already formalized ideas, the poet always takes a chance. He cannot pick them with an eye to posterity, for he has no means of knowing which ideas will endure and which will not. He must write for himself and the readers of his own generation, and for the rest he can only hope. He must, as Day Lewis remarks,[20] "hope for the pure luck that Donne had with the compass legs—that men still use compasses, though they have discarded epicycles and planispheres." For us the identity metaphor in the context of friendship has gone the way of the planisphere. And that is not the worst of it, for it was Shakespeare's habit to think of friendship in terms of both identity and the outmoded theory of the four elements (fire, air, earth, and water) of which all things were thought to be made. The belief was that physical things were made of the heavier elements, earth and water, and things of the mind and spirit of the other two. In Shakespeare's time references to the belief were, of course, immediately understood and spontaneously credited. In a pair of sonnets, numbers forty-four and forty-five, the poet wishes that he were entirely made of the lighter elements so that he could leap the distance to his friend, as his thoughts and wishes, being incorporeal and therefore free of earth and water, were able to do. One imagines that the poems were never vital, but their pretty ingenuity [28] must have been more telling, and their thought more forceful, when the identity metaphor was taken seriously and the content of the idea of the elements was readily available.

Only a small portion of that content is now conveyed to the average reader. The association of tears and water is plain enough to be a perpetual commonplace, and it was hardly fresh when Shakespeare used

[20] Cecil Day Lewis, *The Poetic Image*, Oxford University Press, New York, 1947, p. 92.

it—but it was not empty. Water being then associated with earth and opposed to fire and air, the water-tears conjunction in poetry could carry the suggestion of heaviness and earth in separation from warmth and light. This gave meaning to such passages as that in which Laertes declines to shed tears for his drowned sister: "Too much of water hast thou, poor Ophelia." At the time of its composition the line was not simply the word play it has now become; it then suggested that her body had returned, cold and lifeless, to the heavier elements. But time has taken the content of the line away, and for most of us it is an irritatingly commonplace assertion, suggesting little but crassness in the speaker and forcing the actor to hope that in the richness of the scene the line will pass unnoticed.

Sometimes conceits no longer admired in themselves are effectively employed, for the decay of an idea need not be fatal to its use in a poem, provided the force of the idea *as employed* is not single. The dramatic function of the weird sisters at the opening of *Macbeth* is immediately apparent, quite apart from the spectators' belief or disbelief in witches, because the reality of the thing for which they are the emblem is undeniable to all intelligent playgoers. In a like manner the old conceit of the conflict between the eye and the heart, or the mind and the eye, is used powerfully in the dark lady sonnets because it is there invested with the force of a moral struggle; but in the sonnets written in absence to the young man, the conceit is used ingeniously for its own sake, and time has left little but the ingenuity.[29] Other uses of the conceit, as in sonnet one hundred fourteen, succeed because they are endowed with a collateral intellectuality:

> Or whether doth my mind, being crown'd with you,
> Drink up this monarch's plague, this flattery?
> Or whether, shall I say, mine eye saith true. . . .

Other sonnets written in absence are interesting for what they glance at, for what they give us of the poet's mind.[21] Still others [22] derive their power from the poet's fears for the dissolution of the friendship under the blows of circumstance. These can more appropriately be considered later. The thing to notice here is the relation between the power of the poems and their subject matter. Absence was not in itself a subject which the poet could work into enduring poetry. He writes best in absence when he celebrates the friendship itself, or fears for it, or writes of absence in images which for him were always figures of thought and feeling as well as figures of speech.

[21] See Sonnets 35, 37, 38, 58, 59.   [22] See Sonnets 36, 49, 57.

He saw nature precisely and was always able to find the right words for her loveliness—"proud-pied April," for example. It is to the exercise of this talent that the absence sonnets of widest fame owe their renown. Two of them ("How like a winter" and "From you I have been absent," numbers ninety-seven and ninety-eight) are remembered for passages of unobtrusive melody and lines of easy grace:

> Nor did I wonder at the lily's white,
> Nor praise the deep vermilion in the rose. . . .

It is clearly not the summit of Shakespeare's art, but it is one of his peculiar achievements, this seemingly effortless poetry of nature: "The teeming autumn big with rich increase" and such phrases as "What old December's bareness everywhere." No other English poet has phrases of that quality,[30] and, as far as I know, none of Shakespeare's translators has been able to approximate it in other languages. Shakespeare always wrote well on nature's morning loveliness and her plenitude. Subjects for which he had an affinity, they gave these poems an excellence beyond anything that the contemplation of absence inspired in him. It is one of the most striking *données* of his poetic talent. To it even more impressive powers were shortly to be added.

With writers of stature, the development of style stands in a reciprocal relation to intellectual and spiritual growth. A writer's style can persist unchanged to the end of his career only if he remains minor. In the first years of the 1590's the young Shakespeare, mainly under the influence of Marlowe, formed a style admirably suited to his early powers. The rhythmic unit was the blank verse line, and generally the memorable phrases were those of a Marlovian rotundity, or descriptive passages of his own peculiar loveliness. One could not say of it, as Eliot said of the style of *In Memoriam*, that it was intimate with the poet's depths, for there is nothing in the first works that can properly be called depths. But he soon became conscious of the depths, and a new style had to be evolved to disclose them. By the time he was writing *Richard II*, the first style was already inadequate to the new perception, and was felt to be. He was able to characterize Richard by making him the connoisseur of surfaces and the artist in words, and by bringing him to a realization of the speciousness of appearance —in short, by endowing him with a share of his own sensibility.

Richard's most moving speeches have a greater flexibility than the best verse of the preceding plays, but their metrics are not markedly different. While Richard is less inclined to think in blank verse lengths

than his predecessors, the line is still the rhythmic unit, and the run
on rhythms tend to end at the caesura: [31]

> That rounds the mortal temples of a king
>   For within the hollow crown
> Keeps Death his court, and there the antic sits,
> Scoffing his state, and grinning at his pomp,
> Allowing him a breath, a little scene,
> To monarchize, be fear'd, and kill with looks,
> Infusing him with self and vain conceit,
> As if this flesh which walls about our life,
> Were brass impregnable; and humour'd thus
> Comes at the last, and with a little pin
> Bores through his castle wall, and—farewell king! 23

Or, through its propriety to the character of the hero, the poet makes
effective dramatic use of his ornate style, as in the descent from the
ramparts of Flint Castle, where the magnificent showmanship is both
Shakespeare's and Richard's:

> Down, down I come; like glist'ring Phaeton,
> Wanting the manage of unruly jades.
> In the base court? Base court, where kings grow base,
> To come at traitors' calls and do them grace.24

But at other times the formalism obscures, almost obliterates, the
meaning:

> Ay, no; no, ay; for I must nothing be;
> Therefore no no, for I resign to thee.25

Throughout the play there is little of what we are later to have in
abundance, and toward the end of the play when the theatricality is
over and the inwardness of Richard is the dramatist's first concern,
the disparity between the ornate style and the deeply felt content,
between the achieved style and the newly realized depths, is the concern of Shakespeare's deposed and imprisoned artist-hero. We discover him in [32] Pomfret Castle brooding on the difficulty of putting
his misery into words:

> I have been studying how I may compare
> This prison where I live unto the world,
> And for because the world is populous,
> And here is not a creature but myself,
> I cannot do it; yet I'll hammer it out. . . .26

23 *Richard II*, 3.2.160–170.   24 *Ibid.*, 3.3.178–181.
25 *Ibid.*, 4.1.201–202.   26 *Ibid.*, 5.5.1–5.

With Shakespeare himself it was never hammered out in these terms. His most deeply revealing passages are never in a style which is at once in contrast to and congruent with the depths disclosed. That is the glory of Racine, who in that respect is unchallenged. Shakespeare found a more direct solution.

There is little to suggest the solution in his first works, where in general he searched for depths with Marlovian means, or with his own adaptation of the styles of Marlowe and Spenser. But when the profundity came, when, as in the later tragedies, it was at its greatest, it was sometimes expressed in a style having at once homeliness and splendor, as in Macbeth's "I have supp'd full with horrors. . . ." In his early works he tended to reserve homeliness for prose, a practice he quickly outgrew; indeed, he departed so completely from it that by the time he wrote *King Lear* the rhythmic distinction between prose and verse had disappeared, and the movement from prose to verse is, in the greatest passages, not always to be distinguished by the ear; and when it can be, it is a difference without a distinction in kind. In *King Lear* the unpatterned rhythm of the prose is the pulsing of its spirit, and the verse, if one has got it by heart, cannot be written down again in Shakespeare's lines without consulting the text. The reader is invited to try.

The seeds of this were in Shakespeare from the beginning, and as he learned to write the shoots began to appear. Their [33] growth, in the way of such developments, was not constant. Sometimes purposely, sometimes without apparent awareness, he doubled back upon himself; but there was no stopping the fitful progression. In *Romeo and Juliet* there is early formalism and ornateness, there is fustian, there is sheer aria, and there are promises of things to come: Romeo, dreaming of his love, is greeted by his servant with the news of her death:

> Her body sleeps in Capel's monument,
> And her immortal part with angels lives.

Romeo replies in a speech of startling contrast to the lyric regularity of the servant's lines:

> Well Juliet, I will lie with thee to-night.

The accents have varied values, the rhythm is irregular, the line is just a little in excess of pentameter length. Homely words in their prose order making poetry as revealing of character as any dozen lines in the play! Yet they are not altogether simple, and in as far as they are simple, it is the simplicity of the master of language. The increasing frequency with which such passages appear is the most striking index of Shakespeare's ability to make his art the servant of his insights. It is, in Granville-Barker's phrase, "the power to show us reality behind appearance, or as Shelley said, to lift the veil from the hidden beauty—and, he could have added, the unrecognized horror—of the world." The power is more often demonstrated in the sonnets than in the plays contemporary with them, because, one supposes, of the greater difficulty of expressing perceptions in dramatic form. In any case his most considerable power flowered first in the poems.

What the reader remembers most vividly from the early *Venus and Adonis* are vignettes of nature—bits of natural description, and, above all, Poor Wat, the hare. What stays [34] ineradicably in his mind from the early sonnets is the joy in plenitude, the sadness of mutability, beauty of phrase and beauty of nature, and the virtuosity of such rhythms as,

> Sap check'd with frost, and lusty leaves quite gone,
> Beauty o'er-snow'd, and bareness everywhere.

And while the reader will continue to find these things to the end of the sonnets, it is not long until he also finds: "then hate me when thou wilt," "give not a windy night a rainy morrow," "my love is as a fever," and,

> For I have sworn thee fair and thought thee bright,
> Who art as black as hell, as dark as night.

Examples swarm to be quoted, and in an instant pass from the depiction of homeliness to the unveiling of horror. In this unveiling Shakespeare sometimes displayed the old extravagance of his earlier ornateness. In an almost Strindbergian poem [27] on the power of lust, he writes,

>   . . . lust
> Is perjur'd, murderous, bloody, full of blame,
> Savage, extreme, rude, cruel, not to trust. . . .

It is hortatory rather than persuasive, and there is some sacrifice of power to the exigencies of art. The anticlimactic position of "not to trust" is owing entirely to the need for a rime. But he does not make the sacrifice as often as in the earlier sonnets. He had no sooner mas-

---

[27] Sonnet 129.

tered the homeliness than he employed it concretely and compactly
to give immediacy—the constable, for instance, as the emblem of
death:

> . . . when that fell arrest
> Without all bail shall carry me away. . . .

To us this vivid immediacy of the commonplace is not always as no-
ticeable as it should be, since the dissonance of one age mellows into
the harmony of the next. Time bestows [35] a patina; an image used
successfully in a poem acquires poetic associations. But when Shakespeare's homely images were new they must have been as startling as
Eliot's "patient etherized upon a table" seemed to be just a generation
ago.

Shakespeare's use of this new and startling homeliness (could we
call it the second major aspect of his style?) is of a piece with his
juxtaposition of grandeur and horror. The juxtaposition of comedy
and tragedy had long been a part of the English tradition, but it was
reserved for Shakespeare to make each a part of the other; and we
may see the growth of his poetic use of homeliness in the sonnets.
There could be no purer instance of this development than the juxtaposition of styles in the seventy-third and seventy-fourth sonnets, two
sonnets which comprise one poem. The first ("That time of year
thou may'st in me behold") employs what had long been known to
be the poetic image and the language of poetry. The second concen-
trates on the homely and the ugly and ends in a couplet of the barest
language. There is not a word in the couplet (except perhaps *worth*)
which carries an overtone. Language could not be more completely
stripped of connotation. There is nothing to distract the reader from
bare singleness of the thought. Yet the emotion of the quatrains carries over, and, in its context, the couplet is poetry. It is what he was
later to do, perhaps more magnificently, with Lear's five *nevers*.

> But, be contented: when that fell arrest
> Without all bail shall carry me away,
> My life hath in this line some interest,
> Which for memorial still with thee shall stay.
> When thou reviewest this, thou dost review
> The very part was consecrate to thee:
> The earth can have but earth, which is his due;
> My spirit is thine, the better part of me:
> So then thou has but lost the dregs of life,[36]

The prey of worms, my body being dead,
The coward conquest of a wretch's knife,
Too base of thee to be remembered.
  The worth of that is that which it contains,
  And that is this, and this with thee remains.

The simplest statement of the sonnet's meaning would be, "the essential is best." It is an idea of which Shakespeare never wearied, and nothing more readily recalled its truth to him than the contemplation of poetry. He asks that the sonnets be remembered for their content.[28] He says that it is their subject that makes the poems pleasing, and not what the poet brings to them.[29] He repeats that his powers are not worthy of their theme. And once, after a long silence, he invoked his muse to return again to his friend and "sing to the ear that . . . gives thy pen both skill and argument." [30] The young friend, except for these poems, is now unknown, and Shakespeare has become the greatest of English writers. This admiration for a man we do not know, and this derogation of poetic powers we esteem, may strike us at first as curious. But the sonnets tell of a time when Shakespeare was unknown, or almost so, and the young man was not only well-known, he was, in the poet's eyes, fair, kind, and good. In those days the poet's attitude was not curious; and it is still less so when thought of in relation to his tendency to hold the subject more highly than the means by which it finds expression.[37]

[28] Sonnet 32.   [29] Sonnet 38.   [30] Sonnet 100.

G. Wilson Knight

Symbolism

> O, Love, you be a King. A King.
>
> *The Tragedy of Nan*

W E HAVE SEEN how certain supposed 'conceits' or 'fancies' may be in reality attempts to grapple with some super-thought which baffles expression. The most usual medium for such intuitions is poetic symbolism, and the Sonnets show a rich use of it. Indeed, the weighty realisation of these imaginative solidities sets them apart from the poetry of Donne and Marvell. True, both Donne and Marvell have their imagery and symbols, and some of Donne's recall Shakespeare's. But with the more metaphysical poets the symbol is, as it were, subdued to—in Donne it is often there to be mocked by —the thinking; it grows from a matrix of metaphysical speculation and intellectual gymnastics. In the best Sonnets the thinking is put at the service of the symbol, and sometimes appears, as we shall see, to lag behind it. The result is that whatever 'eternity' Shakespeare succeeds in establishing is far more than a concept, or web of concepts: it flowers from close physical perception, and holds all the colour and perfume of spring.[1]

One feels that it is only with the greatest reluctance, and perhaps even a sense of guilt, that the poet is forced to admit, if he ever does admit, that it is the distilled truth of the boy, the eternal 'idea,' in Plato's sense, that he loves rather than the boy himself; and in so far as he writes of the 'idea' rather than of the thing itself, his writing becomes philosophic rather than strictly poetic; at the best, 'metaphysical poetry,' as with Donne and Marvell. Those are concerned with,

SOURCE: Chapter 3, *The Mutual Flame* (London: Methuen & Co., Ltd., 1955), pp. 58–68.

[1] For a similar judgment see G. K. Hunter's *Dramatic Technique of Shakespeare's Sonnets; Essays in Criticism*, III, ii; April, 1953.

and brilliantly transmit, their own experience of love, but they have
nothing much to say of the loved-one: in Marvell's *Definition of Love*
we cannot even be sure of his or her sex. Since they never realise a
personality [58] outside themselves, we are not forced to join with
them in adoration. But when in Shakespeare we read:

> Why should poor beauty indirectly seek
> Roses of shadow, since his rose is true? (67)

we cannot avoid being half-in-love with the youth ourselves. There
is a more vivid realisation of the loved person in that one little word
'his,' which might well be italicised, than in all Donne's love-poetry.
Nor does Shakespeare confine himself, as, on the whole, you might
say that Michelangelo does, to a few archetypal thoughts. Such
thoughts he has, but they are part only of a closely realised drama,
showing all the variety, and hinting the physical detail, of an actual
experience. Sense-perception is vivid. We enjoy a rich physical apprehension, the flush and bloom of a young life, with all the perfumes
of spring in company, rather as when we read Chaucer's description
of his young Squire. We are aware of nature before we proceed to
metaphysics: if 'this composed wonder of your frame' (59) is a
miracle, it is a miracle born less from our minds than from the 'great
creating Nature' of *The Winter's Tale* (IV, iii, 88). At their greatest
moments the Sonnets are, indeed, less love-poetry than an almost religious adoration before one of 'the rarities of Nature's truth' (60);
that is, one of the splendours of human creation. So, though nothing
but poetry can meet his problem, yet Shakespeare's move from love to
the great poetry of the plays might yet be called, paradoxically, a fall,
a second-best: 'for these dead birds sigh a prayer.'

We shall now list the main associations used by the poet to establish
verbal contact with the miracle which is his theme. About these there
is nothing very abstruse or learned. They are, on the natural plane,
flowers, especially the rose; on the human plane, kingship, with gold;
on the universal, the Sun, with gold; on the spiritual, jewels. Rose,
King, Sun, Gold, Jewels. Our examination need pay slight regard to
the Sonnets' order: we shall use our usual practice of 'spatial' analysis,
seeing the symbols as existent powers in their own right irrespective
of, though of course never contradicting, their particular contexts.[59]

Our first sonnet has 'beauty's rose' (1). One of our finest end-
couplets runs:

For nothing this wide universe I call
Save thou, my rose; in it thou art my all. (109)

The rose as truth is contrasted with shams and vices. The youth's 'true' rose of beauty, in the exquisite passage recently . . . quoted, is contrasted with the false beautifyings of society (67). If faults be present in him, 'roses have thorns, and silver fountains mud' (35). His beauty encloses 'sins' as the rose contains a 'canker' (95). But 'canker' may also mean wild roses, as when 'canker-blooms' are said to have colour without 'the perfumed tincture' of 'sweet roses,' which survive death in distillation, even as the inmost truth of the boy's beauty is distilled by poetry (54). With the rose we may group the lily: 'Lilies that fester smell far worse than weeds' (94). The youth is the 'pattern' of both 'the lily's white' and 'the deep vermilion in the rose' (98). In one sonnet the poet relates, point by point, violet, lily, marjoram and roses, red and white, together with the 'vengeful canker' of destruction, to the separate excellences of his love's beauty (99). In contrast his mistress' cheeks have nothing of 'roses damask'd, red and white' in them (130). It is easy to understand the intense poetic appeal made by the Wars of the Roses to Shakespeare in the three parts of *Henry VI*, so rich in impressions of human loveliness and pathos caught in the shambles of meaningless destruction, all summed by the line, 'The red rose and the white are on his face' (*3 Henry VI*, ii, v, 97).

Next, kingship. Royal images recur, as in the love-poetry of Donne, some of them holding similar connotations. The poet addresses the youth as 'lord of my love,' to whom he sends a 'written ambassage' (26); he is 'my sovereign' and the poet his 'servant' or 'slave' (57). Love-passages in the dramas offer parallels. There is Bassanio's

> There is such confusion in my powers,
> As, after some oration fairly spoke
> By a beloved prince, there doth appear
> Among the buzzing pleased multitude . . .
> (*The Merchant of Venice*, iii, ii, 178)

and Troilus' [60]

> My heart beats thicker than a fev'rous pulse;
> And all my powers do their bestowing lose,
> Like vassalage at unawares encountering
> The eye of majesty.
> (*Troilus and Cressida*, iii, ii, 36)

The lover is abased before a blazing power.

The loved one is royal, and so compared to 'a throned queen' (96). He is 'crowned' with various gifts of nature and fortune (37), especially 'all those beauties whereof now he's king' (63). Like a sovereign, he radiates worth, his eyes lending 'a double majesty' to the rival poets' 'grace' (78); if it were not for certain suspicions, he would be owning 'kingdoms of hearts' (70). This royalty is somehow shared by the lover; having found his own king, he regards all other, more commonplace, grandeurs as poor stuff in comparison. His astronomy, learned from those 'constant stars,' his love's eyes, cannot, and clearly has no desire to, busy itself with the fortunes of 'princes'; it is a different 'art,' prophesying 'truth and beauty' (14). After all, 'great princes' favourites' enjoy an insecure glory in comparison (25); time changes the 'decrees of kings,' but his love is lasting (115); it is in no sense 'the child of state,' and is independent of 'smiling pomp' (124); bearing 'the canopy' means nothing to him, nor does any such external 'honouring' (125). The result is that the poet, through accepted love, becomes himself royal. His mind is 'crown'd' with the wondrous youth, and is accordingly 'kingly' (114); when he is sure of him, he is a 'king,' but when disillusioned, 'no such matter' (87). However depressed he may be in other ways, in so far as his love is assured, it brings such wealth, well-being and power, 'that then I scorn to change my state with kings' (29).

Such symbols act variously as contrasts or comparisons, and apply to either partner of the love-association. Our final impression is of love itself as king, of some super-personality, the Sun of Sonnet 24 . . . , made of, or liberated by, the love of two human beings, as when Donne in *The Ecstasy* writes 'else a great Prince in prison lies.' Love liberates this mysterious sovereign, allows him to realise himself in human terms. This sovereign reality it is which is indicated by the word 'love' of our phrase 'in love with,' Nerissa's 'lord love' of *The Merchant of Venice* (II, ix, 101). It is something, or someone, experienced [61] immediately, 'crowning the present' (115); either that, or known beyond death, as in Romeo's 'I reviv'd and was an emperor' in *Romeo and Juliet* (v, i, 9), and Cleopatra's 'I dream'd there was an emperor Antony,' in *Antony and Cleopatra* (v, ii, 76). The associations are just, since the king, properly understood, holds within society precisely this super-personal and supernal function. In more obviously religious terms we have Henry VI's:

> My crown is in my heart, not on my head;
> Not deck'd with diamonds and Indian stones,
> Nor to be seen.
>
> (*3 Henry VI*, iii, i, 62)

But the Sonnets never engage too far in mysticism, and perhaps our finest example of all, warm with meanings both physical and heraldic, is the line, 'Then in the blazon of sweet beauty's best' (106), where kings are not specifically mentioned at all.

Kingship is naturally golden, and golden impressions recur with similar variations in use. 'Gilded honour' may be 'shamefully misplac'd' (66); poets flatter the youth with 'golden quill' (85); his hair is contrasted with false 'golden tresses' (68); Shakespeare's poetry can make him outlive 'a gilded tomb' (101). More important is his eye 'gilding' the object on which it gazes (20)—eyes in Shakespeare's are active powers, not just passive reflections (p. 37)—and the lovely phrase characterising youth as 'this thy golden time' (3). Stars are 'gold candles' (21).

The Sun is nature's king, and also pre-eminently golden. Throughout Shakespeare king and sun are compared. The Dark Lady's eyes are 'nothing like the Sun' (130); they are 'mourning,' because dark, eyes, and may at the best be compared to the 'morning sun' in a grey dawn, or the evening star (132). With the Fair Youth, the association 'that sun, thine eye' (49) comes easily enough. The successful lover compares himself to the morning 'lark' singing 'hymns at Heaven's gate' (29), though, when things go wrong, 'basest clouds' obscure the Sun, who now rides 'with ugly rack on his celestial face,' and steals to the west disfigured (33); for 'clouds and eclipses stain both Moon and Sun' (35). In our 'transparency' sonnet (24) the Sun functions as the supernal love corresponding to Donne's prince (p. 61). The Sun, 'daily new and old' (76), is [62] visualised in all positions of his diurnal course, with close reference to age. Youth is a 'day' ready to decline (15), and the poet's age just such an hour 'as after sunset fadeth in the west' (73).

We have various clusters of king, gold, and sun. King and gold come together in 'the gilded monuments of princes' (55); and sun and gold, when the Sun's 'gold complexion' is dimmed in the sonnet, 'Shall I compare thee to a summer's day?' (18), or the young man graces 'the day' and 'gilds' the evening in place of stars (28). We may have all three. So 'great princes' favourites' are compared to the mari-

gold opening to the Sun's 'eye' (25). Man's life resembles the diurnal progress of the Sun, who first 'lifts up his burning head' from the orient, everything beneath him doing 'homage' to his 'sacred majesty' as he makes his 'golden pilgrimage,' till finally he 'reeleth' to his setting (7). Love resembles a 'glorious morning' seen to 'flatter the mountain tops with sovereign eye,' kissing meadows with his 'golden face,' and 'gilding' streams with his 'heavenly alchemy' (33).

These impressions are not just decoration. They are attempts to realize in 'black ink' (65) the wonder of youthful beauty at 'this thy golden time' (3); and beyond that, to make real and visible, without relying on abstract terms, that supernal and authoritative Love of which lovers are part only, expressions, voices.

Nor is all this so simple and obvious as it sounds. The Sun is not a necessary, nor even a natural, accompaniment to Shakespearian romance: the Moon is more usual. Shakespeare's heterosexual love-themes are usually moonlit, as with the Balcony scene of *Romeo and Juliet*, the central scenes of *A Midsummer Night's Dream*, and the fifth act of *The Merchant of Venice*, though Portia has 'sunny' locks (I, i, 170). Much of *As You Like It* shows us a shadowed, dappled, world, and in *Twelfth Night* the Sun never dominates until Sebastian's, 'This is the air, that is the glorious sun' (IV, iii, 1). *Antony and Cleopatra* has 'gaudy' nights (III, xi, 182) and Enobarbus' moonlit death, the Sun itself acting rather as a background power than as a present witness, until Cleopatra's dream. Certainly in *Love's Labour's Lost* the Sun is lyrically vivid as a love-accompaniment. But this early play is made on a pattern of its own; it ends with winter; it is full of sonnet-material; and it is exactly this sort of [63] love-poetry that is not repeated. Our first really convincingly sun-impregnated love-scene is the sheep-shearing festival of *The Winter's Tale*.[2]

The Sun is male, the Moon female; the one suggests the intellectual consciousness, the other emotion, the twilit world of romance. When Shelley's Hermaphrodite (= poetry) in *The Witch of Atlas* is fully *awakened*, then we may expect the Sun.[3] When sensual love, whose natural medium, as D. H. Lawrence insisted, is the dark world below consciousness, is our theme, the Sun may, as in Donne's *The Sun Rising*, be an intruder, though, in so far as such a love is vividly and directly lived by day, with a strong physical awareness fully accepted,

---

[2] For an amplification of these judgments, see *The Crown of Life*, III, 102.
[3] For the awakening of Shelley's Hermaphrodite, see *The Starlit Dome*, III, 229; also p. 220 [of Knight, *The Mutual Flame*].

as in *The Winter's Tale*, it may be in place. Normally, we can say that it is far from easy to blend it with a heterosexual love. As an extreme example of a natural tendency, we have the 'woman wailing for her demon-lover' under a 'waning moon' in *Kubla Khan;* and we must remember Lorenzo's and Jessica's list of famous moonlit love-incidents in their 'In such a night . . .' duet (*The Merchant of Venice*, v, i, 1–22). That last act is, in its way, a recovery and a retreat—yet how wonderful a retreat—from the stern compulsions of the greater action.

But it is precisely among those 'stern compulsions' that the Sun is likely to assume poetic centrality. So Theseus, man of power, efficiency, chivalrous courtesy and common-sense, enters with the dawn on the moonstruck world of *A Midsummer Night's Dream;* the heroic idealism of *Julius Caesar* is marked by important passages of sunrise and sunset, before and after the assassination (ii, i, 101–11; v, iii, 60–3); and in *Cymbeline* the royal boys are sun-worshippers (iii, iii, 1–9) and Cymbeline himself 'radiant' (v, v, 476). Shakespeare's kings, in so far as they carry, or claim, true, that is magical, royalty, are regularly given sun-correspondences, as with Richard's comparison of himself to a rising sun:

> But when, from under this terrestrial ball,
> He fires the proud tops of the eastern pines,
> And darts his light through every guilty hole . . .
> (*Richard II*, iii, ii, 41) [64]

Henry VIII is a 'sun' (iii, ii, 416), and so on. All this is fairly clear. But, with the waning of the royalistic and aristocratic valuations, there is less of it in English poetry than you might expect. Milton's Samson-like figure of power-with-virtue at the close of the *Areopagitica* is as a sun-gazing eagle; Keats offers some notable splendours in *Hyperion*, and Coleridge's *Zapolya*, with its youthful hero Andreas, is a complete work constructed from this particular area of the imagination (*The Starlit Dome*, iv, 284–7; ii, 160–78). Byron, perhaps our subtlest sun-poet of all, offers many variations, serious and amusing (*The Burning Oracle*, vi, 256–9, 284). The sombre Tennyson is happiest with the setting sun: you have to be empowered with an innate, virile, humanistic faith to use the sun-symbol with power. Wordsworth once crashed badly (*The Excursion*, iv, 232; *The Starlit Dome*, i, 55).

The Sun tends to assume poetic centrality when our concern is: (i) any fully-*conscious*, or victorious, love, as defined in Biron's great speech in *Love's Labour's Lost* (IV, iii, 290–365); with love-as-power, love virile and victorious; or, (ii) royal power felt magically, almost, we might says, erotically. We may say, more generally, that it fits any strong conviction of power or sexual virility fused with virtue, and it is true that in the Renaissance period it can accompany any love in so far as that love is, as in Spenser's *Hymns*, felt as a sovereign power. But it is clear that a mole love lends itself most readily to the symbol, and indeed we cannot always be sure how far our Renaissance love-lyrists are using heterosexual terms for a homosexual engagement. In such engagements, being as they are denied sexual consummation, sex is forced into consciousness, so that it becomes . . . a matter of 'eyes,' of burning, over-flooding, apprehension; all is strongly idealistic; while the loved object, being male, inevitably assumes the power-properties of male action, aristocracy, and royalty. In his adoration for the loved youth, the two main positive directions of Shakespeare's work are accordingly implicit.[4]

The various natural and cosmic symbolisms of the Sonnets grow from a soil of normal Shakespearian imagery: flowers, crops, and seasons; moon and stars; effects of winter, cloud,[65] storm and tempests; inundation (64); and wrecks (80). The love-quest is a sea-voyage (80, 86), as in *Troilus and Cressida* (. . . and see *The Shakespearian Tempest*, II, 72; IV, 172–4). Stars may be important, sometimes holding astrological significance (14, 15, 26, 116); they may be more directly descriptive or symbolic (21, 132); they are symbols of constancy (14, 116).

We have already reviewed certain impressions of 'gold.' 'Gold' naturally accompanies 'sun' and 'king'; the king's crown, and indeed gold in general, might be called 'solid sunlight.' Gold has for centuries exerted magical radiations and its value, worth and power, its 'virtue' in the old sense, need no emphasis. These properties make it an apt symbol for any high value, or worth.

Love is such a value, and it is regularly in Shakespeare compared to rich metals or merchandise (*The Shakespearian Tempest*, II, 65–9). Throughout poetry precious stones symbolise what may be called 'spiritual value' (*Christ and Nietzsche*, v, 193–5 . . .). All this is powerful in the Sonnets.

The 'rich gems' of 'earth and sea' are regarded as a natural love-

---

[4] For my general placing of the Sun within the integration-pattern, see *Christ and Nietzsche*, IV, 139–46; also pp. 219–20 [of Knight, *The Mutual Flame*].

comparison (21); though cruel, the Dark Lady is 'the fairest and most precious jewel' (131); and the youth's image by night hangs 'like a jewel' before the poet's soul (27), recalling Romeo's 'It seems she hangs upon the cheek of night like a rich jewel in an Ethiop's ear' (*Romeo and Juliet*, I, v, 49). Compared with 'a prize so dear,' the poet's 'jewels' are as 'trifles' (48); even the youth's faults are to be prized as a poor 'jewel' may be on the figure of 'a throned queen' (96); his tears are as 'pearl,' and called 'rich' (34); he is himself costly, a matter of 'riches' (87). One sonnet is packed with suggestions of 'rich,' 'treasure,' 'stones of worth,' 'chest,' and 'robe,' and contains the grand line, 'captain jewels in the carcanet' (52). Most striking of all is:

> Where, alack,
> Shall Time's best jewel from Time's chest lie hid?
> (65)

As elsewhere throughout Shakespeare, such symbols blend with rich merchandise and sea-voyages. Love, it is true, is too [66] rich to be 'merchandis'd' (102), but symbolically the thought may act serenely enough:

> Was it the proud full sail of his great verse
> Bound for the prize of all too precious you . . .
> (86)

Poetry is itself a quest. Apart form all flattery and advantage, it is a spiritual penetration and achievement, in some deep sense a possession, of the mysterious splendour. But the poet is, of course, jealous in a human fashion too: he is like a 'miser' so intent on 'the prize of you,' that he varies between pride of possession and horrible doubts lest 'the filching age' may 'steal his treasure' (75).

Shakespeare's bitter comments on the youth's risking 'infection' from a sinful society (67), with the cutting conclusion 'thou dost common grow' (69), may indeed derive from a questionable jealousy and possessiveness. We need not assume that the young man, who is once specifically said to have survived the temptations of youth victoriously (70), was naturally vicious. In certain moods Shakespeare would, clearly, regard all society as too base for a youth of so infinite and mysterious a worth. His love was to him the inmost centre and furthest aim of all things, its value lying beyond human assessment:

> It is the star to every wandering bark,
> Whose worth's unknown although his height be taken.
> (116)

It was the crowning glory of creation, and more than that. 'Jewels,' as we have said, suggest spiritual values, and this love is also religious.

Our theme (31) is 'dear, religious, love' ('dear' meaning 'of highest value'). It is not 'idolatry' (105)—compare Hector's aspersions on idolatry at *Troilus and Cressida*, II, ii, 56—because it and its object are constant (105). Even though faults be found, even though there be no objective 'image,' to quote Hector, 'of the affected merit' (*Troilus and Cressida*, II, ii, 60), 'Heaven' has somehow decreed in the youth's 'creation' that only 'sweet love' can dwell in his 'face'; he cannot *look* faithless or bad (93). Such beauty, with its 'heavenly touches' (17), exists in its own right; it is itself 'sacred' (115); and the [67] poet complains that, since artifice became the fashion, 'sweet beauty' has no 'holy bower' (127). As it is, the youth's presence is said to 'grace impiety' when he mixes with sinful people (67). Shakespeare's love-poetry, his own 'better part,' is 'consecrate to thee' (74); he has 'hallow'd' his 'fair name' in verses which are as 'prayers divine' (108); and his own love is offered as an 'oblation' (125). The idealised boy is even called 'a god in love,' and 'next my heaven the best' (110). He is the poet's 'better angel' (p. 28). Adoration can go no further.

Such is the experience, or phenomenon, straining the sweetest and grandest symbols, natural, human, and divine, to do justice to 'this composed wonder of your frame' (59). It is pre-eminently an incarnate mystery or miracle, not unlike that symbolised by Dante's Gryphon in the *Purgatorio* (XXXI). The poetry gives us a close-up of the thing itself, not merely, as does Donne, of the supervening and enclosing experience. It is a marvel here and now, 'crowning the present,' even though leaving us 'doubting of the rest' (115). For there can be no permanence. That is our problem: the problem of *Troilus and Cressida, Hamlet, Othello, Timon of Athens, Antony and Cleopatra*. And yet, somehow, we feel that it should, indeed must, be permanent. The poet must say, and we applaud him for saying it, 'Love's not Time's fool' (116), but he fears, and so do we, that it may be. He starts a sonnet with 'To me, fair friend, you never can be old,' but continues:

> Ah, yet doth beauty, like a dial-hand,
> Steal from his figure and no pace perceiv'd.
>
> (104)

Can both be true? One way or another, we shall surely come up against the agony of Troilus: 'This is, and is not, Cressid' (*Troilus and Cressida*, V, ii, 143). On this torturing antithesis, the greatest passages of the Sonnets converge.[68]

Explications

R. M. Lumiansky

Shakespeare's Sonnet 73

IN THEIR DETAILED explication of this sonnet, Wright Thomas and Stuart G. Brown, *Reading Poems*, pp. 744–745, find that the "plain sense" of the first twelve lines is "You know that I am growing old," which is said three different times, once in each of the quatrains. These writers further state that the couplet makes "a direct statement which does not need to be translated into prose." Thus they take the "plain sense" of the whole poem to be "You know that I am growing old; therefore you love me more, since you must soon leave me."

A difficulty in this interpretation is that in line 14 the poet does not speak of his imminent departure from the person to whom the sonnet is addressed; rather, the person addressed will ere long do the leaving. In this connection it is interesting that Massey emended *leave* to *lose* (*New Variorum Shakespeare*, "The Sonnets," 1, 189). It should also be noted that the couplet does not specifically say, as Wright and Thomas state, "you love *me* more," or "you must soon leave *me*." *Me* does not appear in the couplet. The person addressed experiences heightened love for *that*, and the important question in interpreting the sonnet is: To what does *that* in line 14 refer?

It seems to me that the "plain sense" of the sonnet is "You see that I am growing old; therefore, your love for your youthfulness, which you must soon lose, grows stronger." The young person to whom the poem is addressed must inevitably grow old and experience those things which the poet says, in the three quatrains, he is experiencing in his old age. Thus, I think that Sonnet 73 is best understood as a contrast between the melancholy aspects of old age and the joys of youth.

SOURCE: *The Explicator*, VI (June, 1948), item 55.

Edward F. Nolan

Shakespeare's Sonnet 73

MR. R. M. LUMIANSKY (Exp., June, 1948, VI, 55) interprets the sense of *Sonnet* 73 as being: "You see that I am growing old; therefore, your love for your youthfulness, which you must soon lose, grows stronger." It seems to me, however, that the sense is substantially as Thomas and Brown have given it: "You know that I am growing old; therefore you love me more, since you must soon leave me." "Leave," as used here, it should be pointed out, does not mean "to depart from," but rather "to give up" or "to part with." The word has this latter signification in *The Merchant of Venice*, v, i, 172 and v, i, 196, and in the First Folio reading of Gertrude's lines to Hamlet (*Hamlet*, III, iv, 88–91):

> O Hamlet, speak no more:
> Thou turn'st mine eyes into my very soul;
> And there I see such black and grained spots
> As will not leave their tinct.

According to my interpretation, Shakespeare says in *Sonnet* 73: "You know that I am growing old; therefore, you love me more, since you must soon give me up"—i.e., "since you perceive that Death will soon deprive you of me."

As Mr. Lumiansky says, "The important question in interpreting the sonnet is: To what does *that* in line 14 refer?" That the word refers to the speaker, Shakespeare, and not to the addressee's youthfulness, seems to be indicated by the opening lines of *Sonnet* 74. *Sonnet* 73 ends:

> This thou perceiv'st, which makes thy love more strong,
> To love that well which thou must leave ere long.

Sonnet 74 begins:

> But be contented: when that fell arrest
> Without all bail shall carry me away,
> My life hath in this line some interest,
> Which for memorial still with thee shall stay.

SOURCE: *The Explicator*, VII (November, 1948), item 13.

It is admitted, of course, that the present order of the sonnets, in its entirety, is probably not Shakespeare's; but it is equally clear that some of the sonnets seem to be in their right order. The word "But" clearly relates *Sonnet 74* to some preceding sonnet. After the connective "But" we expect a thought in contrast with the thought preceding the conjunction. That is what we find here. In *Sonnet 73*, if my interpretation is correct, Shakespeare says that the addressee will soon have to give him up to Death. "But," he continues in *Sonnet 74*, "be contented." And he explains that though Death may claim his body,

> The earth can have but earth, which is his due;
> My spirit is thine, the better part of me:

And his spirit, embodied in his poetry, will remain with the addressee. It seems to me, then, that *Sonnet 74* is a logical sequel to *Sonnet 73* and that the "me" in line 2 of *74* establishes the reference of the "that" in line 14 of *73*.

Carlisle Moore

Shakespeare's Sonnets 71-74

Mr. EDWARD F. NOLAN has shown (Exp., Nov., 1948, VII, 13) that *Sonnet 73* is better understood when considered in relation to the sonnet which follows it. I should like to suggest that when considered also in the light of the two sonnets which precede it a still fuller meaning emerges. Despite our uncertainty about the correct order of the sonnets, it seems clear that the four sonnets, 71–74, express a complete idea and form a distinct unit. The question arising with *Sonnet 73*, which taken alone has two almost equally plausible meanings, cannot be decided without reference to the whole unit any more than this unit can be considered apart from the whole sonnet sequence.

It is true that the first two lines of *Sonnet 74*,

> Bvt be contented when that fell arest
> With out all bayle shall carry me away . . .

SOURCE: *The Explicator*, VII (October, 1949), item 2.

depend from the last two lines of *Sonnet 73*, but they also furnish a direct and explicit answer to the opening of *Sonnet 71:*

> Noe Longer mourne for me when I am dead,
> Then you shall heare the surly sullen bell
> Giue warning to the world that I am fled . . .

In this first sonnet of our unit Shakespeare urges the young man not to mourn his death nor to attempt to praise him "Lest the wise world should . . . mock you with me after I am gone." For, (*Sonnet 72*) "There is nothing worthy in me and you would have to lie to praise me. I am shamed by my poems, and you should be ashamed to admire them."

Sonnet 73 may now be seen to contain a suggestion of the poet's disillusionment about his own poetry. He is concerned about his old age, but in two of the three metaphors he is further concerned with the deprivations of age, with the dying of his creative powers: (lines 1–4) "You see me in the late autumn of my life, recently stripped of my poetic powers" ("yellow leaves," "Bare rn'wd quiers, where late the sweet birds sang"); (lines 5–8) "You see me at the sundown of my life, all but extinguished by night"; (lines 9–12) "In me you see a fire that is dying of what fed it." Although this metaphor is not perfectly clear I take *that* in line 12 to refer to the fuel which fed the fire and is now ashes in which the fire is dying, i.e. the poet's genius, which fed his powers and now, in old age, is consuming them. The sonnet therefore seems to say: "In me you see the destructive effects of age. I am dying both as a man and as a poet; so it behooves you to love me well, for you will lose me 'ere long'."

This leads directly to the consolation contained in the next sonnet (74) which resolves the problems raised in the other three. The poet urges the young man not to mourn his death because these sonnets will continue, after the death of his body, to express his spirit, "the better part of me" which was "consecrate to thee." Hence the young man does not, after all, lose Shakespeare "ere long," and the meaning of the sequence is complete.

It should be added that this reading does not necessarily exclude other readings. *Sonnet 73* can be interpreted on one level or on several levels at once, like Picasso's faces. It expresses an abstract, philosophical truth; it contains a personal plea for love; and it suggests the poet's declining powers with the approach of old age. But in its setting it is part of a larger meaning and contributes to a noble though somewhat pathetic testament of friendship, of the marriage of true minds, which admits no impediments, or hardly any.

Karl F. Thompson

Shakespeare's Sonnet 129

THE OPENING AND CLOSING statements of the sonnet (cf. EXP., May, 1948, VI, Q17) are generalizations, the first angry in tone, the last resigned. The intervening images shift as lust is imagined as a traitorous counselor, a hunted object and then a hunter. The ever-changing tenses of the verbs contribute a restless, distraught quality to which the resigned melancholy of the final couplet is sharp contrast.

The poet, after stating that "lust in action" (2) is a waste of mental and moral capabilities in an activity that is shameful, describes lust in its pre-operative state. "Till action" (2) must mean "until it becomes action." Lust in the mind or heart, before action, is "perjur'd, murderous, bloody, full of blame" (3). In other words, it is the betrayer within, employing blandishments, urgings, persuasion and compulsion to induce its victim to take action. "Not to trust" (4) sums up the nature of the traitor lust, the crooked counselor that presents the act of lust as unalloyed pleasure.

The act of lust is completed (5) and immediately becomes a source and object of loathing. Line 6, however, reverts to the situation before the completed act. The object of lust is "hunted" and pursued "past reason." The conflict is resumed in line 7 which begins with a repetition of "past reason," an emphasis of the irrationality of desire and ensuing disgust, the knowledge beforehand of the consequences, and the poet's sense of helplessness in the toils of the counselor lust that are for him the maddening aspects of the recurrent drama in which he is involved. He is at once the hunter (6) and the hunted (7) who has taken the poisoned bait, whereupon lust which had been the object of the hunt becomes the hunter, the ensnarer.

In line 12 the time element ("before" and "behind") is stressed to show the recurrence of the emotions connected with lust, a recurrence which has already been indicated in line 10 where the past tense "had" implies the act in the past, the present participle "having" brings it to the present, and the phrase "in quest to have" foretells recurrence. And every part of the cycle is termed "extreme" (10), a word repeated from line 4.

The word "dream" is difficult here. Its normally pleasant associa-

SOURCE: *The Explicator*, VII (February, 1949), item 27.

tions must be discarded before the true connotation, unpleasant dream or nightmare, is sensed. Yet, the introduction here of the ordinarily pleasant connotations which accompany "dream" effects a subtle change in tone: that fretful self-loathing (3-10) is qualified by the melancholy realization (13-14) that experience is no guarantor of wisdom and that men will forever shuttle between this "heaven" and "hell."

The sonnet is, in a way, an answer to Donne's "Ah cannot we, As well as Cocks and Lyons jocund be, After such pleasures?" But Shakespeare's answer is a counsel of surrender, without Donne's ironic attitude toward human passion.

C. W. M. Johnson

Shakespeare's Sonnet 129

THE CENTRAL PROBLEM of this sonnet (EXP., May, 1948, VI, Q17; Feb., 1949, VII, 27) is the establishing of a sound text. That problem has been set forth in a widely admired passage by Laura Riding and Robert Graves, in *A Survey of Modernist Poetry*, London, 1927, pp. 62–75, 79–82. Any reader interested in getting at the meaning of this sonnet should start with the Riding-Graves analysis, based upon the text of 1609 and undoubtedly closer to the poet's intentions than any explication following the usual modernized text. The latter reduces the poem to a mere ranting piece of rhetoric. But the reader is likely to boggle at such insistence upon the reliability of the text of 1609 as he will find in the above analysis, and to conclude that Shakespeare never writ such loose syntax, nor no man ever intended the total effect of his poem to depend upon such disorderly ambiguities.

Hardest to take, and in ascending order of implausibility, are the phrases "blouddy full of blame," "to have extreame," and "and very wo." As for the first, "blouddy" is so obviously parallel with "murdrous" that something is lost if one reads "full as with blood," as do Riding and Graves. In place of a glance at less extreme types of sadism, we are left with nothing but an intensifier out of harmony with the fact that "full of blame" means "blameful." The interpreta-

SOURCE: *The Explicator*, VII (April, 1949), item 41.

tion offered of "to have extreame" ("to have extremes, to have in extreme degrees"—*which?*) really entails, as the authors work it out, the removal of the comma at the end of line 10. The word "extreame" is not an adverb; it probably is the obsolete noun meaning "extremity, distress." Reading "and very wo"—in fact, reading all line 11 as the authors do—results in a flat contradiction of statements of lines 5–7. The only way out seems to be to reject "and" as a corruption. (Would there be any authority for "an"? Cf. Mrs. Quickly's "an fool's-head," *MWW*, I, iii—but her English is not the best!) In line 12 the thought gracefully undergoes the progression the authors are impatient for —suggesting the victim's endless vacillation between disgust and anxiety to get on with further "action."

The Riding-Graves analysis slights a few points not directly connected with the textual problem.

(1.) This is a defining sonnet, linked to the sequence by way of contrast with 126, which offers a definition of love. The theme stated in line 1–2 can be paraphrased: "The gratification of lust involves a shameful waste of one's spiritual energy," i.e., "shameful destruction of one's ego, accretion of guilt," and so on.

(2.) On one level the image in line 7–8 presents the devil employing Renaissance methods to gain his end. There is a pun on "layd"; on this level there is the suggestion that hostility and mutual distrust exist, or should exist, between partners in lust. Further, in suggesting that the bait is poisoned and leads to madness there is an allusion to the effects of the "great pox."

(3) The botched text we read today was devised by editors who read the poem as a statement of one of the eternal verities. While Riding and Graves do not find the same "truth" in the poem, they find others; they seem at times disposed to endorse that theory of poetry. E.g., ". . . Shakespeare has been at pains to show all along, that lust is all things at all times." This needs to be qualified. Reference to lines 5–7 and a proper reading of line 12 should establish that the focus is on the paradox of lust: the victim at the same time despises what he has had and promises himself better luck next time; he remains impaled on the two horns of his dilemma. The poem provides us then not with a "truth," but with an ironic disparity between means and ends, between expectation and realization. As in 116 the propositions are pushed to extremes; they invite disbelief. When we are prepared to read 129 for what it is—a communication of one of many possible emotional attitudes, an orchestration of disgust with "action" —we shall be able to see it as poetry.

Gordon Ross Smith

A Note on Shakespeare's Sonnet 143

Lo, as a careful housewife runs to catch
One of her feathered creatures broke away,
Sets down her babe, and makes all swift dispatch
In pursuit of the thing she would have stay
Whilst her neglected child holds her in chase,
Cries to catch her whose busy care is bent
To follow that which flies before her face,
Not prizing her poor infant's discontent—
So runn'st thou after that which flies from thee,
Whilst I thy babe chase thee afar behind,
But if thou catch thy hope, turn back to me,
And play the mother's part, kiss me, be kind.
   So will I pray that thou mayst have thy *Will*,
   If thou turn back and my loud crying still.

Few of Shakespeare's sonnets have been so much abused and so little understood as No. 143. The Hyder Rollins (1) variorum edition of the sonnets cites Steevens as having called it "lame and impotent," and the poet's distress, "the loud blubberings of the great boy *Will*"; Conrad as having called it "comic," at least to the modern mind; Stopes, "the least dignified of all the poet's figures"; and an anonymous critic, a "mare's-nest" and the "most stupendous wind-egg of them all." E. K. Chambers (2) noted that both J. W. Mackail and J. M. Robertson denied it was by Shakespeare. More recent writers both on the sonnets and on Shakespeare's imagery—Hubler (3), Cruttwell (4), Knight (5), Watkins (6), Smith (7), Spurgeon (8), Clemen (9), Baldwin (10), and Hankins (11)—have either ignored it altogether or given it only passing mention.

An explanation is possible, however, providing one is willing to suspend any assumptions one may have made that Shakespeare's writing could express only the commonplace or dominant thought of his age.*

SOURCE: *American Imago*, XIV (Spring, 1957), 33–36.

---

* Schucking (12) and Stoll (13) once made this assumption dogma for academic critics, but in recent years it has been much called in question. Taylor (14), Doran (15), Harbage (16), Craig (17), Knights (18), and Leech (19) have all expressed doubts, as have many others also.

The entire octet is a Homeric simile fully developed from a very domestic incident: a housewife's temporary neglect of her infant while she chases after "one of her feathered creatures," presumably a goose. The sestet points the parallels: Shakespeare himself is the infant, his mistress is the mother, and some plumed gallant is the goose. Shakespeare hopes his mistress may have her erotic will of the courtly goose providing she then return and comfort Will Shakespeare.

What is most remarkable here is that the sonnet recapitulates the Oedipal attachment and equates it with a mature, heterosexual one. We see as in a photographic montage both the unmanageable, callous mistress and the unmanageable, indifferent mother; the lover's longing for his mistress and the infant's for his mother; the *feeling* of helplessness in the lover and the *fact* of helplessness in the infant; and finally, inconsolable grief in both lover and infant unless the mistress or mother return. Initially, the infantile dilemma appears to be a mere recollection, ancient, pallid, and almost adventitious, and the formal elements of the octet heighten this impression. Only the adult situation as stated in the sestet seems vivid and real. But toward the end of the sonnet the old and the current situations are not only completely combined, but the infantile one becomes dominant. When the lover asks his mistress to play the mother's part, we may surmise that the infantile relationship is rising to submerge the adult, and when in the last line he refers to his own grief as "my loud crying," then the grief of the lover has become identical with the grief of the child; by backward association lover becomes child, and mistress, mother: we arrive at the very identifications since made by Freud.

That these parallels are stated concretely instead of being formulated abstractly and theoretically as in Freud is no proof of accident and therefore nothing to the purpose. The extraordinary shifts of rhythm in line four and lines six and seven, so remarkably echoing the sense, also lack abstract formulation, but are not for that reason to be considered accidental. The central comparison from which the sonnet is wrought must have been intended by Shakespeare, and a Freudian interpretation is the only one that explains why anyone should make such a comparison.

Certain interesting inferences can be made from this interpretation. The first is that the pattern of grief was set in the poet's infancy, and as a response to deprivation it reappeared in maturity and rendered impossible other responses, such as Suckling's, "If of herself she will not love, . . . The devil take her!" From this we may infer that Shakespeare's infantile love for his mother was imperfectly resolved and incompletely repressed, whence its recollection in this sonnet. A comparable view of Shakespeare's personality has been offered by Kanzer (20), who from his study of the plays has declared the central theme of Shakespeare's work to "reflect hysterical defences against incestuous attachment to the mother." Finally, we may infer that from such psychic configurations could issue Shakespeare's marriage to a woman eight years his senior and also the mother-devotion that Jones (21) found in *Hamlet* and Towne (22) in *Coriolanus*.

These inferences are, of course, only speculations. But it is clear that sonnet 143 is perfectly intelligible as an artistic expression of the relationship of the Oedipus complex to mature, heterosexual love.

BIBLIOGRAPHY

1. Hyder Rollins. *New Variorum Edition of Shakespeare's Sonnets*, Phila., Lippincott, 1944. I, 366–367.
2. E. K. Chambers. *William Shakespeare*, Oxford, Clarendon Press, 1930. I, 561.
3. Edward Hubler. *The Sense of Shakespeare's Sonnets*, Princeton University Press, 1952.
4. Patrick Cruttwell. *The Shakespearean Moment*, London, Chatto and Windus, 1953.
5. G. Wilson Knight. *The Mutual Flame*, London, Methuen, 1954.
6. W. B. C. Watkins. *Shakespeare and Spencer*, Princeton University Press, 1950.
7. Hallet Smith. *Elizabethan Poetry*, Harvard University Press, 1953.
8. C. Spurgeon. *Shakespeare's Imagery*, Cambridge University Press, 1935.
9. Wolfgang Clemen. *The Development of Shakespeare's Imagery*, Harvard University Press, 1951.
10. T. W. Baldwin. *On the Literary Genetics of Shakespere's Poems and Sonnets*, University of Illinois Press, 1950.
11. John E. Hankins. *Shakespeare's Derived Imagery*, University of Kansas Press, 1953.
12. Levin L. Schucking. *Character Problems in Shakespeare's Plays*, London, George G. Harrap, 1922.
13. E. E. Stoll. *Shakespeare Studies*, New York, Macmillan, 1927.
14. George Coffin Taylor. "Two Notes on Shakespeare," in *Renaissance Studies in Honor of Hardin Craig*, Stanford University Press, 1941, pp. 179–184.
15. Madeleine Doran. "That Undiscovered Country. A Problem Concerning the Use of the Supernatural in *Hamlet* and *Macbeth*," *ibid.*, pp. 221–235.
16. Alfred Harbage. *As They Liked It*, New York, Macmillan, 1947, pp. 21–39.
17. Hardin Craig. "Shakespeare and the Here and Now," *PMLA*, LXVII (1952) 87–94.
18. L. C. Knights. "On Historical Scholarship and the Interpretation of Shakespeare," *Sewanee Review*, LXIII (1955) 223–240. Answered by Virgil K. Whitaker, "Vindicating the Historical Approach," *The Shakespeare Newsletter*, V (1955) 39.
19. Clifford Leech. "The 'Historical' School," in *Shakespeare Survey 9*, Cambridge University Press, 1956, pp. 9–12.

20. Mark Kanzer. "The Central Theme in Shakespeare's Works," *Psychoanalytic Review*, XXXVIII (1951) 1–16.
21. Ernest Jones. *Hamlet and Oedipus*, Norton, 1949.
22. Jackson E. Towne. "A Psychoanalytic Study of Shakespeare's *Coriolanus*," *Psychoanalytic Review*, VIII (1921) 84–91.

Albert S. Gérard

Iconic Organization in Shakespeare's Sonnet 146

How THE SECOND LINE of this sonnet read when Shakespeare wrote it, we shall never know. Of two emendations recently proposed, one by Hubler:

> Thrall to these rebel powers that thee array,

the other by Sisson:

> Fenced by these rebels powers that thee array,

the latter sounds more truly Shakespearian in that it repeats the conceit of the first line, turned inside out: any centre is necessarily surrounded by what it is the centre of. The first line expresses the natural order of things: the soul as the vital principle within the body; the second formulates the actual order of things: the soul as prisoner of the rebellious body. What we might call the topographical situation is the same, yet the reciprocal relationship between soul and body has been reversed. As so often in Shakespeare's sonnets, the first couplet provides the text, the theme which is going to be developed. And just as the first line is normative and the second factual, so the main body of the sonnet falls into two parts: the next six lines (ll. 3–8) pointing out the absurdity of the actual relationship between soul and body, the last six lines (ll. 9–14) exhorting the soul to react and conform to the ideal.

The central conceit which organizes the poem's imagery is that of

SOURCE: *English Studies*, XLII (June, 1961), 157–159.

the ways in which the soul may choose to use or misuse its resources. This conceit branches off into two iconic trends, one dealing with spending, the other with feeding.

Spending imagery dominates the first part (l. 4: 'costly,' l. 5: 'cost,' l. 6: 'spend,') and in its turn gives birth to a cluster of secondary images, which form a coherent pattern. First the idea of the soul's central position inevitably calls up the opposition between 'within' (l. 3) and 'outward' (l. 4) which remains the main axis of the poem. In connexion with the spending imagery, it is used to express the view that the soul is devoting her resources to the body's unworthy outward ornaments, while nothing is left to feed her inwardness; hence a second subordinate metaphor, that of the body as a house. But the reason why the things on which the soul is lavishing her resources are unworthy is that they are transitory; this is where time intervenes: not only has the soul a 'short lease' (l. 5) on the body, but the body itself is strikingly described as a 'fading mansion' (l. 6); this third trend issues into the lurid death imagery of ll. 7–8.

But the feeding imagery runs as an undercurrent throughout this first part. Since the soul is squandering her wealth away in expensive ornaments for the body, she 'pines' and 'suffers dearth' instead of feeding herself. The image takes a sudden turn in l. 8: whereas the primary duty of the soul is to feed herself, the fact that she chooses to sacrifice her wealth to the body results in the worms eating up her 'charge.'

The central lines of the poem are climactic in mood and in rhythm. While the first two questions fill one couplet each, the third question has a line and a half and the fourth only one half line. The absurdity of the soul's behaviour and its ultimate consequences are pointed out first in the realistic image of the worms and then in abstract terms: 'Is this thy body's end?' The speeding rhythm and the repulsive imagery show that the poet's indignation has reached its apex, while the abstractness of the last question at the same time anticipates the more serene and more philosophical mood of the second part. But there is more in that couplet than meets the casual eye. Huber thinks that 'excess' means 'body,' in the sense of 'excess luggage.' It seems more economical to take the word as a reference to the excess expressly mentioned in such phrases as 'so costly gay,' 'so large cost,' i.e. to the excessive luxury bestowed by the soul upon the body. Nor is the meaning of the word 'charge' obvious; although it must be taken in the archaic sense of expense or cost, it may also have dim moral connotations and refer to the resources entrusted to the soul, who has recklessly wasted them on the body. As to the pronoun 'this' in the last question, it plainly does not stand for 'to be eaten up by worms.' The mood of the question is one of nearly incredulous puzzlement as well as of indignation. The answer must be negative. The question, therefore, means: Is it the body's mission to enable worms to eat up the soul's resources?

While the basic idea of the first two quatrains is that the body's rebellion brings about the triumph of death, the second part of the poem expresses the contrasting and complementary view that subjection of the body will result in triumph over death. The body as 'rebel' becomes therefore the body as 'servant' and the main trends of the imagery undergo significant reversals.

The framework, of course, remains set by the within-without opposition, l. 12 closely corresponding to ll. 3–4. With regard to the time-motif, the 'short lease' of l. 5 is echoed in 'hours of dross' which is forcefully opposed to 'terms divine' (l. 11), the word 'term' unobtrusively recalling the image of a rented house. The spending metaphor recurs with an interesting variation: in the second part, the poet does not speak of 'cost' and 'spending' but of 'buying' and 'selling,' i.e., the soul now gets something worth while in exchange for what she gives away; this is especially true in view of the fact that the soul is no longer spending her own resources, but those of the body ('thy servant's loss,' l. 9).

But the main stream of imagery that flows across the second part of the poem deals with feeding and illustrates the reversal of the body-soul relationship from actual to normative. 'Feed' is repeated thrice. The word 'pine,' which is also repeated, now applies to the body (l. 10). Instead of spending upon the body, the soul now lives upon it (l. 9) and is therefore fed within (l. 12). In the field of actual experience, her charge was eaten up by worms; in the realm of the ideal, her store is aggravated, enriched (l. 10). Verbal parallelisms ('spend *upon*,' 'live *upon*'; 'pine *within*,' '*within* be fed') intensify the reader's perception of the contrast.

Sonnet 146 is a remarkable example of Renaissance organization both in structure and in imagery. With regard to subject matter and theme, it is constructed as a diptych, one panel dealing with things as they are, the other with things as they ought to be. The thought is simple and straightforward: there is no metaphysical ambiguity; even the metaphysical recognition of man's inner contradictions which characterizes Sonnet 129 is absent. According to the principle of 'multiple unity,' each part has its own clearly delineated individuality and rises to its own climax, but both parts are symmetrical and therefore integrated in the higher unity of the whole poem. Not only does each climax deal with death, but the imagic motifs (the inward-outward contrast, the spending and feeding metaphors, the time and death motifs) recur with significant shifts and variations and skilful verbal echoes. There is even a smack of Renaissance préciosité in the pseudo-syllogistic conceit of the final couplet and in the unconvincing play on the word 'death,' which, to one reader at least, unfortunately mar this otherwise finely woven poem.

Hilton Landry

A Slave to Slavery:

Shakespeare's Sonnets 57 and 58

SONNETS 57 AND 58 come at the end of a large and loose group of poems concerning "absence" (Sonnets 43–58), and with Sonnet 56 they may well form a small sub-group.[1] The hortatory opening of Sonnet 56, "Sweet love, renew thy force; be it not said/Thy edge should blunter be than appetite," suggests that the friend's sexual appetite has begun to displace love for the speaker, hence the poet urges a renewal of the strength of the friend's affection. The "sad int'rim" separating them is not a mere absence but rather an estrangement; and with the master-slave Sonnets 57 and 58 the worst fears of Sonnet 48 have been realized, since the speaker is forced to endure full-blown inconstancy and deliberate desertion.

Sonnets 57 and 58 concern a master-slave relationship in which the speaker plays the unhappy role of the slave of love, disliking his servile dependence and the "bitterness" of his friend's absence without being able to escape from emotional domination. His resentment is realized by the sense, tone, and feeling of the Sonnets, by an obvious and bitter irony. Both of them convey the misery of the true and watchful servant and in that respect may be a kind of expanded inversion of Luke xii.35–37:

SOURCE: This essay appeared in an expanded form in Hilton Landry, *Interpretations in Shakespeare's Sonnets* (Berkeley: University of California Press, 1963).

[1] There is only one reference to the sex of the person addressed in the whole group (43–58): Sonnet 54 speaks directly to a "beauteous and lovely youth." (Sonnets 40–42 are addressed to a handsome youth, and there are male references in Sonnet 63.)

Let your loynes be girded about, and your lights burning,
And yee your selves like unto men that waite for their master, when
hee will returne from the wedding, that when hee commeth and
knocketh, they may open unto him immediatly.
Blessed are those servants, whom the Lord when he commeth, shall
finde waking: verely I say unto you, hee will girde himselfe about, and
make them to sit downe at table, and will come forth, and serve them
(Geneva Version, 1600).

In the first of these poems the implications of an initial generalization (in the form of a rhetorical question) are made clear by the par-
ticulars of succeeding lines, and the irony which is directed chiefly at
his friend is also aimed at the poet himself.

> Being your slave, what should I do but tend
> Upon the hours and times of your desire?
> I have no precious time at all to spend,
> Nor services to do, till you require.
> Nor dare I chide the world-without-end hour
> Whilst I, my sovereign, watch the clock for you,
> Nor think the bitterness of absence sour
> When you have bid your servant once adieu.
> Nor dare I question with my jealous thought
> Where you may be, or your affairs suppose,
> But, like a sad slave, stay and think of nought
> Save where you are how happy you make those.
> So true a fool is love that in your will,
> Though you do anything, he thinks no ill.[2]

4

8

12

He begins by asking a question needing no answer: as your abject
inferior, subservient to your will, what ought I to do except be
(always) ready to serve you whenever you want something (whenever you are through satisfying your appetites, your other needs and
longings that have nothing to do with me)? In fact, he continues, I
have no time to spend that seems valuable (to me), and no services
to perform for you until you ask or demand them. (I would like to
have the opportunity to do the things for you that *my* loving friendship prompts me to, but you avoid me until you have some demand
to make and thus cause me to waste a great deal of my time.)

"The hours and times of your desire," built on a formula that is a
hallmark of Shakespeare's style, is deliberately ambiguous, enabling the
poet to refer to different aspects of the same situation. It obviously
points to the friend's demands on the speaker, with "desire" ("wish,
request, demand") looking forward to "require" and "hours and
times" implying the few hours and occasions on which friendship is

[2] Throughout the essay I follow the text of the Crofts Classics edition:
William Shakespeare: Sonnets, ed. H. E. Rollins (New York, 1951).

"served." And despite the silence of the commentators, it also calls attention to the friend's neglect of the poet. In this sense the phrase is equivalent to "your times of pleasure" in Sonnet 58; "desire" ("sensual appetite, lust") anticipates "will," and "hours and times" refers to the "world-without-end" hours and many occasions devoted to the pursuit of pleasure.

The irony of the second quatrain, which bears out my reading of "hours and times" and lines 3-4, is straightforward: I "dare" not curse the tedium of waiting for you, my lord and master, or even think that your absence is bitter. The striking compound in the phrase "the world-without-end hour" (l. 5), used by Shakespeare in only one other place, may remind one of the phrase "world without end" which occurs in the *Gloria Patri* and the hymn *Te Deum laudamus* of the Book of Common Prayer,[3] as well as in Isaiah xlv.17:

Glory be to the Father, and to the Sonne: and to the holy Ghost
As it was in the beginning, is nowe, and ever shal be: world without end.

> We magnifie thee day by day,
>   and world withouten end:
> Adore thy holy name, O Lord
>   vouchsafe us to defend
> From sinne this day, have mercy Lord,
>   have mercy on us all:
> And on us as we trust in thee,
>   Lord let thy mercy fall.

But Israel shall be saved in the Lord, with an everlasting salvation: yee shall not be ashamed nor confounded, world without ende.[4]

Perhaps one or more of these familiar passages suggested the phrase as a vivid means of conveying "everlastingness," the psychological truth that when we are waiting for someone to come or for something to happen, with all our attention and energy directed toward that moment, even an hour seems endless. Here as in *Love's Labor's Lost* (v. ii. 797) Shakespeare thinks of love as "a world-without-end bargain," and because it is, the enslaved speaker cannot hope that he "shall not be ashamed nor confounded world without ende."

[3] The phrase appears in the First Prayer Book of Edward VI (1549) and in all later editions.

[4] The text for these quotations is that of the Geneva Bible (1600). The relevant stanza of the *Te Deum* is quoted in the metrical version of Sternhold and Hopkins, whose versified Psalms were frequently bound up with Geneva and Bishops' Bibles and with the Prayer Book. The Isaiah passage is part of an exhortation to patience.

"World without end" also occurs in Ephesians iii.21 in the Rheims New Testament (1582) and the Authorized Version.

With the last quatrain the speaker's irony returns more forcibly upon himself. I "dare not" consider too carefully with my justifiably suspicious mind where you may be, or form too clear an idea of your affairs, for your sake as well as my own; instead, like a sorrowful and serious "slave" I wait for your return and think of nothing except how happy you make those who are with you—wherever you are. He can't help thinking of what his friend is doing—indeed, in a general way he knows—but to preserve his self-respect he dare not inquire too closely.

Ambiguous in syntax and diction, the couplet summarizes his view of his "slavery." There are at least three ways of taking it: (a) So true a fool is love that in your Will (the poet)/Though you do anything, he thinks no ill; (b) So true a fool is love that, though you do anything, he thinks no ill in your will; (c) So true a fool is love that, though you do anything in your will, he thinks no ill. Since all of these readings are consonant with the poem as a whole, there is no need of favoring any one of them to the exclusion of the others. The Quarto's "Will" invites us to regard it as the poet's name or a play on his name in the manner of Sonnets 135 and 137; so faithful and genuine a fool is love that in the person of your friend Will he thinks there is no harm in whatever you do. In the second "meaning" of the line the constant fool who is the loving speaker thinks the friend's *intentions* are good, or rather not bad, whatever he does. This may also be a way of uttering a hoary commonplace by way of an excuse—that the volitional faculty or rational appetite is always directed at what seems to be the good. According to the third reading, so loyal a fool is love that whatever the friend does that lies within his power of choosing, or in his willfulness or perversity, in his lust, the speaker thinks there is no evil in it.

Setting aside the significance of "fool" for the moment, it is clear that "true" denotes "loyal, constant, faithful" as well as "real, or genuine." Neither sense can be dispensed with, for although the speaker intends the phrase to convey strong self-reproach (So big a fool am I), the fool's loyalty to his friend is the basis of their relationship. Playing on the poet's name, "will" has all these senses: "the volitional part of the rational soul, the power of choosing and willing; choice, wish, pleasure, desire; intention; wilfulness or perversity; lust." Both "anything" and "he" are emphatic, and "ill" signifies "(moral) evil, sin; harm, injury." There is an implicit disparity between what he, as opposed to others, thinks of his friend's intentions and actions. As a "true" fool he may see no personal injury, no sin against friendship in them, but others who can see things objectively probably regard them as both morally evil and injurious to the speaker.

Here and elsewhere in the Sonnets the fool is one who has been made a fool of (by Love or Time), who is somebody's or something's dupe or sport: "Love's not Time's fool" (116); "the fools of Time" (124); "Thou blind fool, Love, what dost thou to mine eyes/That they behold and see not what they see?" (137). On the most obvious level, then, the speaker qualifies as a fool because he is "stupid" enough to be duped by love, which is traditionally blind. He is also a servant or slave, a talker, and a condoner of sin, roles which further entitle him to be called "fool." In relation to his "sovereign" he is something like a court fool—a privileged familiar who can say almost anything, but nevertheless a mere servant. Much as he dislikes his situation, as a slave he can only think and talk about it, complain at length but take no action. In this respect he is a talker (rather than a doer), and to talk is characteristic of the fool, as both etymology and the Bible suggest. "Fool" derives from a Latin word for "bellows" which in late Latin became "windbag, fool," and a number of passages in Proverbs and Ecclesiastes remind us that "a fool . . . is full of words." In the Bible "fool" often signifies "sinner," a sense that fits the poet to the extent tht he sins in condoning "ill," corrupting himself by salving the friend's "amiss":

> To connive and wink at your friend's weaknesses, to gloss them over and to be taken in by them, even to admire and love his worst faults as if they were virtues—doesn't this look like folly? (Erasmus, *Praise of Folly*, tr. L. F. Dean, p. 57.)

Yet in the final analysis perhaps it is the friend who is the fool and the speaker who is wise, for in the Socratic view to know you are a fool is a sign of wisdom.

Pooler describes the equivocal Sonnet 58 as a "complaint in the form of an assertion that he has no right to complain"; Empson agrees that it is "two-faced in idea." [5]

> That god forbid that made me first your slave
> I should in thought control your times of pleasure,
> Or at your hand th' account of hours to crave,
> 4   Being your vassal bound to stay your leisure!
> O, let me suffer (being at your beck)
> Th' imprisoned absence of your liberty;
> And patience, tame to sufferance, bide each check
> 8   Without accusing you of injury.
> Be where you list; your charter is so strong

[5] William Empson, *Seven Types of Ambiguity*, 2d ed. (1947), p. 54. Empson's brief comments, concentrating on ll. 7 and 11, are vitiated by his taking the Quarto punctuation too seriously. It is hard to "make sense" of the Quarto's comma after "tame," and though the syntax of l. 11 is somewhat ambiguous, it makes the quatrain unnecessarily tautological to regard "your time" as a subject of "belong."

That you yourself may privilege your time
To what you will; to you it doth belong
12   Yourself to pardon of self-doing crime.
        I am to wait, though waiting so be hell;
        Not blame your pleasure, be it ill or well.

It opens with a statement put in an ironic, almost sarcastic optative mood: may the god (of love) that first made me your "slave" forbid that I should, *even in thought,* control the occasions of your "pleasure," the times devoted to enjoyment, amusement, gratification (whether sensuous or sensual), to doing whatever you want to do; or that I should beg for an accounting of how you spend your time, for I am only your servant, obliged to wait till you are unoccupied.

The ironic optative continues in the second quatrain, which apparently stresses the poet's patient servility while it reveals a painful awareness of his grievances. Since I am at your command, let me bear with patience and constancy the pain of imprisoning absence resulting from your freedom and libertinism; and may my patience, submissive to suffering and pain, endure each rebuke or taunt without accusing you of wrong or insult. Four words in these lines ("suffer," "patience," "sufferance," and "bide") [6] combine the notions of experiencing something which causes pain and grief and putting up with, making the best of it. The ostensible emphasis is on toleration, a necessary condition of "slavery," but the speaker's sense of injury is equally prominent. Of course the friend has the "liberty" to be absent, the freedom to do what he wishes, even if absence imprisons the poet by keeping him from his friend. Yet if the friend flaunts his liberty by devoting his absences to libertinism, then it is natural for the speaker to feel wronged ("check," "injury," "crime"). "Check" signifies "taunt" as well as "rebuke or reproof," and in view of the implications of "pleasure" and "liberty," it probably glances at the term from falconry meaning "stoop for baser game" and "the baser game itself."

In the third quatrain the friend's rights, already recognized in the references to liberty and pleasure, temporarily come to the fore. The poet says, be where you please; do what you want with your

[6] "Suffer"—"to bear with patience and constancy; to bear or undergo pain or distress"; "patience"—"suffering or enduring (pain, etc.) with calmness"; "bide"—"to face, encounter; suffer, endure; tolerate, put up with"; "sufferance"—"distress, pain, suffering; endurance; permission, toleration, acquiescence." C. T. Onions gives the last sense, "permission," as the definition of "sufferance" in his *Shakespeare Glossary* (2d ed., rev., Oxford, 1919). "Tame" has the senses "submissive, meek, subdued; servile or spiritless," and "tame to sufferance" may be read at least three ways: subdued to pain; submissive to the point of endurance; servile to the point of acquiescence.

time; forgive yourself for any sin you commit and any injury you do to yourself. As "list" and "will" look backward (and forward) to "pleasure," so "charter" and "privilege" look back to "liberty," for its senses include "franchise, privilege, right" as well as "freedom" and "libertinism." "Charter," signifying "right or privilege," may also suggest a "contract" between them, a contract favoring the friend because the speaker's love is so great. Indeed, it is the depth of the poet's love even more than the friend's character that makes one a fool and a slave and gives the other the prerogatives of a king.

The summarizing couplet states the requisites of the poet's position as he derives them from his experience: he is to wait and suffer and to suffer in silence. He must "wait," even if it is a veritable hell of anxiety and misery to do so; he must not find fault with the friend's choice, with the gratification, whether good or bad, that keeps the friend from him even though it may be a rebuke or insult. "Wait" has three senses which sum up the speaker's role with marvelous economy —"to wait for, to keep watch, to be on duty or ready to serve"; for he is at once the anxious loving friend, the ineffectual observer-guardian of his friend's behavior ("For thee watch I whilst thou dost wake elsewhere,/From me far off, with others all too near"), and his friend's willing (and unwilling) servant.

Appendices

Bibliography

THE WORKS LISTED BELOW are arranged chronologically by decade from 1800 to 1960 and, for the most part, consist of essays and books which are wholly devoted to the sonnets. The year 1800 was arbitrarily chosen because very little in the way of full-length essays was written before then. The chronological arrangement should enable interested readers to trace the various lines of the sonnet scholarship and criticism.

Two works deserve to be placed in a category by themselves. The first is Hyder Edward Rollins, *A New Variorum Edition of Shakespeare: The Sonnets*, 2 volumes, Philadelphia: J. B. Lippincott Co., 1944. Volume 1 contains the text of the sonnets, along with variations suggested by a multitude of scholars and critics. Volume 2 contains 12 appendices, along with a bibliography and a general index. The appendices deal with such problems as textual authenticity, the date of composition, Mr. W. H., the rival poet, and so on. It is an invaluable reference work.

The second is Samuel Aron Tannenbaum, *Shakespeare's Sonnets* (*A Concise Bibliography*), New York: Elizabethan Bibliographies, 1940 (Elizabethan Bibliographies, No. 10). It lists the sonnet literature more fully than any other similar work and should be consulted by those who may need a more complete bibliography than is listed below.

1800–1819

DRAKE, NATHAN. *Shakspeare and His Times.* 2 vols. London: T. Cadell and W. Davies, 1817.

"PUDOR, PROH." "On Shakspeare's Sonnets." *Blackwood's Magazine,* III (August, 1818), 585–588.

STOCKDALE, PERCIVAL. "Drake's *Shakspeare and His Times.*" *Monthly Review,* LXXXIX (August, 1819), 357–372.

1820–1829

J., Y. "Shakspeare's Poems." *New Monthly Magazine*, VII (1823), 470–476.

SKOTTOWE, AUGUSTINE. *The Life of Shakspeare*. London: Longman, Hurst, Orme, Brown, and Green, 1824.

COLERIDGE, HARTLEY. "Shakspeare a Tory and a Gentleman." *Blackwood's Magazine*, XXIV (August, 1828), 570–583. [Reprinted in his *Essays and Marginalia*. 2 vols. London: E. Moxon, 1851. I, 113–147.]

BROUGHTON, JAMES. "Shakspeare's Poems." *The Gentleman's Magazine*, XCIV (March, 1829), i, 225–226.

CAMPBELL, THOMAS. "The Sonnets of Shakspeare." *New Monthly Magazine*, XXVI (no month, 1829), 577–583.

1830–1839

RICHARDSON, D. L. "On Shakspeare's Sonnets, Their Poetical Merits, and on the Question to Whom They Are Addressed." *The Gentleman's Magazine*, n.s., IV (September, 1835), 250–256; (October, 1835), 361–369.

BOADEN, JAMES. *On the Sonnets of Shakspeare*. London: T. Rodd, 1837.

BROWN, CHARLES ARMITAGE. *Shakspeare's Autobiographical Poems*. London: J. Bohn, 1838.

1840–1849

BARRETT, WENDELL H. "Shakspeare's Sonnets." *American Whig Review*, VI (September, 1847), 304–309.

HART, J. S. "Shakspeare's Sonnets." *Sartain's Union Magazine*, V (September, 1849), 153–157.

1850–1859

ANONYMOUS. "Shakspeare's Minor Poems." *Fraser's Magazine*, LII (October, 1855), 398–411.

BATHURST, CHARLES. *Remarks on the Differences in Shakspeare's Versification*. London: J. W. Parker & Son, 1857.

WHITE, R. G. "The Sonnets of Shakspeare." *Westminster Review*, LXVIII (July, 1857), 116–137.

1860–1869

NEIL, SAMUEL. *Shakspeare, A Critical Biography*. London: Houlston and Wright, 1861.

Bibliography

ALGER, W. R. "Shakspeare's Sonnets and Friendship." *Christian Examiner,* LXXIII (November, 1862), 403–435.

CORNEY, BOLTON. *The Sonnets of William Shakspere: A Critical Disquisition Suggested by a Recent Discovery.* London: F. Shoberl, 1862.

MASSEY, GERALD. "Shakspeare and His Sonnets." *Quarterly Review* [American Edition], CXV (April, 1864), 224–250.

HITCHCOCK, ETHAN ALLEN. *Remarks on the Sonnets of Shakspeare.* New York: J. Miller, 1865.

HUNT, LEIGH, and S. ADAMS LEE. *The Book of the Sonnet.* Boston: Roberts Brothers, 1867.

BUDD, THOMAS D. *Shakspeare's Sonnets with Commentaries.* Philadelphia: J. Campbell, 1868.

SIMPSON, RICHARD. *An Introduction to the Philosophy of Shakspeare's Sonnets.* London: N. Trübner & Co., 1868.

1870–1879

BROWN, HENRY. *The Sonnets of Shakspeare Solved.* London: J. R. Smith, 1870.

DOWDEN, EDWARD. *Shakspere: A Critical Study of His Mind and Art.* London: H. S. King & Co., 1875.

FLEAY, F. G. "On the Motive of Shakspere's Sonnets (1–125)." *Macmillan's Magazine,* XXXI (March, 1875), 433–445.

HILLARD, KATE. "On the Study of Shakspeare's Sonnets." *Lippincott's Monthly Magazine,* XV (April, 1875), 497–506.

BRAE, A. E. "Shakspeare's Sonnets." *Lippincott's Monthly Magazine,* XIX (June, 1877), 761–762.

SPALDING, T. A. "Shakspere's Sonnets." *The Gentleman's Magazine,* CCXLII (March, 1878), 300–318.

SWINBURNE, ALGERNON CHARLES. *A Study of Shakspeare.* London: Chatto & Windus, 1879.

1880–1889

TYLER, THOMAS. "The Date of Shakspeare's Fifty-Fifth Sonnet." *Athenaeum* (September 11, 1880), 337–338.

ANONYMOUS. "New Views of Shakespeare's Sonnets: The 'Other Poet' Identified." *Blackwood's Magazine,* CXXXV (June, 1884), 727–761; CXXXVII June, 1885), 774–800; CXXXIX (March, 1886), 327–350.

MORGAN, APPLETON. "Whose Sonnets?" *The Manhattan,* III (May, 1884), 441–451.

DAVIS, HORACE. "Shakspere's Sonnets." *Overland Monthly,* 2nd Series, XI (March, 1888), 245–259.

WILDE, OSCAR. "The Portrait of Mr. W. H." *Blackwood's Magazine,* CXLVI (July, 1889), 1–21. [Published later in book form and greatly lengthened. The latest edition is London: Methuen & Co., 1958.]

1890–1899

STOPES, CHARLOTTE C. "Shakspeare's Sonnets." *Jahrbuch der deutschen Shakespeare-Gesellschaft*, XXV (1890), 185–204.
——————. "Shakspeare's Sonnets, 'W. H. and the Dark Lady.'" *Poet-Lore*, II (September 15, 1890), 460–480.
TYLER, THOMAS. *Shakespeare's Sonnets*. London: D. Nutt, 1890.
WENDELL, BARRETT. "Shakspere's Sonnets." *William Shakspere*. New York: Charles Scribner's Sons, 1894. Pp. 221–237.
ARCHER, WILLIAM. "Shakespeare's Sonnets. The Case against Southampton." *The Fortnightly Review*, LXVII (December 1, 1897), 817–834.
LEIGH, G. A. "The Rival Poet in Shakespeare's Sonnets." *Westminster Review*, CXLVII (February, 1897), 173–187.
LEE, SIR SIDNEY. "Shakespeare and the Earl of Pembroke." *The Fortnightly Review*, LXIX (February 1, 1898), 210–223.
——————. "Shakespeare and the Earl of Southampton." *Cornhill*, LXXVII (April, 1898), 482–495.
GOLLANCZ, ISRAEL, ed. *Shakespeare's Sonnets*. London: J. M. Dent, 1898.
WYNDHAM, GEORGE, ed. *The Poems of Shakespeare*. New York: Thomas Y. Crowell, 1898(?).
BUTLER, SAMUEL. *Shakespeare's Sonnets; Reconsidered and in Part Rearranged* . . . . London: Longmans, Green and Co., 1899. [Reprinted as volume 14 in *The Shrewsbury Edition of the Works of Samuel Butler*, London: Jonathan Cape, 1923–1926.]

1900–1909

MC CLUMPHA, C. F. "Parallels between Shakespeare's Sonnets and *Love's Labour's Lost*." *Modern Language Notes*, XV (June, 1900), 168–174.
——————. "Parallels between Shakespeare's Sonnets and *A Midsummer Night's Dream*." *Modern Language Notes*, XVI (June, 1901), 164–168.
PRICE, THOMAS RANDALL. "The Technic of Shakspere's Sonnets." *Studies in Honor of Basil L. Gildersleeve*. Baltimore: The Johns Hopkins University Press, 1902. Pp. 363–375.
MC CLUMPHA, C. F. "Parallels between Shakespeare's Sonnets and *Romeo and Juliet*." *Jahrbuch der deutschen Shakespeare-Gesellschaft*, XL (1904), 187–203.
KLEIN, DAVID. "Foreign Influence on Shakespeare's Sonnets." *Sewanee Review*, XIII (Fall, 1905), 454–474.
LOUNSBURY, THOMAS R. *The Text of Shakespeare*. New York: Charles Scribner's Sons, 1906.
LUCE, MORTON. *A Handbook to the Works of Shakespeare*. London: G. Bell and Sons, 1906.
RALEIGH, SIR WALTER. *Shakespeare*. London: Macmillan and Co., 1907.

Bibliography

LANIER, SIDNEY. *Shakspere and His Forerunners.* New York: Doubleday, Page and Co., 1908. [Contains sonnet lecture delivered in 1879.]

LEE, SIR SIDNEY. "Ovid and Shakespeare's Sonnets." *Quarterly Review*, CCX (April, 1909), 455–476. [Reprinted in his *Elizabethan and Other Essays.* Oxford: Clarendon Press, 1929. Pp. 116–139.]

1910–1919

BATES, E. S. "The Sincerity of Shakespeare's Sonnets." *Modern Philology*, XIV (April, 1910), 129–152.

PLATT, ARTHUR. "Edward III and Shakespeare's Sonnets." *The Modern Language Review*, VI (October, 1911), 511–513.

DE MONTMORENCY, J. E. G. "The Mystery of Shakespeare's Sonnets." *Contemporary Review*, CI (May, 1912), 737–742.

PALMER, GEORGE HERBERT. *Intimations of Immortality in the Sonnets of Shakspere.* Boston: Houghton Mifflin Co., 1912.

ACHESON, ARTHUR. *Mistress Davenant and the Dark Lady of the Sonnets.* London: B. Quaritch, 1913.

BLATT, W. M. "A New Light on the Sonnets." *Modern Philology*, XI (1913), 135–140.

CHAMBRUN, CLARA LONGWORTH DE. *The Sonnets of William Shakespeare.* New York: G. Putnam's Sons, 1913.

MASSON, DAVID. "The Sonnets." *Shakespeare Personally.* Edited by Rosaline Masson. New York: E. P. Dutton and Co., 1914. Pp. 191–238. [A lecture given in 1895.]

SHAW, GEORGE BERNARD. "Preface" to *The Dark Lady of the Sonnets. Misalliance, The Dark Lady of the Sonnets, and Fanny's First Play.* London: Constable and Co., Ltd., 1914. Pp. 203–230.

GRAY, H. D. "The Arrangement and Date of Shakespeare's Sonnets." *PMLA*, XXX (1915), 629–644.

ALDEN, RAYMOND M. "The 1710 and 1714 Texts of Shakespeare's Poems." *Modern Language Notes*, XXXI (May, 1916), 268–274.

BYVANCK, W. G. C. "Reading Shakespeare's Sonnets." *A Book of Homage to Shakespeare.* Edited by Sir Israel Gollancz. London: H. Milford, 1916. Pp. 468–472.

Wisconsin Shakespeare Studies by Members of the Department of English of the University of Wisconsin. Madison, Wisconsin: University of Wisconsin Press, 1916. [Contains "An Obsolete Elizabethan Mode of Rhyming," by R. E. N. Dodge, pp. 174–200; and "Shakespeare's Sonnets and Plays," by Arthur Beatty, pp. 201–214.]

GRAY, H. D. "Shakespeare's Last Sonnets." *Modern Language Notes*, XXXII (January, 1917), 17–21.

CARPENTER, B. F. "Shakespeare's Sonnets: To Whom Dedicated?" *Catholic World*, CVI (January, 1918), 496–507.

MORGAN, APPLETON. "What Meres Knew about Shakespeare's Sonnets." *Catholic World*, CVII (May, 1918), 235–246.

1920–1929

BAYFIELD, MATTHEW A. *A Study of Shakespeare's Versification.* Cambridge: Cambridge University Press, 1920.

ORD, HUBERT W. *Chaucer and the Rival Poet in Shakespeare's Sonnets.* London: J. M. Dent & Sons, Ltd., 1921.

ACHESON, ARTHUR. *Shakespeare's Sonnet Story 1592–1598.* London: B. Quaritch, 1922.

ALDEN, RAYMOND M. "The Poems." *Shakespeare.* New York: Duffield & Co., 1922. Pp. 105–146.

ADAMS, JOSEPH QUINCY. *A Life of William Shakespeare.* Boston: Houghton Mifflin Co., 1923.

EMERSON, O. F. "Shakespeare's Sonneteering." *Studies in Philology*, XX (April, 1923), 111–136.

FORT, JAMES A. *The Two Dated Sonnets of Shakespeare.* London: Oxford University Press, 1924.

NOYES, ALFRED. "The Origin of Shakespeare's Sonnets." London *Bookman*, LXVII (December, 1924), 159–162.

BECKWITH, ELIZABETH. "On the Chronology of Shakespeare's Sonnets." *The Journal of English and Germanic Philology*, XXV (April, 1926), 227–242.

FORT, JAMES A. "Thorpe's Test for Shakespeare's Sonnets." *The Review of English Studies*, II (October, 1926), 439–445.

BRAY, SIR DENIS. "The Art-form of the Elizabethan Sonnet Sequence and Shakespeare's Sonnets." *Jahrbuch der deutschen Shakespeare-Gesellschaft*, LXIII (1927), 159–182.

DAVIES, RANDALL. *Notes upon Some of Shakespeare's Sonnets.* Kensington: Cayme Press, 1927.

RIDING, LAURA, and ROBERT GRAVES. "William Shakespeare and E. E. Cummings." *A Survey of Modernist Poetry.* London: William Heinemann, Ltd., 1927. Pp. 49–82. [Extensively revised and published as "A Study in Original Punctuation and Spelling," in Robert Graves, *The Common Asphodel*, London: Hamish Hamilton, 1949. Pp. 84–95. Reprinted on pages 161–172 of the present volume.]

FORT, JAMES A. "Further Notes on Shakespeare's Sonnets." *Library*, 4th Series, IX (December, 1928), 305–325.

―――――――. "The Date of Shakespeare's 107th Sonnet." *Library*, 4th Series, IX (March, 1929), 381–384.

―――――――. *A Time Scheme for Shakespeare's Sonnets.* London: The Mitre Press, 1929.

MURRY, JOHN MIDDLETON. "Concerning Sonnet 107." *New Adelphi*, II (March, 1929), 251–254.

1930–1939

CHAMBERS, SIR E. K. *William Shakespeare. A Study of Facts and Problems.* 2 vols. Oxford: Clarendon Press, 1930.

Bibliography

EMPSON, WILLIAM. *Seven Types of Ambiguity.* London: Chatto & Windus, 1930. [See the 2nd, revised edition, 1947, pp. 50–56; 113–138. A 3rd edition appeared in 1953.]

LYNCH, ARTHUR. "The 'Onlie Begetter' of Shakespeare's Sonnets." *Review of Reviews,* LXXX (April, 1930), 307–312.

WILSON, KATHERINE M. "Shakespeare's Sonnets." *Calcutta Review,* 3rd Series, XXXVII (November, 1930), 179–197; XXXVIII (January, 1931), 46–70.

JONSON, G. C. A. "Shakespeare's Sonnets." *Poetry Review,* XXII (July, 1931), 274–292.

STROUP, THOMAS B. "Biron and the 116th Sonnet." *Philological Quarterly,* X (July, 1931), 308–310.

TANNENBAUM, SAMUEL ARON. "The Copy for Shakspere's Sonnets." *Philological Quarterly,* X (October, 1931), 593–595.

KNIGHTS, L. C. "Shakespeare's Sonnets." *Scrutiny,* III (September, 1934), 133–160. [Reprinted in *Explorations,* London: Chatto & Windus, 1946; pp. 40–65. Reprinted on pages 173–197 of the present volume.]

SPURGEON, CAROLINE F. E. *Shakespeare's Imagery and What It Tells Us.* Cambridge: Cambridge University Press, 1935.

BROOKE, TUCKER. *Shakespeare's Sonnets.* London: Oxford University Press, 1936.

EVANS, WILLA MC C. "Lawes' Version of Shakespeare's Sonnet CXVI." *PMLA,* LI (March, 1936), 120–122.

NISBET, ULRIC. *The Onlie Begetter.* London: Longmans, Green and Co., Ltd., 1936.

WELLS, HENRY W. "A New Preface to Shakspere's Sonnets." *The [N.Y.] Shakespeare Association Bulletin,* XII (April, 1937), 118–129.

RANSOM, JOHN CROWE. "Shakespeare at Sonnets." *Southern Review,* III (January, 1938), 531–553. [Reprinted in *The World's Body,* New York: Charles Scribner's Sons, 1938; pp. 270–303. Reprinted on pages 198–218 of the present volume.]

DARBY, ROBERT H. "The Date of Some Shakespearean Sonnets." *Jahrbuch der deutsches Shakespeare-Gesellschaft,* LXXV (1939), 135–138.

SANDERLIN, GEORGE. "The Repute of Shakespeare's Sonnets in the Early Nineteenth Century." *Modern Language Notes,* LIV (June, 1939), 462–466.

1940–1949

MIZENER, ARTHUR. "The Structure of Figurative Language in Shakespeare's Sonnets." *Southern Review,* V (Spring, 1940), 730–747. [See pages 219–235 of the present volume.]

KENYON, JOHN. "Shakespeare, Sonnet CXI." *Modern Language Notes,* LX (May, 1945), 357–358.

CLARKSON, PAUL S., and CLYDE T. WARREN. "Pleading and Practice in Shakespeare's Sonnet XLVI." *Modern Language Notes,* LXII (February, 1947), 102–110.

BANKS, THEODORE H. "Shakespeare's Sonnet No. 8." *Modern Language Notes,* LXIII (December, 1948), 541–542.

BERKELMAN, ROBERT. "The Drama in Shakespeare's Sonnets." *College English*, X (December, 1948), 138–141.

CARTER, ALBERT H. "The Punctuation of Shakespeare's Sonnets of 1609." *Joseph Quincy Adams Memorial Studies.* Edited by Giles E. Dawson and Edwin E. Willoughby. Washington: Folger Shakespeare Library, 1948. Pp. 409–428.

LUMIANSKY, R. M. "Shakespeare's Sonnet LXXIII." *Explicator*, VI (June, 1948), item 55. [Reprinted on page 269 of the present volume.]

NOLAN, EDWARD F. "Shakespeare's Sonnet LXXIII." *Explicator*, VII (November, 1948), item 13. [Reprinted on pages 270–271 of the present volume.]

HOTSON, JOHN LESLIE. *Shakespeare's Sonnets Dated and Other Essays.* New York: Oxford University Press, 1949.

————. "When Shakespeare Wrote the Sonnets." *Atlantic Monthly*, CLXXXIV (December, 1949), 61–67.

JOHNSON, CHARLES W. M. "Shakespeare's Sonnet CXXIX." *Explicator*, VII (April, 1949), item 41. [Reprinted on pages 274–275 of the present volume.]

MOORE, CARLISLE. "Shakespeare's Sonnets LXXI–LXXIV." *Explicator*, VIII (October, 1949), item 2. [Reprinted on pages 271–272 of the present volume.]

STARNES, D. T. "Shakespeare's Sonnet 60: Analogues." *Notes and Queries*, CXCIV (October 15, 1949), 454.

THOMPSON, KARL F. "Shakespeare's Sonnet CXXIX." *Explicator*, VII (February, 1949), item 27. [Reprinted on pages 273–274 of the present volume.]

1950–1959

ABEND, MURRAY. "Two Unique Gender Forms in the Shakespeare Sonnets." *Notes and Queries*, CXCV (July 22, 1950), 325.

BALDWIN, T. W. *On the Literary Genetics of Shakespeare's Poems and Sonnets.* Urbana: University of Illinois Press, 1950.

GOLDSMITH, ULRICH K. "Words Out of a Hat? Alliteration and Assonance in Shakespeare's Sonnets." *Journal of English and Germanic Philology*, XLIV (January, 1950), 33–48.

HARBAGE, ALFRED. "Dating Shakespeare's Sonnets." *Shakespeare Quarterly*, I (April, 1950), 57–63.

HOTSON, LESLIE. "The Date of Shakespeare's Sonnets." *Times Literary Supplement* [London], June 2, 1950, p. 348.

————. "More Light on Shakespeare's Sonnets." *Shakespeare Quarterly*, II (April, 1951), 111–118.

HUBLER, EDWARD. *The Sense of Shakespeare's Sonnets.* Princeton: Princeton University Press, 1952. [Reprinted on pages 236–256 of the present volume.]

MC NEAL, THOMAS H. " 'Every Man out of his Humour' and Shakespeare's 'Sonnets.' " *Notes and Queries*, CXCVII (August 30, 1952), 376.

SMITH, HALLETT D. "The Sonnets." *Elizabethan Poetry.* Cambridge, Mass.: Harvard University Press, 1952. Pp. 131–193.

Bibliography

LEWIS, C. S. *English Literature in the Sixteenth Century*. Oxford: Clarendon Press, 1954. Pp. 502–508.

PETERSON, DOUGLAS L. "A Probable Source for Shakespeare's Sonnet CXXIX." *Shakespeare Quarterly*, V (Autumn, 1954), 381–384.

CRUTTWELL, PATRICK. "Shakespeare's Sonnets and the 1590's." *The Shakespearean Moment*. New York: Columbia University Press, 1955. Pp. 1–38.

KNIGHT, G. WILSON. "Symbolism." *The Mutual Flame*. London: Methuen & Co., 1955. Pp. 58–68. [Reprinted on pages 257–266 of the present volume.]

MICHEL, LAURENCE. "Shakespeare's Sonnet CVII." *Journal of English and Germanic Philology*, LIV (April, 1955), 301–305.

FOX, CHARLES A. O. "Thomas Lodge and Shakespeare." *Notes and Queries*, new series, III (May, 1956), 190.

SISSON, C. J. *New Readings in Shakespeare*. 3 vols. Cambridge: Cambridge University Press, 1956. Vol. I.

SCHAAR, CLAES. "Shakespeare's Sonnets L–LI and Tebaldo's Sonnet CVII." *English Studies*, XXXVIII (October, 1957), 208–209.

SMITH, GORDON ROSS. "A Note on Shakespeare's Sonnet 143." *American Imago*, XIV (Spring, 1957), 33–36. [Reprinted on pages 276–279 of the present volume.]

BERRY, FRANCIS. " 'Thou' and 'You' in Shakespeare's Sonnets." *Essays in Criticism*, VIII (April, 1958), 138–146.

CLARKE, ROBERT F. "An Emendation of Sonnet 146." *Shakespeare Newsletter*, VIII (May, 1958), 11.

HERBERT, T. WALTER. "Sound and Sense in Two Shakespeare Sonnets." *Tennessee Studies in Literature*, III (1958), 43–52.

DAVIS, JACK M., and J. E. GRANT. "A Critical Dialogue on Shakespeare's Sonnet 71." *Texas Studies in Literature and Language*, I (Summer, 1959), 214–232.

HUBLER, EDWARD. *Shakespeare's Songs and Poems*. New York: McGraw Hill Book Co., 1959.

TAYLOR, DICK, JR. "The Earl of Pembroke and the Youth of Shakespeare's Sonnets." *Studies in Philology*, LVI (January, 1959), 26–54.

1960–1962

BARBER, C. L. "An Essay on the Sonnets." *The Sonnets of Shakespeare*. The Laurel Shakespeare. New York: Dell, 1960. Pp. 7–33.

——————. "Shakespeare in His Sonnets." *Massachusetts Review*, I (Summer, 1960), 648–672.

GÉRARD, ALBERT S. "The Stone as Lily: A Discussion of Shakespeare's Sonnet XCIV." *Jahrbuch der deutschen Shakespeare-Gesellschaft*, XCVI (1960), 155–160.

LEISHMAN, J. B. "Variations on a Theme in Shakespeare's Sonnets." *Elizabethan and Jacobean Studies*. Edited by Herbert Davis and Helen Gardner. Oxford: Clarendon Press, 1960. Pp. 112–149.

MAY, LOUIS F., JR. "The *Figura* in Sonnet 106." *Shakespeare Quarterly*, XI (Winter, 1960), 93–94.

ROGERS, E. G. "Sonnet CXXX: Watson to Linche to Shakespeare." *Shakespeare Quarterly*, XI (Spring, 1960), 232–233.

ROSTENBERG, LEONA. "Thomas Thorpe, Publisher of 'Shake-Speare's Sonnets.'" *Papers of the Bibliographical Society of America*, LIV (First Quarter, 1960), 16–37.

SCHAAR, CLAES. *An Elizabethan Sonnet Problem: Shakespeare's Sonnets, Daniel's Delia, and Their Literary Background*. Lund: C. W. K. Gleerup, 1960.

SOUTHAM, B. C. "Shakespeare's Christian Sonnet? Number 146." *Shakespeare Quarterly*, XI (Winter, 1960), 67–71.

STIRLING, BRENTS. "A Shakespeare Sonnet Group." *PMLA*, LXXV (September, 1960), 340–349.

BLACKMUR, R. P. "A Poetics for Infatuation." *Kenyon Review*, XXIII (Autumn, 1961), 647–670.

GÉRARD, ALBERT S. "Iconic Organization in Shakespeare's Sonnet CXLVI." *English Studies*, XLII (June, 1961), 157–159. [Reprinted on pages 279–282 of the present volume.]

LEISHMAN, J. B. *Themes and Variations in Shakespeare's Sonnets*. New York: Hillary House, 1961.

RADLEY, VIRGINIA L., and DAVID C. REDDING. "Shakespeare: Sonnet 110, a New Look." *Shakespeare Quarterly*, XII (Autumn, 1961), 462–463.

GREEN, A. WIGFALL. "Significant Words in Shakespeare's Sonnets." *University of Mississippi Studies in English*, III (1962), 95–113.

GRUNDY, JOAN. "Shakespeare's Sonnets and the Elizabethan Sonneteers." *Shakespeare Survey*, XV (1962), 41–49.

HUBLER, EDWARD, editor. *The Riddle of Shakespeare's Sonnets*. New York: Basic Books, 1962.

MAHOOD, M. M. "Love's Confined Doom." *Shakespeare Survey*, XV (1962), 50–61.

NEARING, HOMER, JR. "Shakespeare as a Nondramatic Poet: Sonnet XXIX." *Shakespeare Quarterly*, XIII (Winter, 1962), 15–20.

NEJGEBAUER, A. "Twentieth-Century Studies in Shakespeare's Sonnets, Songs, and Poems. 2. The Sonnets." *Shakespeare Survey*, XV (1962), 10–18.

SCHROETER, JAMES. "Shakespeare's Not 'To-Be-Pitied Lover.'" *College English*, XIII (January, 1962), 250–255.

The Authors

ROBERT GRAVES   English poet and novelist. During World War I began to write poetry. After the war attended Oxford, graduating in 1926. Subsequently taught for two years at the University of Cairo. Settling later on the island of Majorca (where he now lives), he operated, with the aid of Laura Riding, the Seizin Press. The Press, discontinued during the Spanish Civil War, published a number of his and Miss Riding's books. Among his novels are *I Claudius* (1934) and *Count Belisarius* (1938). His volumes of poetry include *The Treasure Box* (1919), *John Kemp's Wager: A Ballad Opera* (1925), *Collected Poems, 1914–47* (1948), and *Homer's Daughter* (1955). His works on mythology are *The White Goddess* (1948) and *The Greek Myths* (2 volumes, 1955).

LAURA RIDING   American poet and critic. Began writing while a student at Cornell University. In 1924 awarded a prize of $100 by the Fugitives, a group of poets who believed in a return to an agrarian society. Went to Europe in 1925, where she met Robert Graves; in collaboration with him, she wrote *A Survey of Modernist Poetry* (1927) and *A Pamphlet Against Anthologies* (1928), among other works. She is now married to Schuyler Jackson, with whom she is preparing *A Working English Dictionary*. Her volumes of poetry include *Four Unposted Letters to Catherine* (1930), *The Life of the Dead* (1933), *Poet: A Lying Word* (1933), and *Collected Poems* (1938).

L(IONEL) C(HARLES) KNIGHTS   English critic and scholar. Educated at Cambridge; member of the editorial board of *Scrutiny*, 1932–1953. Now professor of English at the University of Bristol. Visiting professor at the University of Pittsburgh, 1961–1962. His books include *Drama and Society in the Age of Jonson* (1937), *Explorations* (1946), and *Some Shakespearean Themes* (1959).

JOHN CROWE RANSOM   American poet, critic, teacher. Educated at Vanderbilt University; later a Rhodes Scholar. Returned to Vanderbilt after World War I. A member of the Fugitives (others: Robert Penn Warren, Allen Tate, Donald Davidson, Merrill Moore). Edited *The Fugitive*, 1922–1925. In 1937 went to Kenyon College as professor of poetry. From 1939 to his retirement he edited the *Kenyon Review*. His volumes of poetry include *Poems about God* (1919), *Chills and Fever* (1924), *Grace after Meat* (1924), and *Selected Poems* (1945). His critical works include *The World's Body* (1938) and *New Criticism* (1941).

ARTHUR MIZENER American scholar, teacher. Educated at Princeton and Harvard. Has taught at Yale, Wells, and Carleton; now professor of English at Cornell. Has published widely in such reviews as the *Kenyon*, the *Southern*, and the *Partisan*. Author of *The Far Side of Paradise* (1951), a critical biography of F. Scott Fitzgerald.

EDWARD (LORENZO) HUBLER American Shakespearean scholar, teacher. Educated at Princeton University, where he now teaches. Has taught also at Franklin and Marshall College and the University of Rochester; has been visiting professor at Haverford College and at the Universities of Bordeaux, Toulouse, and Algiers. With Thomas Marc Parrott he has published *Shakespeare, Twenty-Three Plays and the Sonnets* and *Shakespeare, Six Plays and the Sonnets*.

G(EORGE) WILSON KNIGHT English critic and teacher. Turned to literature after having taught mathematics for five years. In 1931 appointed to a professorship at Toronto University. Since 1946 has been at the University of Leeds. Interested primarily in the production of Shakespeare's plays and the criticism surrounding them. His works include *The Shakespearian Tempest* (1932), *Principles of Shakespearian Production* (1936), and *Essays in Interpretation of Shakespeare's Final Plays* (1947).

R(OBERT) M(AYER) LUMIANSKY American scholar, teacher. Educated at the Citadel, the University of South Carolina, and the University of North Carolina. Formerly dean of the Graduate School, Tulane University; now professor of English, Duke University. Has published widely. His works include *"The Canterbury Tales" in Modern English* and *Of Sondry Folk: The Dramatic Principle in "The Canterbury Tales."*

EDWARD F. NOLAN American scholar, teacher. Educated at the University of Florida and Princeton. Has taught at Presbyterian College and is now professor of English at the University of South Carolina. Interested mainly in Shakespeare studies. Has published "Verdi's *Macbeth*," which appeared in *Renaissance Papers* for 1954.

CARLISLE MOORE American scholar, teacher. Educated at Princeton. Now teaches at the University of Oregon. His major interest is in nineteenth-century English fiction. Currently at work on Carlyle's development as an artist. Works include *Carlyle and Fiction* (1940).

KARL F(REDERICK) THOMPSON American scholar, teacher. Educated at Yale. Has taught at Oberlin and Michigan State University. Contributor of articles on Renaissance literature and Shakespeare to *PMLA, Shakespeare Quarterly, Comparative Literature,* and others.

C(HARLES) W. M. JOHNSON American critic. Educated at Emory University and the University of Chicago. Has taught at the University of Minnesota; now lives and works in New York City. Contributed an article on Proust to William Van O'Connor's *Forms of Modern Fiction* (1948).

GORDON ROSS SMITH American scholar, teacher. Educated at Columbia and Pennsylvania State University, where he now teaches. An associate bibliographer of the Modern Language Association and compiler of *A Classified Shakespeare Bibliography, 1936–1958*, published in 1963. His articles have appeared in *Shakespeare Quarterly, American Imago, Literature and Psychology,* and *College English*.

ALBERT S. GÉRARD Belgian scholar, teacher. Has taught at the University of Elisabethville, Katanga Province, Congo. Lives in Seraing, Belgium. Has published widely on Shakespeare in *Jahrbuch der deutschen Shakespeare-Gesellschaft, English Studies,* and others.

HILTON LANDRY American scholar, teacher. Educated at Harvard, where he studied under I. A. Richards and Hyder Rollins. Teaches at the University of California at Davis. His *Interpretations in Shakespeare's Sonnets* has recently been published.

Exercises

I BIBLIOGRAPHICAL

In order not to overload the facilities of your library, works other than the sonnets and authors other than Shakespeare have been included in the following exercises.

1. Compile a bibliography for one of Shakespeare's plays, limiting yourself to a five-year period. For example, you might choose *Othello* for the period 1920–1925.
2. Work up a bibliography on a character from one of Shakespeare's plays, again limiting the time span. Example: Iago, 1935–1940.
3. Work up a bibliography on a single work by one of the following authors, limiting yourself to a ten-year period: Christopher Marlowe; Thomas Dekker; Thomas Heywood; John Webster; George Chapman; Ben Jonson; John Marston; Thomas Middleton; Henry Howard, Earl of Surrey; Sir Philip Sidney; Thomas Wyatt; Edmund Spenser; Samuel Daniel.
4. Compile a bibliography for one of the following: Thomas Thorpe, Francis Meres, John Benson, George Steevens, Edmond Malone, James Boswell (the younger).

II THEME TOPICS
BASED ON THE SONNETS

1. On the basis of your own choice of the most and the least successful of Shakespeare's sonnets, write an essay analyzing the differences between Shakespeare at his best and at his worst. Examine the relationship between the qualities that make the worst sonnets bad and those that make the best good.
2. Observe how important the sentiment of revulsion is to the sonnets—how often Shakespeare expresses disgust with himself, with those he loves, or with the way of the world. Read through the sequence again, noting all the poems that deal with these themes. Then write an essay on the distinguishing characteristics of the

group—on their imagery, their diction, and any other pertinent elements.

3. It is usually supposed that the many references in Shakespeare's sonnets to a young male friend have to do with a single person. If you see no objection to this supposition, write an essay on the young man, including, if possible, both a psychological analysis and a physical description. If you see inconsistencies in the sonnet sequence that make it impossible to accept such an inference, write an essay refuting the theory that a single person is involved and distinguishing the several men from one another.

4. It is often assumed that the scattered allusions to a woman the poet loves refer to a single "dark lady." If you find no inconsistencies invalidating this assumption, write an analysis of the woman (cf. topic 3). If you do find inconsistencies, write an essay demonstrating that several women are involved.

5. Make a list of the sonnets in which the sex of the person addressed or discussed is unmistakable. Then write an essay on the differences between those written to or about a man and those written to or about a woman, discussing differences of tone, diction, imagery, and anything else worthy of comment.

6. Analyze in detail the ways Shakespeare uses any of the following devices, showing the psychological effects achieved by his use of the device in question: (a) antithesis; (b) paradox; (c) oxymoron; (d) jingle (an approximate repetition of sounds as in "hew all Hews").

7. Analyze Shakespeare's recurrent use of images drawn from accountancy, commerce, and law. Write a unified essay illustrating their function in the sonnets and explaining his use of such images in a sequence of poems largely concerned with love.

8. Discuss the place of the "war with time" theme in the sonnets.

9. Read one of the following sonnet sequences and compare it to Shakespeare's, including in your essay a discussion of the image of himself that each poet projects: (a) Sir Philip Sidney's *Astrophel and Stella;* (b) Edmund Spenser's *Amoretti;* (c) Michael Drayton's *Idea;* (d) Samuel Daniel's *Delia.*

10. Compare sonnet 138 or 144 to its variant draft published in *The Passionate Pilgrim.* Arrive at some conclusion about the priority of the drafts of the sonnet you have chosen and write a unified essay presenting your argument.

III THEME TOPICS
BASED ON THE ESSAYS AND EXPLICATIONS

1. Select a sonnet and compare the original with a modernized version. If your instructor assigns a short theme, you will have to

limit yourself to a single aspect in your comparison. For example, you may be able to discuss the effect of a single change in punctuation or spelling. Of course, should your instructor assign a long theme, you will be afforded the chance to develop your comparison fully. For this assignment, re-read the Graves-Riding essay.

2. In his essay, L.C. Knights remarks, "In the sonnets no image is *merely* decorative, as in Romeo's 'Two of the fairest stars in all [the] heaven . . .'" (p. 188). Examine four or five sonnets in the light of the above remark; then write a theme in which you agree or disagree with Knights, citing the sonnets you have examined.

3. Write a theme based on the following statement by Knights (p. 189): "when ambiguity occurs in successful verse it is valuable in much the same way as successful imagery is valuable, as representing a heightened, more inclusive and more unified form of consciousness." Document your theme by citing passages from one or more sonnets.

4. Re-read section 2 of John Crowe Ransom's essay (pp. 200–203), in which the thesis is that "generally [Shakespeare's sonnets] are ill constructed." Then write a theme agreeing or disagreeing with Mr. Ransom, paying particular attention to the structural aspects of the sonnets that are commented on.

5. Write a theme in which you discuss Mr. Ransom's contention (pp. 204–205) that the kind of poetry Shakespeare writes in the sonnets is saved by "metric," which "persuades us . . . that this is a poetry of wonderful precision, when logically it is a poetry of wonderful imprecision, and the only precision it has is metrical, therefore adventitious."

6. Mr. Ransom, in discussing Shakespeare as a metaphysical poet, says (p. 208) that we are surprised "to find no evidence anywhere that Shakespeare's imagination is equal to the peculiar and systematic exercises which Donne habitually imposed on his." In a theme discuss what you think Mr. Ransom means, using a sonnet by Shakespeare and one by Donne to support your position.

7. Arthur Mizener, in refuting a point made by Mr. Ransom, says of sonnet 73 "that the success of Shakespeare's compound metaphor does not depend on the strict logic of its vehicle" (p. 221). Analyze another Shakespeare sonnet, making the same point.

8. Re-read section V (p. 235) of Arthur Mizener's essay; then write a theme in which you show that one of Shakespeare's sonnets establishes the pattern that Mr. Mizener claims for them.

9. In "Form and Matter," Edward Hubler points out instances of poor lines in the sonnets and quotes Ben Jonson's famous answer to the statement that Shakespeare had rarely blotted (i.e., erased) a line: " 'Would that he had blotted a thousand.' " Write a theme

in which you discuss a number of lines or images from the sonnets that you think ought to have been blotted.

10. Analyze one of the sonnets on absence, none of which Mr. Hubler claims "is among Shakespeare's distinguished poems" (p. 248; numbers of sonnets in question are given in footnote 19). Try to work your analysis in such a way as to prove or disprove Mr. Hubler's position. Do not choose sonnets 57 or 58, since they are analyzed in Hilton Landry's article (which you would do well to re-read in this connection).

11. Re-read the opening paragraph of G. Wilson Knight's essay, particularly the last two sentences. In an essay of your own, discuss what you take Mr. Knight to mean, using relevant passages from one or more of the sonnets to make your point.

12. Discuss sonnets 59 and 60 in terms of Mr. Knight's statement (p. 258) that "the Sonnets are, indeed, less love-poetry than an almost religious adoration before one of 'the rarities of Nature's truth' (60); that is, one of the splendours of human creation."

13. Write an explication of sonnet 73, continuing the argument as it runs from Lumiansky to Nolan to Moore. Note also that Mizener and Ransom comment on the sonnet.

14. Do the same with sonnet 129, taking the argument from Graves and Riding to Thompson to Johnson.

15. Write a theme on the extent to which you think Freudian analysis of poetry is valid. In this connection, re-read Gordon Ross Smith's article.

16. Write a short essay on sonnet 146 in which you elaborate on or rebut Gérard's thesis.

17. In the light of what Hilton Landry has to say of sonnets 57 and 58, reconsider Mr. Hubler's view of the friendship sonnets (see topic 10) and base a theme on your reconsideration.

Index of Sonnets by First Lines

Index of Sonnets by First Lines

Appendices

Index of Sonnets by First Lines